Ethnography of an Interface

Technologists frequently promote self-tracking devices as objective tools. This book argues that such glib and often worrying assertions must be placed in the context of precarious industry dynamics. The author draws on several years of ethnographic fieldwork with developers of self-tracking applications and wearable devices in New York City's Silicon Alley and with technologists who participate in the international forum called the Quantified Self to illuminate the professional compromises that shape digital technology and the gap between the tech sector's public claims and its interior processes.

By reconciling the business conventions, compromises, shifting labor practices, and growing employment insecurity that power the self-tracking market with device makers' often simplistic promotional claims, the book offers an understanding of the impact that technologists exert on digital discourse, on the tools they make, and on the data that these gadgets put out into the world.

YULIYA GRINBERG holds a PhD in Sociocultural Anthropology from Columbia University, New York, and specializes in digital culture. Her teaching addresses the social impact of technological innovation, automation, big data, and the future of work. Her writing has been published in top academic journals such as *Anthropological Quarterly* as well as in popular forums including the Committee for the Anthropology of Science, Technology, and Computing (CASTAC) and the Ethnographic Praxis in Industry Conference (EPIC) blogs.

"Grinberg's masterful ethnography brings a new perspective to quantified self technologies, exploring how the technology designers' fissured and unstable working conditions inform what designers think should matter when quantifiying. Brimming with new insights, she connects the dots between the designable and the personal in this eminently teachable book."

— Ilana Gershon, *Rice University*

"An incisive look into the making of self-tracking technologies. Grinberg unearths all the hopes, desires, networks, and labor that go into building the tools and startups of the Quantified Self movement. This book is a must-read for anyone interested in metrics, tracking, and digital capitalism."

— Angèle Christin, *Author of* Metrics at Work, *Stanford University*

"QS, the translation of self into quantifiable data, is a model for technological optimism. Wearable and sensor-enabled devices promise to optimize humans. Silicon Valley has long pursued this dream. Enthusiasts imagined these objects as the ideal interface between the body and the wider world. Grinberg thoughtfully documents how this nascent social movement morphed into the self-tracking market more than a decade later. She tracks people, practices, and metaphors to reveal a darker story. Unkept promises, entrepreneurial precarity, and emotional labor mark the present reality of this technological sector."

— Jan English-Lueck, *San José State University*

Ethnography of an Interface

Self-Tracking, Quantified Self, and the Work of Digital Connections

YULIYA GRINBERG

CAMBRIDGE
UNIVERSITY PRESS

CAMBRIDGE
UNIVERSITY PRESS

Shaftesbury Road, Cambridge CB2 8EA, United Kingdom

One Liberty Plaza, 20th Floor, New York, NY 10006, USA

477 Williamstown Road, Port Melbourne, VIC 3207, Australia

314–321, 3rd Floor, Plot 3, Splendor Forum, Jasola District Centre, New Delhi – 110025, India

103 Penang Road, #05-06/07, Visioncrest Commercial, Singapore 238467

Cambridge University Press is part of Cambridge University Press & Assessment, a department of the University of Cambridge.

We share the University's mission to contribute to society through the pursuit of education, learning and research at the highest international levels of excellence.

www.cambridge.org
Information on this title: www.cambridge.org/9781108832809

DOI: 10.1017/9781108966047

When citing this work, please include a reference to the DOI 10.1017/9781108966047

First published 2025

Cover image: Malte Mueller/fStop/Getty Images

A catalogue record for this publication is available from the British Library

A Cataloging-in-Publication data record for this book is available from the Library of Congress

ISBN 978-1-108-83280-9 Hardback
ISBN 978-1-108-96575-0 Paperback

"In reality every reader is, while he is reading, the reader of his own self."

– Marcel Proust, *Remembrance of Things Past, Volume 3*

Contents

Preface

On a frosty January night in 2016, Chris Dancy and I line up outside of the McKittrick Hotel in New York City for the premier of the new Showtime documentary series *Dark Net*. The episode to be screened that evening, called "Upgraded," stars Dancy and documents his avid embrace of digital self-monitoring. As we wait, I steal a sidelong glance at the invitation he had sent to my phone a few weeks earlier. A delicate face set with plump lips, eyes covered by an electronic circuit board as though it were a mask, spreads across my screen (Figure 1). Promising a night of technophilic mystery, the tagline running across the forehead of the person pictured on the image reads, "Dangerous. Seductive. Illuminating." The provocative and intimate premise echoes in the series scheduling. Slated to run on Showtime at eleven in the evening, the marketing evokes the scopophilic pleasure of "Showtime After Hours" that has turned the cable station into a pop culture phenomenon during the 1990s and early 2000s.

The burlesque qualities of the promotional materials seem mirrored in the venue chosen for the series premier. The show *Sleep No More*, described by one reviewer as "synonymous with intrigue," plays at the McKittrick Hotel most nights. During the performance, the audience walks about the set as they uncover important clues, becoming part of the act. Although the McKittrick Hotel is billed as an original venue that dates back to the 1930s, it was constructed for the show on the site of a former warehouse. The feigned authenticity of the hotel contributes to the sense of mystery and discovery the audience is meant to experience both during Sleep No More and the screening of Dark Net.

The performance space is also just to the side of the main thoroughfare filled with restaurants and buildings that now border the winding Manhattan High Line where voyeurism has become the area's main draw. Once dominated by abandoned factory buildings and auto shops, the neighborhood – now that the

Figure 1 Poster for *Dark Net*. Showtime. "The Dark Net" used with permission. ©2024 SHOWTIME Networks Inc. All Rights Reserved.

High Line, a former elevated rail line, has been reclaimed as a designer park – boasts rows of high-end condominiums with floor-to-ceiling glass windows that tower over the elegantly landscaped tracks. Perched several stories above the street, the High Line has upgraded pedestrians' ability to see and to be seen. Walking its span of nearly two dozen blocks from Gansevoort to 34th Street, the thrill of looking inside private windows placed all too close to the former tracks, and being seen walking down its stylish rows, constitutes the main pleasures of the park's experience. The series *Dark Net* connects with this exhibitionist infrastructure once again. By naming Dancy's episode "Upgraded," Showtime slyly implies that contemporary self-tracking devices have similarly improved the perceptual faculties of the people using them.

Popular media outlets such as Showtime continue to hype the revelatory capacities of wearable gadgets. And yet, the transgressive potential of these devices is at odds with the vagaries of the self-tracking industry that this book

explores, which is marked by breakdown, employment precarity, and entrepreneurial uncertainty. By concentrating on the experiences of those involved
in the business of self-tracking, and mainly on the work of US-based developers of wearable computing who participate in the international forum known as
the Quantified Self (QS), this book examines how technological ambition,
employment anxieties, and new forms of entrepreneurial sociality configure
contemporary commercial wearable devices and self-tracking applications. QS
offers a means of interfacing with these otherwise unseen business realities.
In evaluating how QS works as a community, that is, how the forum variously
reflects and sustains the work of those developing this technology, this book
surfaces the social conventions, occupational exigencies, and personal compromises that animate the possibilities and promises of a data-driven life.

Acknowledgements

This book represents the culmination of a long personal and intellectual journey, one whose roots extend in multiple directions. A significant portion of this journey can be traced back to the years I spent at Columbia University, a time marked by rigorous thinking, writing, and learning. It would be an understatement to say that I am deeply grateful for the intellectual environment at Columbia, which allowed me to cultivate a rich scholarly life. My years in the Department of Anthropology were transformative, expanding my thinking in ways I never would have imagined.

First and foremost, I am profoundly indebted to my dissertation advisor, Marilyn Ivy. Your mentorship has been invaluable throughout my time at Columbia and beyond. Your rigorous critique of my work and the thoughtful guidance you provided over the years have consistently pushed me to challenge myself as a scholar and grow as a writer. I also owe a debt of gratitude to my dissertation committee members for their steadfast support and constructive feedback, which played a crucial role in my early writing. This book owes much to their formative guidance. Brian, I am deeply appreciative of the many conversations we shared, where your door was always open for rich, stimulating dialogue. Your incisive commentary opened new avenues of thought and revitalized my writing at every turn. Nadia, your pointed questions and astute direction helped me refine and clarify my ideas. I am equally grateful for the thoughtful feedback from my external dissertation readers, Matthew Jones and Dennis Tenen. Your early input was instrumental in shaping my dissertation and continued to inform my thinking throughout the writing of this book. I must also acknowledge the Wenner-Gren Foundation for providing early research support that was pivotal in shaping the ideas and findings that inform this book.

Throughout the writing process, I also benefited from the expert guidance of five anonymous reviewers who provided insightful feedback at various stages of this project. Your keen suggestions were invaluable and helped me develop my ideas to their fullest. I am also grateful for the anonymous feedback from reviewers at *Anthropological Quarterly*, where an earlier version of Chapter 3 was published under the title 'The Data Multiple: Seeing Double in Digital Entrepreneurialism' in the Fall 2021 issue. Your expert feedback has had a lasting impact on this project as well. I am likewise grateful to the editors, content managers, and project managers at Cambridge University Press, particularly Lauren Cowles, whose feedback played a key role in refining this manuscript, Clare Dennison, Arman Chowdhury, and Dhivyabharathi Elavazhagan, who helped steer this book to publication, and Pete Gentry whose attention to detail and commitment to precision enhanced the quality of the final product. I additionally appreciate the sabbatical support from Drew University, which allowed me the time and space to focus on the final stages of writing. The intellectual conversations with my colleagues at Drew have further enriched this work and kept me motivated throughout the process.

I would not be where I am today without the early guidance of Timothy Malefyt, who first encouraged me to pursue anthropology and whose mentorship I've valued deeply over the years. I am also grateful to Robert Morais, whose support and mentorship have been instrumental in the ensuing years. Your guidance has provided me with both intellectual and personal direction, and I have benefited greatly from your wisdom. I am also truly thankful to my interlocutors in the tech sector, who made my research possible by taking the time to meet with me, engage in thoughtful discussions, and share their insights. I particularly appreciate the conversations and the encouragement from Dawn Nafus. Our early discussions, along with your writing, have influenced my own thinking. And a big thanks to my friend Mark Fox for helping me get started on this journey, not least with your incisive copy editing of an early version of this book.

Finally, I am profoundly thankful to my family for their support throughout this long journey. My sister, Emily Besidski, you have always been a sounding board for ideas. Your creative guidance and writing advice have been especially valuable during this process. My parents and my parents-in-law, thank you for your continued encouragement and, of course, for helping with my children so that I could focus on my writing. Biata Kekhman, your unwavering enthusiasm has been a constant source of encouragement. My grandmother, Gita Baytman, who has been a steady guide throughout my entire life – your boundless energy, strength, humor, and wisdom are always with me. To my partner in everything, Eugene Grinberg, thank you for always believing in me. And to my kids, Clara and Robert, you have been there from the very beginning, and I am constantly amazed by the smart, compassionate, and thoughtful young people you have become. I have learned so much from you and with you. You are my inspiration.

Introduction

The camera slowly scans Chris Dancy's face, first focusing on a profile of his bespectacled eyes, then quickly switching to a frontal shot to examine his contemplative expression at close range. Seconds later, the angle shifts again, the panorama now filmed as though from behind Dancy's shoulder. The foreground looks blurry to start with. But once the lens adjusts, the viewer clearly sees the nearby cityscape at which Dancy longingly gazes. All the while, the video sequence is layered with a voice-over in which Dancy intones predictions of a proximate digital future in a self-assured and measured baritone:

> Humans, over the next twenty years, will evolve into something greater than a biological species. We'll become part machine, part software, and part flesh. That simply means that we will be all connected at once. Right now, I am the world's most connected person. But you will be soon. We'll all be connected. Traditionally, the interface was a keyboard and mouse or screen. But over the last five years, we have been noticing that biology and behavior has become the interface. See, being connected isn't just about the things you put on your body to stay fit, it's about all the things in your life that you connect to ... knowingly, or unknowingly ... and your relationship with that information. In the future, we'll download habits and environments. We'll actually upgrade ourselves as we become apps. This digital duality that exists between "are you online or offline?" is something that's a relic of the past. We are all online all the time ... I believe this will happen in our lifetime. I believe we are entering not an Internet of Things but an Internet of Humanity. (Dancy, 2017)

The film is brief, only two minutes long. But at the point when credits would typically roll, the clip is revealed as an extended commercial for the Swedish telecommunications company Telia Carrier. "Carrier Declaration # 6: Power to the User" reads the penultimate frame before cutting to the company logo. The video's length indicates that it was intended for more casual and viral online

1

viewing rather than for scheduled TV ad placement that, given the steep price of airtime, rarely exceeds thirty seconds.

Telia Carrier released Declaration # 6 in 2017 as one part of a larger advertising campaign featuring technophiles like Chris Dancy as well as mavericks and daredevils such as domino artist Lily Havesh (Declaration # 1: Be a Control Freak) and Sven Yrvind (Declaration # 2: Challenge Everything). Havesh has attracted a large following with elaborate domino chain reaction videos that she films and shares online. Yrvind has earned accolades for crossing oceans in the world's smallest boats. As people who, according to company advertising, have all used telecommunication in unexpected ways to reach their goals, these record setters act as fitting ambassadors of the firm. Their extreme hobbies underscore that Telia Carrier is likewise located on the edges of technological possibilities, taking telecommunication to new lengths and uncharted territories.

Yet, even as Dancy anticipates the enduring quality of digital connections, the advertising campaign he starred in has not stretched quite as far. Telia Carrier, which has also since rebranded as Arelion, has by now taken the hyperlinks supporting the footage on its website offline. Advertising is a cyclical business, and major corporations develop new campaigns on an annual basis to guard against "wear out," the point at which commercials begin to loosen their grip on the fickle attention spans of potential consumers.

By placing this commercial on his personal website, Dancy has extended the film's promotional life and message. Here, it occupies a prominent place at the head of his "About" page, though it now mainly advertises Dancy himself. The video adds visual interest to the adjacent content summarizing Dancy's varied exploits, such as a short biography that introduces him as "the most connected man on earth." For impatient readers eager to cut to the chase, Dancy has also added a byline that includes some of his other credits: "Featured on Showtime's *Dark Net*, the cover of *Businessweek*, interviewed by the *Wall Street Journal, NPR*, the *BBC, Fox News* and *Wired*. Purveyor of *TED* talks. Subject of *TED* talks" (Dancy, 2017). Visitors may follow the web links embedded in the publication titles to read each piece in full. But for those rapidly scrolling through the content, an excerpted quote from NPR Marketplace set in bold and an oversized font screams the punchline: "You probably know someone like Chris Dancy, but not really. Chris Dancy is arguably the most quantified self in America, probably the world."

People like Dancy frequently figure in the popular press as emblems of a data-driven future, as those who simply operate on the leading edge of coming digital trends. I first learned about Dancy in just such an editorial and was equally intrigued by his apparent commitment to wiring himself with countless sensors and the voluminous digital records that this activity has produced as by the publicity he has garnered for these efforts.

This book focuses on the promises and failures of such digital connections. But it takes a slightly different tack in studying them. To date, the bulk of popular and academic commentary on the subject have concentrated on the social implications of these emerging digital practices.[1] And little wonder. Even though popular media outlets often paint Dancy's preoccupation with data as both rare and extreme, data collecting is an activity that has become mainstream. Until recently, credit cards, online browsing patterns, government censuses, and medical records have been the main sources of consumer, citizen, and patient information – archives that have largely been kept in specialty hands. Yet, affordable digital sensors have dramatically expanded the scope of information that a nonspecialist public can personally gather. In the United States, where the bulk of my ethnographic fieldwork has been based, it is now easy to find clothing, watches, and jewelry embedded with miniature biosensors that measure a seemingly expanding range of attributes, including blood glucose levels, stress, sleep quality, and mood. This set of devices is commonly described as wearables, or wearable technology (WT). Supplementing these are the sensors placed in objects of everyday use, such as refrigerators, coffee makers, mattresses, showers, cars, mirrors, and door locks, to name just a few, that collect information about one's whereabouts, household habits, and patterns of use. Such gadgets have become collectively known as the Internet of Things (IoT).[2]

This book shifts the lens to direct attention onto the makers of wearable and IoT tools to investigate the forms of labor and capital that organize contemporary self-monitoring technology and the digital imaginary. In particular, drawing on five years of ethnographic fieldwork with US-based developers of these applications and with those who participate in technophile forums such as the Quantified Self (QS), the book evaluates the work and influence of the people who introduce such gadgets into the social sphere. Chiefly, this monograph pursues two related goals: it looks to understand the world of digital professionals in the self-tracking arena through QS, and to examine QS as an effect and performance of the consumer wearables and IoT market. Dancy plays a vital role here, still. As "the most quantified self in America" if not "the world," he is not only an avid technology user who most vividly embodies the wired future, as popular and academic observers often emphasize. He is also an experienced information technology (IT) professional. Even his website indicates that his avowed commitment to self-monitoring is as promotional as it is personal. As the website catalogues his digital exploits, it also advertises his consulting services.

Technologists laboring in the self-tracking arena are guardians and care-takers of these devices in a compounded sense. They are people who create the digital ecosystems that support contemporary data gathering. They are also more than the makers and marketers of digital tools. Their beliefs about data, social views, perspectives on personal analytics, as well as their professional ambitions and anxieties affect how this technology becomes embedded into the everyday. Looking at the way technologists interact with and within QS offers valuable insight into the forms of work and desire that shape the business of self-tracking. Studying how their involvement with the forum intersects with the pressures and practices of the self-tracking market also offers novel means for engaging with the politics of digital representation and the transformations in digital entrepreneurialism that are shaping digital practices today. Doing so ultimately underscores the deeply qualitative, disorderly, and situated nature of digital tools.

Interfacing with Digital Entrepreneurialism

Digital professionals are notoriously difficult to study ethnographically. Not only does research with technologists generally require "studying up" (Nader, 1974 [1969]), but it often involves navigating professional settings protective of proprietary ideas and therefore wary of outsiders. As a result, the technology sector largely remains an empirical "black box" (Pasquale, 2015). Even those who can be considered industry "insiders" only ever enjoy limited and situated insight into corporate practices, and therefore they themselves continue to experience access as "a protracted, textured practice that never really ends" (Seaver, 2017).

Sherry Ortner (2010) has offered one solution to studying elite and ethnographically elusive spaces by theorizing a mode of research she has called, invoking a computer metaphor, "interface ethnography." Computers have long served as tools to think with, not just as instruments to work with. They have become "metaphors for the mind, for culture, for society, for the body, affecting the ways in which we experience and conceive of 'real' space," writes media scholar Wendy Hui Kyong Chun (2011, p. 65). In the context of computing, the interface typically describes a platform or a mechanism that allows people either direct access to computer functions or to servers located far away from the people using them. The graphical user interface (GUI), first used in a computer developed by Xerox PARC in 1973 but popularized by Apple in the 1980s, refers to the former. These companies developed the technology and iconography that computer users today largely take for granted: visual shortcuts such as folders, windows, and desktops to represent otherwise complex mechanical operations, thus allowing lay users to more easily engage with computer processes. The web interface describes what technologists often call the "front end" of computer programs, such as the app or web page that allows people to interact with information that is in fact located on distant servers. Although Ortner (2010) uses the term "interface" in a more general sense, she subtly draws on the computer interface for meaning. Interface ethnography, she writes, involves participant observation conducted "in the border areas where the closed community or organization or institution interfaces with the public" (p. 213). In other words, it connects researchers with otherwise inscrutable and difficult to reach subjects in the same way that computer interfaces proffer untrained users access to obscure and remote computer functions.

Ortner (2010) has turned to this style of research to study reclusive Hollywood. While she found it difficult to penetrate the rarefied settings that made up this industry discursively and spatially – the production studios, the movie sets, the exclusive celebrity circles – she was able to negotiate access to this protected sector through public functions such as screenwriting classes, film festivals, and industry panels that featured renowned actors, writers, and producers. These events provided "halfway" access to otherwise restricted professional environments (p. 219). Even though these sites were physically "disconnected," they remained "structurally/culturally connected" to what Ortner understood as the broader Hollywood "community" (p. 221).

In many ways, my work has likewise been enriched by participation in "halfway" activities where the technology industry presents itself to the public. Countless conferences, speaking engagements, and talks organized by industry insiders make it possible for outsiders like myself to interface with digital executives beyond their restricted workplaces. These events are often publicized through technologists' social media accounts. Typing keywords like "wearables," "self-tracking," "Internet of Things," and "personal data" into the search windows of event-organizing platforms such as meetup.com has put me in touch with an even larger number of workshops, seminars, presentations, and events staged by and for professionals in the wearables and self-tracking arena. Following Sherry Ortner, I attended dozens of such events in New York City, Boston, Washington, DC, and San Francisco between 2012 and 2017. I met many of my interlocutors in meetup groups.[3] In addition, I attended several industry conferences along the East and West Coasts centered on wearable computing and personal data, including Strata Hadoop NYC 2014 and 2015, Wearables and Things 2014, Wearables Tech Expo 2015, Wearables 2.0, KDD 2014 (Knowledge Discovery and Data), the Consumer

Electronics Show 2015 and 2016, and the Microsoft Hardware Workshop 2016. These experiences yielded connections that led to the opportunity to spend several weeks in the office of a small New York City startup working on developing a wearable device and to collaborate on a small project with another team working on a wearable prototype. These interactions were complemented by interviews with staff members – communication directors, developers, and marketing leads – of several other startup firms.

Gatherings of this sort – made all the more common by the growing popularity of event-organizing platforms such as meetup.com – are promotional as much as they are informational. Increasingly, they create the means for the expanding "entrepreneurial" digital workforce to foster business relationships, secure credentials, and even attract occasional media attention made necessary by a virtually connected but progressively fractured employment environment (see Martin, 1994; Rosenblat, 2018; also Chapter 4).[4] These venues provide access to computer engineers, product managers, data analysists, and entrepreneurs involved in the development of self-tracking tools as well as to the technological imaginary, professional challenges, and industry tensions that shape this work. My research with experts in these settings also rendered the concept of interface ethnography literal. Many of the people with whom I interfaced in forums such as these were tasked with developing the mechanical and metaphorical bridges between self-tracking technologies and their users. My interface ethnography involved fieldwork with those who create the computer interfaces through which people confront self-tracking devices, their personal data, and the world.

Among this set, QS, a global forum most often associated with digital enthusiasts and tech early adopters such as Dancy, has served as the principal interface with the help of which I negotiated the mechanics of the self-tracking market. A forum such as QS, however, is more than another keyhole through which to peer into a hard-to-see world. QS has offered distinct analytic advantages compared to the other set of industry activities I engaged with throughout my fieldwork. In contrast to the typically short-term and ad hoc business functions I've attended, the long-running and recurrent nature of QS activities has provided consistent and extended access to the beliefs and practices of those who shape our digital experiences. More, while most other forums I visited were explicitly promotional, spaces to openly advertise both devices and the people selling them, QS's reputation largely as a user community offered alternative ways to engage with technologists' perspectives, concerns, and professional predicaments. Participating in the goings-on of QS thus supplemented my engagements with official and sporadic industry functions that socialize the makers of self-tracking applications and wearable tools.

What an analysis of QS and its relationship to the tech sector makes possible to see is likewise of interest to how digital capitalism works more broadly. In this book, I interpret QS as a central network that manifests how the so-called quantified self technologies, as wearable and sensor-enabled devices have also come to be popularly known, operate and become situated by their makers. I also look to the forum as a pivotal instrument for processing the forms of performance, despair, and desire that animate the digital economy. Chiefly, QS serves as an interface between the public promises of self-tracking developers and the business dynamics that shape both the gadgets and the technologists making them. Interacting with the language, participants, and organizing activities of QS has thus helped me to place the often-critiqued glib and worrying public assertions about the functions of self-tracking applications and wearable gadgets issued by technologists elsewhere into the context of their makers' personal ambitions and professional challenges. It's for these reasons that, in contrast to Ortner who has viewed interface ethnography as research that skirts the edges of the field site, I have come to appreciate QS as a key portal to digital entrepreneurialism rather than only one of its many peripheral touch-points.

Establishing New Connections

Readers familiar with QS may first find the forum an unlikely interface with the conditions of possibility that make the self-tracking sector work. Commentators generally interpret QS in the following three ways. They see it as a digital trend with worrisome social effects and as a gathering of at times eccentric "early adopters" of wearable tools such as Chris Dancy. Or else, they approach it as a collective of motivated patients, citizen-scientists, and technologists who are operating on the margins of neoliberal health policies. This coverage shares a common focus: those examining the social implications of QS connect the collective with emerging patterns of device use, regarding it as a lens onto the varied challenges of the digital future and as a field site that proffers ethnographic access to the people already living it. Popular media, much like Talia Carrier did in its advertising, may only simplistically highlight the exotic quantity of such applications as they mark their inevitable quality. However, even as scholars offer more nuanced commentaries, they too emphasize the broad-reaching consequences of QS in a way that situates it largely as a social barometer rather than as a vector of the technology sector. In these accounts, QS is not inherently an interface but rather a social gathering of data fetishists and a methodological approach that refers to the practice of monitoring and measuring various aspects of one's life with self-tracking technology.

The books *The Quantified Self* by Deborah Lupton (2016) and *Self-Tracking* by Dawn Nafus and Gina Neff (2016) epitomize some of these scholarly positions. Nafus and Neff interpret QS as a grassroots community that has coalesced in the spaces opened up by neoliberal policies, particularly in the chasm created by inadequate healthcare that has compelled advocates, tinkerers, and frustrated patients to take their health into their own hands by digital means. Lupton, for her part, examines those who participate in forums such as QS as representatives of a more general and passive social type. The expression "quantified self," she argues, does not only characterize the organizing activities of tech aficionados. She adapts the phrase to describe more diffuse social tendencies. While Nafus and Neff discuss participation in the activities of QS as voluntary, driven more by a common exasperation with the limits of healthcare and people's desire to overcome them, Lupton uses the expression in this expanded sense as a provocation. She sees "quantified self" as a label that all people generating data increasingly wear, whether they want to or not. The "quantified self" thus appears in Lupton's work as a significantly more docile identity, one that generally characterizes technology users interpellated by an expanding number of opportunistic "quantapreneurs" developing self-monitoring tools.[5]

, Historians of science such as Rebecca Lemov (2017) have additionally explored the longer historical tail of such digital practices. In particular, Lemov has drawn a red thread between notational customs of personages such as Benjamin Franklin – an American polymath who often epitomizes the liberal, religious, economic, and scientific concept of the self-made and self-regulating man and who memorialized his pen-and-paper self-tracking habits in his autobiography – and the data-collecting practices of people like Chris Dancy. This work places Dancy's digital monitoring and his participation in the organizing activities of forums such as QS in the context of a wider history of the responsible and self-choosing subject. This account also highlights the specifically American character of modern digital enthusiasm as it stresses its connection with notions of self-sufficiency and the American ideal of the self-made man.

As Chapter 1 explores, Gary Wolf and Kevin Kelly, the two men who first coined the expression "quantified self" as a headline in 2007 when they were developing a story about trends in self-tracking for *Wired* magazine, a popular technology publication where they both worked as editors, and who have since built QS into an organized network of in-person meetings, conferences, and online discussion forums, readily invite and even set the tone for these associations, particularly in establishing QS as a gathering space for intrepid technophiles who continue to follow in the footsteps of historical figures such as Benjamin Franklin. The QS origins story reaffirms the expression as a handle that has helped to name the longstanding social interest in digital data that many, like Lupton, now see in deterministic terms: as all but inevitable. And it bolsters the representations of people like Dancy, who display a deep commitment to digital self-tracking, as forbearers of these trends. In interviews, Dancy often endorses this view himself. A 2014 article published by mashable.com, for example, quotes him as ominously proclaiming, "I'm just like you, but in the future" (Murphy, 2014b).

This popular and academic appraisal of QS and its participants has clear merit, especially as the latter often situate group activities within a social and historical framework that zooms out past its image as a quirky gathering of digital acolytes. This discourse has also consistently highlighted that plenty of QS participants have been patients, data activists, lawyers, nonbusiness aspirational computer nerds, athletes, and even people who don't use digital tools to track. It likewise bares noting that these accounts often do recognize the forum's connections with the tech sector. The idea that QS has been friendly to professionals and innovators in the self-tracking arena is indeed common knowledge. Not least because the group emerged from the heartland of the technology sector itself: Silicon Valley.

The associations between QS and the tech sector that I examine in this book, however, are of a different sort. While observers have focused attention on QS as an emblem of or as a gateway to a quickly approaching digital future with storied roots, these accounts typically don't dwell on the business dynamics that have manufactured it as a point of interest, even if they regularly acknowledge technologists as its regular fixtures. Discussions of QS therefore remain largely disconnected from broader realities of digital entrepreneurialism and the role forums such as QS have played within them.

Against the common sense of this analysis, I focus specifically on the experiences of technologists who have taken on a large share of the work associated with organizing and managing this collective as a "community." These are the contributors who have made it possible for me to interface with some of the central dynamics shaping the self-tracking market and digital practices today. This book also goes beyond an assessment of the group as a forum with techy appeal to examine it both as a product of digital capitalism and as one of its levers. In particular, by examining its connection to the tech sector, to the industry's concept of the consumer, and to the forms of labor that organize the digital economy, this book offers another way to understand why the forum has been endorsed as a meeting ground for technophiles. Looking at

QS in this way highlights the rise of what I call the *extracurricular entrepreneurs* and offers a more nuanced account of the manner in which digital fetishism overlaps with work in the tech sector. When thus evaluated as a gateway to the vagaries of digital labor, QS offers a unique vantage point from which to analyze the neoliberal, fragmented, and turbulent environment within which sensor-enabled tools are made.

Negotiating the Interface

Just like the computer interface, however, QS is not a straightforward mechanism for access. While technologists generally welcome the interface as an apparatus that has opened the computer up for use by a nonspecialist public, media scholars have expressed suspicion and anxiety over screens that regulate our everyday. Interfaces disguise politics, misrepresent intentions of their makers, and mask the conditions within which they were produced. While they gesture to a specific context and even reflect social values and constraints, they often remain mute on the actual labor powering their existence. Similarly, QS is not a direct lens to the key factors impacting the function and the social reception of contemporary self-tracking technology.

Media theorist Wendy Hui Kyong Chun (2011) is among the early scholars who have analyzed the interface as an instrument based only on the fantasy of direct manipulation. Although the interface remains "steeped in a nostalgic view of machines as transparent" (p. 75), she examines it as a navigational tool that inhibits control as much as it promotes it – that hides as much as it reveals. In particular, Chun relates the function of the interface to ideology. Like ideology, it produces its subjects; it interpellates people by hailing "you as a potential user of the system" (p. 83). So, while the interface facilitates interactions, it does so by regulating the terms of engagement. As a dissembling system of displays, it is additionally difficult to fully process. It may direct the gaze and stimulate the mapping of associations between people and machines, but its surfaces disconnect users from the mechanical, social, and political logics that organize it.

Chun presents her reading of the interface as "an argument against commonsense notions of software" rather than as a critique of software as such (2011, p. 92). In the book *Interface*, cultural theorist Brandon Hookway (2014) challenges this common sense further by exploring the additional contradictions of the interface as a mechanism of access. Hookway's project is as philosophical as it is historical, and it's one where he explores the interface as a "relation with technology rather than as a technology in itself" (p. ix). Like

Chun, he sees it as a mechanism that both enables and conditions agency. He also looks beyond the interface as a self-evident technology that simplifies human–machine interactions and examines it as a context-specific "entanglement of power, agency, and subjectivity" (p. 31) that remains conditioned by social, political, and economic realities. Importantly, Hookway recognizes the interface as a "disputed zone" (p. ix). Information channeled through the interface doesn't just flow freely from one side to the other as water does when conducted over an aqueduct. He interprets the interface as a border that acts as a "site of contestation between human beings and machines as much as between the social and the material, the political and the technological" (p. ix). Describing the interface as a threshold experience, Hookway stresses its liminal quality. He emphasizes its function as a technology of negotiation and transformation as much as translation.

I draw on these scholarly interventions to think about additional qualities of QS as an interface to the self-tracking market. In my reading, QS is not only an industry-adjacent forum that acts as a convenient ethnographic access point to otherwise elusive tech sector insiders. Nor is it simply a figurative screen that brazenly puts wearable entrepreneurialism on display. QS is a prism that constructs as it refracts digital knowledge and offers alternative perspectives on the dynamics that power the development of self-tracking tools. Analyzing QS in this way has allowed me to understand how this forum both refracts and creates some of the rhetorical, social, and professional connections necessary to make wearables entrepreneurialism work.

For example, like the computer interface that negotiates the relationship between device users and internal computer functions, I argue that QS serves as an interface between technologists' aspirations and practices. Chapters 2 and 3 explore these dynamics by analyzing how the notion that QS constitutes a community of people invested in digital self-tracking has both sustained and screened out technologists' broader relationship to data, digital representation, and the imagined users of these devices.

The disjuncture between ambition and application is already audible in the contrasts between technologists' public commentaries on the body, which they themselves at times compare to the computer interface, and the more complex perspectives on personal data and corporeality that often surface in candid conversations. On the one hand, it's common to hear digital professionals describe the body, the skin, or as Dancy has put it in the transcript that opened this chapter, "biology and behavior," as both literal and figurative interfaces that facilitate communication between machines and people. A commentary published in an industry report prepared by a New York market research firm PSFK offers another instance of this manner of speaking:

With the emergence of smaller, more advanced sensors, the opportunity to embed technology in clothing allows for an integrated approach. If you think of the *skin as an interface*, clothing becomes the instrument to communicate with the body. This creates an unobtrusive and intelligent design, minimizing distraction. By integrating technology in clothing, it no longer serves as an intrusion, creating a seamless flow of communication. As a result, the wearer experiences a deeper connection with themselves. (Whitehouse, 2016, emphasis mine)

A wearable device developer I met at a tech conference further explained the benefit of apparel with embedded sensors: "Clothing is already something that is very intimate," he observed. "Now, what if clothing could communicate as a friend to tell you about moments you were not aware of?"[6]

Such talk connects wired outfits and accessories with interpersonal intimacy. In these examples, the skin as an interface also serves a dual function. It links bodies with "smart" wearable devices as much as it offers people direct connections with their own "biology and behavior." In these configurations, the skin is described as an interface that conducts information across borders much like the computer interface is popularly viewed as an entry point to obscure technological processes for lay computer users (see also Ruckenstein and Pantzar, 2017). Fetishizing the skin as an interface allows devices placed on or near to the body to be hyped as providing, as the PSFK article claims, "a seamless flow of communication" without obstruction. The physical proximity of wearable devices to one's body is also an element that connotes emotional closeness, resulting in descriptions of wearable tools as objects that come to know someone "personally."[7]

These invoked human–machine interactions are both familiar and new. They once again mechanize the body while humanizing technology (Rabinbach, 1992; Crary, 1999).[8] And in doing so, they ascribe more agency to devices than to the people using them.[9] Yet, these industry perspectives also represent a departure from the way engineers or artists developing early WT at the tail end of the twentieth century and at the start of the twenty-first initially conceptualized these gadgets. For example, members of the MIT Lab "Borg" club, such as engineers Steve Mann and Thad Starner, first saw promise in the conspicuous nature of bulky wearables and proudly wore their gear as armor.[10] The more irreverent ideas developed by technologists and fashion designers in the decades that followed were also conceived as playthings that facilitated entrance into the extraordinary (Ryan, 2014). Cultural theorist Anne Cranny-Francis has noted that for these inventors, the period constituted a "straight-out erotics of power . . . which offered . . . freedom from mundane physical reality" (Cranny-Francis, 2008, p. 267, quoted in Ryan, 2014, p. 70). Today, technologists commenting on the social potential of wearable devices instead aim to minimize visibility of these devices so as to amplify their impact. "Once you have more than one thing, you start to look like, you know, Batman. It's a little disruptive," noted one digital executive I interviewed.[11] Thus adorned, the person's body becomes a caricature rather than an informatics conduit. In his opinion, shared by many others, only technology that disappears from view and thus becomes "invisible" can properly channel personal information.

Critical data scholars frequently emphasize that such remarks reveal digital professionals as people who share only liberal and positivist understandings of data and corporeality (Lupton, 2013; Jurgenson, 2014; Morozov, 2014). From these perspectives, forums such as QS, whose tagline after all plainly calls for "Knowledge through Numbers," only epitomize the reductive social imaginations of those using these devices as they reflect the limited perspectives of those selling them. The idiosyncrasies of the technology sector, however, contravene such neat divisions, as Chapter 2 explores. Looking beyond the popular language digital executives use to describe both bodies and data and at the more candid discussions that take place in forums such as QS helps to reveal that wearable devices and personal information take shape in the tension of professional ambitions, commercial imperatives, and entrepreneurial anxieties. If skin has become an "interface," as developers at times have claimed, I evaluate how these developers do not just approach skin as an unproblematic conduit that can neatly interact with digital devices placed on its surface. They understand data and the bodies that produce them as inherently contested and multiple.

QS likewise serves as an interface between technologists and the technology sector itself. The interface, as Hookway highlights, does not only connect people with machines; it refers to a site of negotiation between people. Similarly, I look at QS as one mechanism through which device makers negotiate the professional arena. For participating technologists, the forum acts as a threshold experience. It renders their labor compatible with the demands and challenges of digital work. In the processes of making compatible, QS regulates appearances as it brings opposing forms of expression into communication and into service of one another. QS thus affects necessary transformations.

For example, as Chapter 3 examines closely, the notion that QS chiefly brings together self-tracking aficionados that has shaped its status as a community in the popular and academic imaginations is not just at odds with the practical realities of QS as a forum that convenes large numbers of technologists producing these gadgets. The staging of QS as a hobby rather than as a professional community has a meaningful role in the business sector itself. It facilitates the conversion of self-tracking devices from "solutions in search of a problem" into gadgets that are responding to observable consumer demand. As Chapter 4 elaborates, technologists "hustling with a passion" benefit from the forum's hobbyist framing in other ways as well. As a collective that putatively fosters and showcases digital enthusiasm, QS helps transform the extracurricular activities of those working in the technology sector into vehicles of entrepreneurial passion that has become increasingly necessary for professional success.

Chapters 5 and 6 explore additional associations between QS and the tech sector. On the one hand, forums such as QS play an important social function for a flexibly and insecurely employed workforce for whom QS provides access to vital opportunities for networking, reputation building, and credentialing. Indeed, the relationships and connections that participants come to form through their engagements with this forum offer support in a capricious digital market. On the other hand, when QS acts as a mechanism of professional self-realization, it helps to further press worker sociality and desire into the service of tech capitalism as it subtly regulates who can and cannot take advantage of QS as an instrument of career development. These chapters act as an interface to the troubled promises of inclusion that affect the organizing activities of QS, digital labor, and the way self-tracking devices work.

Has Digital Critique Run Out of Steam?

As I analyze how technologists developing wearables and IoT devices leverage QS to configure notions of data and transform digital self-monitoring into meaningful work, my research serves as an interface between recent debates within digital anthropology and critical data studies, and the practical realities of the self-tracking market. The contemporary proliferation of data and data-monitoring devices has certainly drawn enormous scholarly attention. The bulk of this analysis, however, has remained focused on the societal impact of digital tools that are perceived as equal parts formidable and inept, rather than on the entrepreneurial settings and frameworks that continue to produce these tools.

One crucial vector of this critique, and one that has received the lion's share of media attention, is scholarship addressing questions of privacy. In these studies, Jeremy Bentham's figure of the panopticon continues to loom large. Bentham's design called for prison cells to be arranged around an observation tower to create the sense that the actions of prisoners were perpetually surveilled by a guard whether anyone occupied the post or not. Theorists concerned with privacy in the digital "age" use this image to suggest that those who routinely use digital devices now sit in the position of the prisoner: our actions are similarly perpetually at risk of scrutiny by an invisible witness. David Lyon, the premier scholar of surveillance studies, warned as early as 1994 that increased computing capacities have drastically improved mechanisms of surveillance. "Precise details of our personal lives are collected, stored, retrieved, and processed every day within huge computer databases belonging to big corporations and governments," he wrote in the aptly titled book *Electronic Eye: The Rise of Surveillance Society* (p. 3). The questions Lyon raised three decades ago at the dawn of personal computing have only intensified in recent years with the spread of wearable and self-tracking devices. Under the premise that someone – or something – could always be watching virtually every action of every day, theorists have raised alarm at the way improved computing and processing power has produced capabilities for people to be monitored with growing precision and continuity, and on a vastly enlarged scale (Richards and King, 2013; Dijck, 2014; Beer, 2018). Media scholars Finn Brunton and Helen Nissenbaum (2015) have thus proposed that strategies of "obfuscation" now offer the only refuge for people subject to perpetual digital monitoring. Given that most of these tools are developed by private companies and not public government entities, legal scholars have also expressed concern that the mechanisms powering social surveillance are shifting further away from civic discourse or critique (Pasquale, 2015).

The uses to which powerful corporate conglomerates or government entities increasingly put personal data of ordinary, and especially of vulnerable, citizens are necessary to think about. However, data do not capture nor transcribe experience unproblematically. The personal information that digital devices now produce continues to be shaped by history, politics, and social perceptions. A number of studies have therefore examined the social nature of data-driven bodies, building as they have done so on research within anthropology of the body that has long demonstrated that somatic experience is as social as it is biological. Scholars working in this vein have considered how self-monitoring tools produce the "self-as-database" (Schüll, 2016, p. 8), construct an "informed body" (Viseu and Suchman, 2010), or configure "algorithmic identities" around parameters stipulated by advertisers (Cheney-Lippold, 2011). This literature resonates with concerns of scholars who connect digital monitoring with the growing rise of surveillance and biopolitical regimes. Yet, in continuing to explore digitized bodies and selfhoods as man-made constructs, this scholarship only further emphasizes that "raw data is an oxymoron" (Gitelman, 2013).

A related body of work has also considered that information systems and wearable devices produce more than algorithmically regulated subjects. For instance, authors attentive to the social life of data have documented the complicated and the oftentimes "ambivalent" (Schüll, 2016, 2019; Ruckenstein and Schüll, 2017; Kristensen and Ruckenstein, 2018) agency of digital device users. Challenging narratives of certain digital control, this work points to the multiple shortcomings and affordances of machines (Nafus and Neff, 2016), the frequent inconsistencies implicit in device use (Ruckenstein, 2014; Lazar et al., 2015; Elsden et al., 2016; Tamar and Zandbergen, 2017), as well as the different ways creative use of data by individuals inevitably subverts technologists' biopolitical aims (Ellerbrok, 2011; Nafus and Sherman, 2014). As this literature reclaims user agency, it also calls attention to what many feel data professionals seem unable to acknowledge: that "real data is all leaks, or better put: real data is all context" (Dumit and Nafus, 2018, p. 270).

Relatively few studies, however, have ethnographically explored the professional settings where these devices – and ideas about digitization – are constructed. Several scholars have of course already considered the "institutional context" within which digital data circulate and take shape (Christin, 2020) and the "ways in which organizational histories become embedded in the objects ... [technologists] create and produce" (Flynn, 2010, p. 42). An additional set of studies has also focused on the spaces adjacent to the office, such as the university programs where data scientists are trained (Lawrie, 2019), or on the freelance labor of those toiling in the shadows of algorithmic processes (Rosenblat, 2018; Gray and Suri, 2019; Irani, 2019). As these projects examine "designers and design process" (Schüll, 2012, 2016; Berg, 2017; Ruckenstein and Schüll, 2017; Knox and Nafus, 2018), they open up fresh opportunities to evaluate professional settings that are otherwise decried as impenetrable and opaque.

My research complements and builds on these emerging debates. By highlighting the layered relationship of technologists to data and the self-tracking market, I emphasize how people contribute to the workings of seemingly impersonal and automated technological systems. This work therefore further stresses that digital devices can only ever produce "partial truths" (Clifford, 1986), that is, situated and incomplete information rather than irrefutable facts. This study additionally looks beyond the office or the data-science classroom to evaluate the impact of extracurricular activities, such as QS, on the way tech executives facilitate and agitate for the data-driven future. My research also responds to an empirical shortage. Despite the growing scholarly attention to professional settings in which contemporary digital devices are made, there still exist few book-length accounts of the way "experts make and remake data," as Hannah Knox and Dawn Nafus recognize in the introduction to their edited volume *Ethnography for a Data-Saturated*

World (2018, p. 11). This book offers an extended ethnographic study of the experts creating self-tracking technology and the industry dynamics that affect their work.

This monograph likewise aims to overcome a familiar analytic divide. Critical data scholarship largely continues to maintain a rigid boundary between those who produce and work with data in the commercial sphere and those who either use wearable devices in daily life or critique their operations in the academic domain. Following a mode of analysis that first emerged in science studies (see Latour, 1988; Bourdieu, 1999 [1975]; Cetina, 1999), this literature tends to expose those who professionally engage with data as unwitting participants in the production of fictions and as naive operators who believe that they are constructing undisputed facts. Technologists' seemingly simplistic views on digitization are then placed in stark contrast to the vital complexity introduced by ordinary device users or by scholars in the social sciences and the humanities. And often, academic contributors inaugurate only themselves as people capable of seeing intricate assemblages and webs of significance, or of fanning out the practical multiplicity of only apparently stable and fixed people and things. Scholarly accounts thus become the chief interface between the narrow views held by digital professionals and the more nuanced realities of digital practices.

But, to paraphrase Bruno Latour, this mode of digital critique may have presently run out of steam. Latour asks the related question, "Why Has Critique Run Out of Steam?" in a 2004 essay that responds to the larger threat of conspiracy theorists who even then were beginning to adopt the doubting posture of the critical social scientist. Rather than wholly condemn the appropriation, however, Latour wonders if it is the expected function of critique, not just its proper messenger, that needs to be addressed as well. At one point, he even sarcastically if matter of factly highlights the absurdity of scholarly analysis that sharpens boundaries between critics and their subjects. Satirizing what he sees as a preposterously lofty position of those who believe that their chief role is to debunk the theories wrongly held by others, Latour writes: "When naïve believers are clinging forcefully to their objects, claiming that they are made to do things because of their gods, their poetry, their cherished objects, you can turn all of those attachments into so many fetishes and humiliate all the believers by showing that it is nothing but their own projection, that you, yes you alone, can see" (p. 239). While social scientists writing in this vein have long worked to deduct misguided thinking, Latour suggests that the better strategy may be to add something. Echoing his broader work, he advocates for scholarship that resurfaces rather than severs connections, for work that multiplies associations even between critics and their subjects. "The critic," Latour concludes, "is not the one who debunks, but the one who assembles" (p. 246).

My work is invested in establishing new connections between critical data scholarship and digital entrepreneurialism by demonstrating that more complicated professional agency is at stake in the making of commercial wearables and in the management of their futures. With QS acting as a central interface to volatile entrepreneurial dynamics, this book reconciles the business conventions, compromises, shifting labor practices, and growing employment insecurities that power the self-tracking market with device makers' often simplistic promotional claims to better understand the impact that technologists exert on digital discourse, on the tools they make, and on the data that these gadgets put out into the world. In thus leveraging QS as a key mechanism for engaging with tech executives, their ongoing predicament, and their social influence, this book hopes to bridge some of the scholarly divide between analysts and digital practitioners.

Structure of the Work

To begin evaluating the interaction of "quantified self," the concept, and Quantified Self, the collective, with digital entrepreneurialism, it's necessary to first understand the influence of QS's originators, Kevin Kelly and Gary Wolf, on this construct's form and function. Chapter 1 reviews how the two writers have coined the term quantified self and established the group as an expression of what Wolf has called the "culture of personal data" (Wolf, 2009). While the founders defer to the explanatory power of culture in situating the collective within the technological imaginary, this chapter examines how their own personal backgrounds as journalists and *Wired* magazine editors have shaped the semantic meaning of "quantified self" as a catchphrase that refers to the means and outputs of digital self-tracking and especially to QS as a community of technophiles. Although the role the forum has come to play within the commercial self-tracking sphere analyzed in this book does not fully align with its originators' intentions, the framing they established has set the tone for many of the ways the collective has become socialized in the technological arena as well as how it has come to work within it.

The three chapters that follow broadly explore how the concept of the "quantified self" as a trope of personal data and the notion that QS primarily constitutes a user community "interoperates," to use a tech industry term, with the sector's notion of the technology user, personal data, and technologists' own parameters of professional identity. Chapter 2, for example, looks closely at the way digital executives talk about data in forums such as QS, among others. These exchanges reveal the contradictions, professional obfuscations, and hyperbole that continue to shape the self-tracking sector. Digital professionals may occasionally enfold concepts such as "the quantified self" into promotional "pitch theater" to stage self-monitoring devices as gadgets that produce faithful and objective data. My interactions with practitioners in these settings, however, point to the more varied social, legal, and fiscal advantages professionals reap from representing digital self-tracking and the data these devices produce as both plastic and precise. This chapter argues that the surface impression that technologists relate to data and modes of self-monitoring in reductive terms has to be weighed against ways tech executives pursue both digital ambiguity and objectivity as a meaningful corporate strategy.

Chapters 3 and 4 investigate QS as a collective that more specifically exemplifies some of the novel forms of sociality that support digital entrepreneurialism. These chapters analyze QS as one of a growing cadre of social devices that press worker sociality and desire into service of tech capitalism. In particular, these chapters examine QS as an interface that connects extracurricular entrepreneurs hustling with a passion with two figures central to the self-tracking sector: the desirous consumer for whom digital professionals innovate, and the devoted entrepreneur whose impassioned labor sustains this work.

Chapter 3 details how business executives have interacted with QS as a site that materializes a particular consumer "segment" and consumer "demand" in ways that accord with the often binary and voyeuristic principles of consumer-centric design. QS offers visibility into ways technologists produce the distance they seek between themselves and their customers. However, the manner in which they interact with the forum also testifies to the involved role digital professionals frequently play in formulating consumer desire.

The participation of tech executives in collectives such as QS likewise belies their intentions to occupy the position of a professional participant observer who is simply looking in on an emerging social scene. Chapter 4 looks at the way technologists have leveraged QS to cultivate a professional identity of a digital devotee. In particular, this chapter analyzes how the popular staging of QS as a space for private explorations of self-tracking makes it possible for technologists to recoup their business-driven engagements with the forum as hallmarks of their personal, not just of a more general, passion for self-quantification. Innovation is often enough framed as a product of masculinized heroics and individual acts of daring. Examining QS as an instrument of professional development refocuses attention on the feminized modes of free and affective labor that continue to move the tech industry forward. As these chapters explore the forum both as a mechanism and as a mirror of these professional imperatives, they highlight the knottier role desire plays in the digital economy.

The remaining chapters analyze QS as a device that further renders the labor of tech executives compatible with the demands of digital work and in the process creates new associations between technologists, tech hobbyists, and wearable gadgets. Chapter 5, for example, investigates "seamlessly" networked self-tracking tools as symbols of idealized professional mobility and looks to QS as a forum that responds to and registers these business challenges and ambitions. Technologists tend to fetishize frictionless digital mobility. Conversations with digital professionals who participate in forums such as QS indicate, however, that the appeal of well-networked devices speaks less to the emerging realities of WT or to consumer "needs and wants" (a concern thematized in Chapter 3) than to the ideals of lasting and sustainable tech sector careers that are often punctuated by instability and breakdown. These are the additional entrepreneurial desires that motivate the making of self-tracking technology and become inadvertently embedded in its design. QS also acts as a practical source of mutual aid that facilitates the desired connectivity and agility of working bodies. This chapter thus investigates QS as an interface that reconciles the technological fantasy and its repetitious recital with the difficulties tech executives themselves face in their personal lives and professional work.

Chapter 6 ultimately analyzes QS as a gateway to the notions of difference that continue to shape the tech sector and therefore the devices that derive from it. As it considers the structural inequality that still constrains technological innovation, this chapter also analyzes QS as a site more specifically connected to the forms of privilege that impact how entrepreneurial extracurricular labor is converted into business advantage. It emphasizes that the modalities of participation that have rendered QS a community of tech acolytes unevenly regulate who can benefit from the group's role as an instrument of professional transfiguration, connection, and access.

In the Conclusion, I consider how QS has evolved since I completed my research in 2017. The composition and social function of this collective have been partially reshaped by its original organizers who have continued to focus group activities on citizen science and academic research. Groups such as QS have also been affected by the COVID-19 pandemic, which has altered the nature and function of in-person post-work socializing more broadly. Nevertheless, the industry practices, challenges, and promises refracted through the QS interface in this book remain germane as they speak to some of the central dynamics that continue to impact the self-tracking market and the devices that emanate from it, if now in a different guise.

Makers of wearable and self-tracking applications are often criticized in popular and academic domains for conceiving of digital connections as unduly enduring and strong. By contrast, this monograph explores the multiple forms of insecurity and failure that shape entrepreneurial imaginations and digital possibilities. In particular, in analyzing QS as an interface between confident entrepreneurial assertions and the practical challenges of digital work, the book illuminates how technologists often knowingly invest in and work to stave off digital ambiguity as they seek to profitably operate in the tension between clarity and doubt. Viewed through this prism, the purported hubris of these professionals and their reputed blind faith in the stability of the data-driven future dissipate. Instead, the digital connections technologists make return as fragile and fraught.

1

Quantified Self and the Culture of Personal Data

The origin of the Quantified Self (QS) offers one important framework for understanding this "community" as a central interface with the self-tracking market. This chapter examines how QS was first established as a window onto the digital future and as a hub for self-tracking acolytes. This history provides an entry point for analyzing how this forum has come to interact with the digital arena to situate its function as a lens that reflects the tech sector's inner workings.

As Gary Wolf, an amiable and soft-spoken journalist, has frequently described it, QS emerged from discreet beginnings. It was initially conceived as a caption in 2007 when he and Kevin Kelly were exploring emerging trends in digital self-tracking for a magazine story. "Geolocation, individualized social media, analytics, the availability of processing capacity, and really small packages that people could use personally" were all things that started gaining traction in the first decade of the twenty-first century, Wolf noted when I interviewed him and asked about the group's genesis (Wolf, 2016). To get a better grasp on these early initiatives and to sharpen the angle through which they planned to write about them, they first tackled the title for the pending article, ultimately settling on the expression "Quantified Self" as a headline placeholder.

This was a standard "journalistic practice," Wolf explained.

> Very often when you're talking about an idea for a story, you do ask, well, "what's the headline like?" ... And so "quantified" is really a synonym, in a way, for computing. Quantified is the language of computing – explicit. Quantified means explicit, and formal, in some sense – technological. And then "self" is the synonym for personal. And it's very ambiguous and really useful in that way. So, when we put that name on it, in a sense and I think, in fact I know, I was the one to say the name first, but it wasn't with the sense of "I now pronounce the name," it was more like, "OK, that's a terrible name for a thing but it's a descriptive name for what we're doing." (Wolf, 2016)

Initially, to catalogue the "tracking systems popping up almost daily," they also registered quantifiedself.com as a website, as Wolf later narrated in the article "Know Thyself: Tracking Every Facet of Life, from Sleep to Mood to Pain, 24/7/365" that was published in *Wired* magazine in 2009. However, they quickly recognized that self-monitoring technology was not the main story. Rather, the burgeoning quantity of gadgets collecting lifestyle and bio data indicated to them that a *"new culture of personal data* was taking shape," as he noted in the same publication (Wolf, 2009, emphasis mine). This new culture, according to Wolf, was marked by a seemingly unlikely social enthusiasm for metrics. In this first expose, he explained it this way:

> For a long time, "to be turned from warm flesh into cold arithmetic" was considered "a terrible thing . . . But two years ago, my fellow *Wired* writer Kevin Kelly and I noticed that many of our acquaintances were beginning to do this terrible thing to themselves, finding clever ways to extract streams of numbers from ordinary human activities."

From the perspectives of its founders, QS transformed from a news story and into a "community" of technophiles at the forefront of the culture of personal data in 2008, when Wolf and Kelly decided to bring a few people together for a conversation about emerging techniques and technologies of self-monitoring at Kelly's Pacifica, California, home (Wolf, 2016). "Come share your experiences/tools/advice about self-tracking, self-experiment, life-logging, personal data collection. Feel free to bring devices you are using, questions you have, or technical problems in need of solution," read the initial announcement (Wolf, 2008). That first gathering was received with enthusiasm and initiated a set of conversations that spilled out beyond a magazine article. Kevin Kelly left a note on the QS meetup page opening the door for a follow-up gathering, writing, "I was blown away by the energy and fire-power of this group of pioneers. I learned tons, and more importantly, wanted to hear from each of you. Will have to do that again. Thanks to all for making the trip to Pacifica."

Arrangements were soon made to meet again in the Bay Area, and Steven Dean suggested starting a similar discussion group on the East Coast. By now, speaking about how QS went from a single gathering convened in Kelly's house to a "community," a sprawling "movement" even, of self-tracking advocates who regularly assemble in more than 100 chapters in as many cities across the United States and abroad has become a cornerstone of the QS story, one typically recounted for participants at each new QS event.

Wolf and Kelly may point to the explanatory power of culture to account for the attention and interest the forum has received from the start, and characterize the technologically curious that they have assembled as something of a discovery. They may at times even attribute agency to the name itself, as Wolf on one occasion did when he stressed the moniker's gravitational pull:

> That name just became … it did a ton of work. And it still does a lot of work. And the ambiguity of the name. The fact that it puts two things together that in a way are not supposed to be together, but that in a way are very much together in our lives – technology, computing, formal expression, data, with self, personal. That's the work. (Wolf, 2016)

In this retelling, the opposing polarities of the words "quantified" and "self," terms that reenact the apparent conflict between "objective" data and "subject-ive" experience, were what drew people in as though by some invisible force, and, as he told me at another point in our conversation, attracted those "who want that and share that point of view to come towards that name" (Wolf, 2016). Echoing Wolf's framing of QS both as a captivating concept with its own force field and as a label that unified otherwise discreet activities, one QS participant explained to me, "Self-tracking was an idiosyncratic habit, but in naming it, it became a practice as well as a community. By naming it, Gary Wolf and Kevin Kelly brought an entire community to light" (Peter, 2015). Another described QS as a serendipitous idea that gained traction because its originators just happened to "hit a cultural nerve of sorts" (John, 2016).

Certainly, the act of naming does a lot of work, as these comments highlight. Yet its impact is also different than what the forum's organizers and observers often emphasize. For one, these commentaries overlook that naming is itself a creative action, one that blends recognition with invention (Butler, 1997; Markell, 2003). More, the QS origins story obscures that naming does not happen in a vacuum. It is a social event conditioned by its broader context. If the name did a lot of work, it was not simply because Wolf and Kelly effectively labeled a set of practices that were already there. In recognizing digital self-tracking as a burgeoning trend and in giving these tendencies a name, the two journalists helped to constitute as much as to note QS as a phenomenon on the rise. In particular, as this chapter describes, its force as a concept that characterized a specific orientation toward personal data and one that signaled some of the early appeal of self-tracking was shaped and sus-tained by Wolf and Kelly's shared utopic cyber-imaginary, their professional roles as detached purveyors of stories, their specific deployment of the concept of "culture," as well as the formal structure they established for QS-themed activities. Interfacing with this history provides one way to address the col-lective's influence within the tech sector and, vis-à-vis this position, to lever-age QS as a lens onto the organizing dynamics and travails of digital entrepreneurialism.

By examining some of the origins of QS as a construct and as a community, and especially the mediating influence of its founders, Gary Wolf and Kevin Kelly, we can begin to understand QS less as an auspicious sign of an emerging or of a hitherto submerged culture of personal data but more as a product and as an instrument of the technology sector itself. As the ensuing chapters will explore, it is when configured as an idea connected to digital enthusiasm that QS attracts technologists whose participation and commentary offers insights into the ways digital practitioners conceive of digitization and imagine their consumers as they work to function profitably in the gaps in knowledge, in the spaces between certainty and truth. It is also when articulated as a community of digital acolytes that QS interacts with the forms of entrepreneurial sociality that mediate the contemporary technological arena and thus reflects the larger value of social and digital connections in the digital economy.

Branding QS

Wolf and Kelly may present their roles as originators of QS humbly, mostly as well-placed media professionals who offered an effective "descriptive name" and a stage for social and technological processes well on their way. However, in recognizing and publicizing QS as a community of self-tracking acolytes, they have also followed a well-trodden techno-utopian path first forged by the writer and Silicon Valley luminary Stewart Brand.[1] Brand's vision of computing and manner of working partially shaped Wolf and Kelly's rollout and informal branding of QS, ultimately determining some of its tech industry function.

Brand is best known as the editor of the *Whole Earth Catalog*, as the convener of the early virtual forum the Whole Earth 'Lectronic Link (WELL), and ultimately as the co-founder of the now popular technology magazine *Wired*. His influence, however, extends beyond publishing. Historian Fred Turner credits him with transforming the computer, which was formally a bureaucratic tool, into a valued personal device by fueling and consolidating the technological imaginations of a group of "libertarian, lifestyle tinkerers" that Turner has called the "New Communalists" (2008).

As Turner writes, for much of the 1960s and the 1970s, computers "loomed as technologies of dehumanization, of centralized bureaucracy and the rationalization of social life" (Turner, 2008, p. 2). Youth groups in particular widely denounced Cold War–era technocracy inaugurated by cyberneticians two decades earlier. In 1964, students even took to the streets of the University of California, Berkeley, to condemn the calculative logic heralded by mid-century computers. "I am a UC student. Please do not fold, bend, spindle or mutilate me," one person wrote on a posterboard to register his rejection of the bureaucratic mechanism that increasingly reduced people to numbers, to little more than information patterns in a machine (Turner, 2008, p. 2).

By organizing what Turner has called "a network forum – spaces where members of these communities came together [and] exchanged ideas and legitimacy" (Turner, 2008, p. 72) – Brand reshaped these sentiments and united the New Communalists around a cybernetic technological imaginary. The New Communalists joined the New Left in vocally denouncing hierarchical structures and bureaucratic control. They were young adults who aimed to embody the romantic American frontier mentality by literally taking to what they imagined were the edges of civilization as they retreated to communes spread across the United States. Yet, following Brand, they also heartily embraced technology as a means of transforming their lives. As they read the works of cyberneticists like Norbert Wiener and Buckminster Fuller and of media theorists such as Marshal McLuhan disseminated by Brand, they began to embrace a "cybernetic vision of the world, one in which material reality could be imagined as an information system" (Turner, 2008, p. 5). Spurred by these ideas, they started to see promise in cybernetic concepts of information. For this group, Turner writes, "the cybernetic notion of the globe as a single, interlinked pattern of information was deeply comforting" (p. 5). Cybernetics offered them a "vision of a world built not around vertical hierarchies and top-down flows of power, but around looping circuits of energy and information" (p. 38). While they first induced this alternate consciousness through unconventional communal living arrangements, drugs, and music, with Brand's guidance, the New Communalists came to seek the experience of disembodiment and unity in the workings of computer technology itself.

In the manner of Benedict Anderson's (1983) "imagined community," Brand's network forums initially took shape textually. He built early enthusiasm around cybernetic ideas through the publication of the *Whole Earth Catalog* in the 1960s, where he circulated reading lists alongside articles about new gadgets. Even when the *Catalog* ceased publication in 1972, Brand continued to bring innovators, technophiles, and the countercultural credo together through the quarterly *Whole Earth Review* (a publication that Brand started in the 1980s to revive his iconic catalogue in magazine form), and later virtually, through the WELL. By 1993, he had taken this worldview – one that media theorists Richard Barbrook and Andy Cameron (1996) later termed "Californian ideology" – to *Wired* magazine, which he had co-founded together with Kevin Kelly, one of his early hires at the *Whole Earth Review*.

Brand's influence on the technological imaginary was as impactful as it was long-lasting. Turner notes that he had offered "key frames through which both the public and professional technologists sought to comprehend the potential social impact of information and information technologies" (Turner, 2008, p. 6). It was through materials and products circulated by Brand that cybernetic ideas about personal computing and the disembodied nature of information eventually entered popular discourse. By the 1980s, as smaller computers that could be used in the home flooded the market, the imagery of technological disembodiment emerged as the central conceptual frame of this technology, an idea that later extended to the World Wide Web. Under Brand's influence, these machines were welcomed both as other-worldly and decidedly intimate.

The way Wolf and Kelly positioned themselves, self-tracking, and QS in the public domain bears the distinct hallmarks of Brand's legacy. They clearly subscribed to Brand's techno-utopian, collectivist vision. Kelly in particular has built a career eulogizing the internet as a "collective hive mind" (Kelly, 1994) as he followed in Brand's footsteps. In the 1999 book *New Rules for the New Economy: 10 Radical Strategies for a Connected World*, he continued to enthusiastically, if now anachronistically, summarize the looming implications of a digitally connected future, writing: "The net is not just humans typing at one another on AOL, although that is a part of it and will be as long as seduction and flaming are enjoyable. Rather, the net is the total collective interaction of a trillion objects and living beings, linked together through air and glass" (Kelly, 1999, p. 13). Kelly's writing persistently highlighted the unifying nature of online interactions that, as it were, tended toward community-building as though by default. Wolf held similarly idealistic views, an orientation that he made clear in QS's founding gathering. "Wolf: reporter, utopian," the journalist simply summarized in the evening's icebreaker exercise, which asked attendees to identify themselves in a handful of words (Roberts, 2008).

The very same cybernetic understanding of humanity as disembodied information and computing as a personal rather than institutional tool that shaped Brand's view of technology now also echoed in the way Wolf and Kelly spoke of digital self-tracking and articulated the relationship of forums such as QS to it. Like the New Communalists who, following Brand's lead, personalized the computer, Wolf and Kelly pronounced QS both as the domain and as the credo of the motivated tinkerer who now aimed to personalize digital self-monitoring. Where the New Communalists embraced the calculative infra-structure formally reserved for corporations alone, "Quantified Selfers," Wolf and Kelly declared, saw potential in turning the bureaucratic mechanisms of self-monitoring onto themselves. This group, they maintained, embraced digital data heartily rather than viewed it suspiciously. And so, like the New Communalists who privatized formally bureaucratic tools such as the computer, contemporary technophiles were now eagerly wresting self-tracking away from industry. As they reported on this phenomenon, they started noting in their writing and public commentary that some of these people were starting to come together in forums such as QS.

In one of the first features covering QS, Wolf gave voice to the core question motivating QSers:

> Corporate executives facing down hostile shareholders load their pockets full of numbers . . . [But] in the cozy confines of personal life, we rarely used the power of numbers. The techniques of analysis that had proven so effective were left behind at the office at the end of the day and picked up again the next morning. The imposition, on oneself or one's family, of a regime of objective record keeping seemed ridiculous. A journal was respectable. A spreadsheet was creepy.
>
> . . . We use numbers when we want to tune up a car, analyze a chemical reaction, predict the outcome of an election. *We use numbers to optimize an assembly line. Why not use numbers on ourselves?* (Wolf, 2009, emphasis mine)

In this report, those who are starting to ask if it may not be better to "use numbers on ourselves" are positioned as an intellectual vanguard who, like the New Communalists once did, are taking these measures because they are questioning and pushing against existing social norms rather than conforming to them. The question "why not use numbers on ourselves" also reads as a solicitation to the reading public to join this forward-thinking group by taking up self-monitoring devices themselves.

In 2015, Wolf opened the QS conference convened in San Francisco with a similar though even more concise message. Now conflating the name of the forum that gathered those interested in self-tracking tools with the self-tracking devices themselves, he probed the crowd rhetorically before answering the question himself: "What is computing? Forty years ago, computers were our managers, but now we see computers as personal. QS is in a sense *very* personal computing."[2] By relating self-tracking devices to personal computers that preceded them, this speech enacted a teleological direction for digital monitoring. Implicitly, it placed QS – and QSers – at the forefront of inevitable social and technological developments. Doing so normalized and naturalized both QS and the self-tracking public that was expected to follow suit.

In a speech Kelly gave at the first QS conference in 2011, where he identified himself as "one of the founders of this tiny (but expanding) subculture," he kept close to the same theme, noting:

Through technology we are engineering our lives and bodies to be more quantifiable. We are embedding sensors in our bodies and in our environment in order to be able to quantify all kinds of functions. Just as science has been a matter of quantification – something doesn't count unless we can measure it – now our personal lives are becoming a matter of quantification. *So, the next century will be one ongoing march toward making nearly every aspect of our personal lives – from exterior to interior – more quantifiable.* There is both a whole new industry in that shift as well as a whole new science, as well as a whole new lifestyle. (Kelly, 2011, emphasis mine)

Here, Kelly speaks as someone who already sees the future, confidently declaring that it will be "more quantifiable." He also places those who constitute the "tiny (but expending) subculture" as leading the troupes on a steady "ongoing march" toward it. Like Wolf, he casts QS both as an obvious expression and as a frontrunner of this future.

Notably, industry and science are in this commentary read as symbiotic developments, although it remains unclear whether Kelly sees commercial activity as a driver of this emerging lifestyle or, vice versa, he views the lifestyle as motivating the emergence of the industry and science of self-tracking. The ambiguity speaks to his and Wolf's own roles as QS originators. They tend to present the trend toward self-quantification as a diffuse phenomenon on which they were merely reporting and to situate the meeting spaces of QS as a setting where representatives of this new lifestyle have started congregating. Wolf said as much when he recalled the first gathering:

It was so undramatic and we really – this was a long time ago – we thought, let's just think about it a little bit. Let's do some blog posts. Kevin was the one who said, let's put it up on Meetup. And he has a really nice workspace in his house in Pacifica. So, we said – let's invite people to come. And it was really more about us learning more and us cultivating some journalistic sources and *people just showed up.* (Wolf, 2016, emphasis mine)

In this excerpt, Wolf Notes that people "just showed up" as "journalistic sources" carrying "fascinating" stories. The two magazine editors didn't so much help constitute QS as a phenomenon as offer a "workspace" for it. This comment defaults to casting the original organizers as reporter-explorers who, in the mode of Western narratives of discovery, fortuitously happened upon a hidden treasure.

And yet, as its founders and popularizers, they also played a functional role in creating it. As we have seen, their reporting gave specific language and shape to this "tiny subculture." Their influence also went beyond journalistic savvy and foresight. In cohering QS as a technophile community of people bravely claiming tools of industry for their own devices, Wolf's and Kelly's reputations and contacts mattered too, just as they did in Brand's own network forums. Turner recognized that the attitude the New Communalists adopted in respect to computing did not derive exclusively from the information circulated by Brand. His vibrant personality as well as his own eclectic relationships played a defining role in resituating the computer as a desirable, personal device. Leveraging these associations, Brand routinely planned conferences, meetings, and virtual gatherings to socialize the politically, technologically, and economically influential few. These encounters fostered innovation and enthusiasm along with useful language and relationships. In identifying Brand's impact on the views of the New Communalists and later on the rhetoric that surrounded personal computing and the early internet, Turner highlights that Brand and his associates were not simply journalists in the conventional sense. They developed their careers and reputations by "building the communities on whose activities they were reporting" (2008, p. 7). Their impact stemmed from the technological imagination and the productive collaboration that they helped generate.

Likewise, in first putting QS on meetup.com, in opening the doors to Kelly's own home, and in facilitating the expansion of QS into a wide network of in-person events and conferences in the years that followed, the QS founders helped to actively create the very community, not just the vocabulary to describe it, that they originally sought to discover as journalists. In doing so, they exerted personal influence on the form QS as a community would take and therefore on its social and industry uptake. Perhaps anticipating this impact, Tim Ferriss, then already a rising life-hacking "guru" (Reagle, 2019; see also Chapter 5),[3] scribbled in the last few lines of the notes he took at the first gathering, which he later shared on his own blog: "Kevin + Co – want to start a movement" (Ferriss, 2013).

As well-networked reporters, their involvement and connections with reputable media outlets contributed to the credibility and legitimacy of the digital practices they wrote about. Kevin Kelly, who by 2007 was an established Silicon Valley veteran in his own right, promoted QS on his personal website, kk.org, which catalogued interesting gadgets in the spirit of the *Whole Earth Catalog*, and through numerous podcasts and speeches he delivered at tech conferences where he was routinely invited to reflect on the digital future. Kelly's professional stature legitimized QS as it introduced both the concept and the forum to a larger audience. People I spoke with routinely pointed to Kelly's blog and social media presence as the means by which they learned about and became interested in QS.

Although Kelly may have been the more recognized and celebrated name to start with, Wolf's affable personality as well as his ease, humility, and graciousness in person and on stage likewise helped to expand interest in the group as it fueled attendance and media curiosity in self-tracking. "Gary Wolf, who is one of the organizers, is probably one of the best moderators I've seen," noted one participant I spoke with, echoing a broader sentiment. "He does such a good job. He is so attuned . . . I mean, he alone is one of the reasons I keep coming back to the meetup," noted another. His skill as a moderator created visibility for QS and helped to turn it into a newsworthy phenomenon. It was also Wolf's expertly crafted features in mainstream publications such as *Wired* and *The New York Times*, as well as the talks he gave at popular conferences like TED, which have accrued more than one million views as of this writing, that helped to enter the concept of the "quantified self," and the notion that it represented a broader social appetite for personal data, into the popular, academic, and corporate discourse. By the time this reportage appeared in print, Wolf and Kelly had already expanded QS beyond a website that kept track of emerging self-tracking applications and into a network of in-person meetings and online discussion forums for people who saw virtue in a "data-driven life," as Wolf described it in *The New York Times* feature (Wolf, 2010). As they continued to report on the culture of personal data, they also routinely highlighted QS as a key forum that showcased it.

Following their lead, pundits, news organizations, and academics began including references to the "quantified self" in their own analyses, often referring readers to visit their local QS meetup to see the simmering cultural passion for themselves.[4] This coverage continued to alternate between using the expression as a classificatory label for an emerging set of mobile applications and digital gadgets, as a term describing the emerging "digital doubles," and as a catchy handle for a global hub that unified all those seeking "Knowledge through Numbers," as the slogan that started appearing next to QS-branded content proclaimed.

Wolf and Kelly have endorsed QS largely as a cultural byproduct. Yet, the techno-utopian narrative they skillfully adapted and the personal media and industry connections they leveraged also anchored the early semantic meaning of QS as a community that organized the representatives of an emerging metrics-forward lifestyle. As they reported on self-tracking trends, they drew on their own experience and social capital as journalists in establishing QS as a descriptive term of a new set of digital gadgets, their digital residue, and as the tip of a cultural zeitgeist iceberg. So conceived, "quantified self" as a label and QS as a forum functioned as "dream machines as well as practical tools for seeing," to borrow Anna Tsing's (2007, p. 159) terminology for describing the creative function of entrenched categories. Their creation produced what Andreas Hepp (2020) has also called the "imaginative 'haze' within which ideas and concepts of technological development are able to emerge and spread" (p. 934).[5] It is in this capacity, as the forthcoming chapters will explore, that QS has served more as a mechanism that materializes some of the inner processes of the self-tracking market rather than as a figurative screen that plainly puts an emerging set of digital gadgets and social practices on display.

The Culture of Personal Data

QS's role as an interface to the self-tracking market is also rooted in its construction as a circumscribed community modeled on a dated concept of culture. By now, anthropologists have variously reckoned with the way "culture" has historically functioned as a closed-circuit idea that, when mobilized as a unit of analysis that is fixed, stable, consistent, and geographically specific, has in many ways come to signify the exact opposite of what it was originally developed to represent (see Clifford, 1988; Trouillot, 2003). This view of culture, however, and more recently of "community," as something stable and thing-like, continues to dominate media and, as we will see in Chapter 3 in particular, the business imaginary. Primarily, in conceiving of "quantified self" as a name of a specific "subculture" or "culture of personal data," and later in socializing QS as a "community" that showcased it, Wolf and Kelly conceptualized QS as just such a limited construct. "Community" in this formulation is interchangeable with the concept of culture as "something out there" (Trouillot, 2003, p. 101) and as a social aggregate whose limits are asserted as self-evident.

This categorization isolates the concept but avoids paying attention to what Trouillot has called, in relationship to the rigid idea of culture that he criticized, its broader "context of deployment" (2003, p. 107). In addition to their specific contributions as media professionals and content creators described above, Wolf's and Kelly's positions as journalists prefigured QS as an expression of a distinct cultural phenomenon, from the get-go. Even as they helped to organize QS and developed the terms by which to understand it, their expected roles as detached purveyors of stories lent QS and the "culture of personal data" it apparently represented a sense of independence, singularity, and coherence. Indeed, the distant posture is resonant in Wolf's narration of the first gathering at Kelly's home where "people just showed up" bearing their self-tracking stories as narrative gifts. From that end, his description of that evening reads as an account of a classic moment of ethnographic entry.[6] This framing activates a voyeuristic gaze where the culture of personal data can be accessed by crossing symbolic and geographic thresholds and can thus be appreciated as a distinct and remote curiosity.

In-person meetups have further formalized QS as a circumscribed phenomenon. As sites that one may visit, they help render QS and the culture of personal data placeable and discoverable, rendering them a discrete social unit one can locate, witness, and analyze. Localized events also subtly endorse the notion that QS, as anthropologist Martin Ortlieb (2010) had noted of the earlier concept of culture, is "ontologically grounded: it is as you find it" (p. 187). As sites that literally "pin down" (Ortlieb, 2010, p. 186) QS and the culture of personal data, these gatherings create stability and fixity around modes of monitoring and forms of organizing that are in fact much more fluid and socially complex. Meetups thus help endorse QS and the culture of personal data as something singular and self-contained, as a social aggregate that can be mapped and identified. This invoked solidity of QS further authenticates the forum as a concrete cultural spectacle.

The stabilizing role of place-based events is telegraphed online as well – for instance, through the page listing all of the cities that have hosted QS meetups to date documented on the group's formal virtual home, quantifiedself.com. Shown scattered across more than 100 cities and thirty countries throughout North America, Europe, Asia, and Oceania, these site-specific events help enact a wider geography of QS. They at once affiliate the forum with these concrete destinations and inaugurate QS as a broader whole that can be mapped and grasped by following its many nodes. While thus invoking QS as an "international community" and heralding the culture of personal data as an expanding and diffuse occurrence, this list helps realize the particularity of QS through allusion to territory.

The idea that QS was a traceable community on the model of culture has additionally been shaped by the aesthetics of home. The figure of home – and in particular, Kelly's California home, a location that has since become a cornerstone of the QS origins story – has played a role in anchoring and segregating QS as a distinct community. "Home" in this context certainly draws on the Silicon Valley mythology of the house-bound garage, which in the founding lore of Technorati such as Microsoft's Bill Gates and Apple's Steve Jobs often sets the stage for acts of unrestrained ingenuity and creativity. Home, moreover, connects QS and "community" activities with famed gatherings such as the Homebrew Computer Club – a group of Silicon Valley DIY computer geeks who met intermittently between 1975 and 1986 to exchange parts and information, occasions that are said to have laid the groundwork for the development of the first personal computer. Indeed, QS participants I spoke with routinely drew connections between contributors to QS and the

Homebrew Computer Club members. Although many of the Homebrew Computer Club participants, such as Steve Jobs and Steven Wozniak, eventually themselves became tech giants, at the time they were seen – and saw themselves – as tech industry outsiders whose passions and creativity were first brewed at home and in informal networks like the Homebrew Club.

Home did not only classify QS as an innovative, albeit masculinized, workshop of ideas in the manner of the startup garage. It also played a symbolic role similar to the part the figure of the frontier performed for the New Communalists. Even though most of the events I attended between 2013 and 2017 were held in corporate offices and professional conference venues (see Chapter 4), ritualistic recollections by organizers and participants of the homegrown roots of QS continued to re-imbue these events with a symbolic domesticity that worked to reaffirm QS as a "real" community.

A photograph Kevin Kelly took of this first gathering (Figure 1.1) unwittingly epitomizes the way the idea of home has colored the decidedly more formal business setting and tonality of subsequent QS functions. In this image, the mismatched dining chairs and floor-to-ceiling bookcases filled with paperbacks convey domestic intimacy, even if in the foreground a speaker dressed in a shirt can be seen giving a talk before a small, seated, all-male audience who are likewise mostly clothed in business casual attire. The scene is furthermore softened by the candid nature of the shot and by the quality of the photograph

Figure 1.1 Photo – Kevin Kelly (Roberts, 2008).

itself. Likely the result of poor lighting, when seen in color, the picture appears as though it has the patina of age, which helps to give the shot a nostalgic and homey air. This distinct point of origin authenticates QS even as, or perhaps especially as, most events are held in corporate offices and when key forum communication has been expertly curated by skilled magazine editors. While the stylish tech office and the personal involvement and endorsement of Silicon Valley luminaries helped to certify QS as a credible and attention-worthy gathering (as I discuss further in Chapter 4), its homegrown roots served to ratify it as a genuine, grassroots phenomenon.

Vendors and Members

Finally, it has been Wolf and Kelly's formal structuring and curation of group activities, over which they exercised significant control, that further shaped the manner in which QS could be recognized as a placeable locus of the culture of personal data (see also Hepp, 2020). For example, from the start, Wolf and Kelly have made personal stories, rather than business pitches, the cornerstone of QS gatherings. Wolf describes this as a setup that emerged organically, fashioned, in part, after a response one person offered during that first evening convened at Kelly's home. Wolf recalled:

> Pointing to someone who had recently walked through the door, I remember Kevin said, "OK, you came in last, so you get to go first." And instead of saying, "my name is and I'm from here," he said, "OK, I can show you something." And he opens up his computer and shows us a fifteen-minute by fifteen-minute breakdown of how he spent his last year. And that was just a moment. He just decided that's how he wanted to introduce himself. (Wolf, 2016)

The rest of the group followed suit, making small, impromptu presentations about their self-monitoring projects. This tactic laid the foundation for a structure that has since defined QS activities.

However, this format, Wolf also recognizes, was likewise shaped by his and Kelly's professional backgrounds:

> Kevin and I have some experience with culture – the way things evolved culturally online. So, I think we did have a little bit of a head start of how to keep things interesting for ourselves. You know, let people do whatever they wanted, but create a clear framework that articulated, that allowed people to ask themselves "do I belong under this label or do I not belong." (Wolf, 2016)

Their experience as content creators and magazine editors certainly taught them ways to organize and lay out information for maximum engagement and clarity. These days, QS events are centered around a set of presentations that Wolf and Kelly have titled "Show & Tell." While QS meetups frequently begin or end with a "Demo Hour" (a small tech showcase), the Show & Tell talks are generally narrativized as the explicit site and purpose of community organizing.

The hierarchy between the Demo Hour and the Show & Tell is emphasized in the contrasting treatment of these activities during QS events. The Demo Hour miniaturizes the tech conference showcase. Here, vendors stand next to promotional displays of self-tracking gadgets as people move about the room casually sampling or examining products. Given that the Demo Hour takes place either at the start or at the tail end of each meetup, lights are kept on and refreshments are generally available for this portion of the night, amplifying the atmosphere of the Demo Hour as a precursor to or as the finale of the main event. At the Demo Hour, novel technology is served up as a sideshow, along with wine and appetizers.

In contrast to the Demo Hour, which is anchored by the marketing of technology vendors, the Show & Tell features three or four presentations focused on the self-tracking experiences or "experiments" of QS "members." To further mark the presentations as the proper site of QS organizing, leaders of local groups typically use this time to make formal introductions and announcements. A brief explanation of QS often follows for the benefit of those who are in the room for the first time, remarks that typically review for the newcomers the story of QS as a community on the rise organized by dedicated members the world over invested in the possibilities of self-tracking. Meeting hosts also frequently use this time to lead a small icebreaker exercise to stimulate a sense of conviviality within the group. Following the example of the original meeting convened in Kelly's home, these typically involve expressing in a few words what drew someone to QS that night, a query that solicits visitors to express their interest in QS and self-tracking in personal rather than business terms. Given that any one meeting has a large number of new participants, this activity also renews the sense of community that otherwise remains frayed as people cycle in and out of the group on a regular basis. After these formal greetings, speakers are introduced and take their turns at the head of the room to talk about their personal experiences with tracking their data.

That the personal stories of group members rather than the exhibition of vendors are said to constitute the central activities of QS is further highlighted by the different formats of the Demo Hour and the Show & Tell talks. Unlike the Demo Hour, which features companies openly hawking their wares, Show & Tell presenters are always asked ahead of time to speak in the first person and to discuss their experiences with data collection as a personal discovery rather than as a sales pitch, even if, as often ends up being the case, that activity has also led the presenter to develop a service or a tool that the talk surreptitiously promotes. Still, couching the talk in intimate tones helps maintain the desired partition between the personal and the professional. Although delivering a talk about one's self-tracking experiences is not a requisite part of engaging with QS – one may simply sit in the audience and listen – in distinguishing between the style of delivery of the Demo Hour and that of the Show & Tell, the latter is further marked as a site for members, while the former is designated as a space for vendors.

"Member" of course is a purely symbolic designation. There is no formal recruitment process. Belonging is very loosely defined. "Joining" QS simply involves attending one of the many events, or signing up through meetup.com to receive email updates about forum activities. There are also no formal membership dues. On occasion, organizers of local events do ask for contributions to help offset small expenses such as food and drinks, and conferences charge an admission fee to subsidize the venue rented for the occasion. By and large, however, "member" rhetorically installs the desired sense of group cohesion. It is a label that generates rather than just conveys a sense of inclusion. It helps to produce and ascribe belonging.

The partitioning may have emerged organically. However, it has been sustained through active gatekeeping maintained by the curatorial labor of the organization's "elite" (Hepp, 2020). Far from constituting QS as a spontaneously assembled collective of motivated tinkerers and self-tracking enthusiasts, these interventions sometimes explicitly and other times subtly configure the "community" narrative and function. For example, modeling a conversation an organizer might have with an interested presenter, Wolf explained to me:

> As long as they want to give a talk in the first person, that's kind of our rule. So, if they want to talk about self-tracking, they can get up and talk about it. [But if they say,] "I have an idea for how I can help millions of people with my inventions though of course I never tried it and it's not really me that I'm talking about," then usually we try to say, "Look, there are a lot of meetups for tech entrepreneurship. Maybe that's a better place to go and give that talk." But if someone wants to talk in the first person about what they are doing with their own data, we're open. (Wolf, 2016)

And although QS is not a registered trademark and therefore open to public uptake, Wolf keeps tabs on how the term is mobilized through online search functions, and when necessary gently censors its application. As Wolf described to me,

Having this kind of thing [QS], that's kind of a "non-proprietary" trademark is how
I would call it. Like it's clearly a thing. And we can search for it, and we can know,
"are you identifying yourself as part of Quantified Self?" But we don't like to send
people letters – if they do something with it that we don't like and say . . . well
actually we do, but they are not legal letters. I might send them a note and say,
"I don't see that as very similar to what other people are doing in Quantified Self.
Is there another name you can use that would be less confusing?" . . .

If someone wants to do a meetup "Getting More Productivity out of Your
Employees through Wearables: Quantified Self as a Tool of Management" – this is a
meshing together of real examples; it's a synthetic example, but stuff like that
happens – I might send them a note and say, "That seems very much like a
managerial, administrative kind of technology, an enterprise thing. It's all very
much – there is a lot going on. But Quantified Self is a real community, with real
people all over the world, [who] are doing a thing – which is talking about
themselves using data. And when you call How Do You Get More Work out of
Your Employees Using Wearables, Quantified Self, you're just inviting a lot of
friction and confusion. So, what if you didn't?" (Wolf, 2016)

The distinction Wolf makes in this composite example between those selling
an "administrative kind of technology, an enterprise thing" and QS as a "real
community with real people all over the world . . . talking about themselves
using data" is apt. It echoes the qualitative difference between "members" and
"vendors" that the structure developed by Wolf and Kelly seeks to maintain.
Therefore, even though QS was comprised of a large number of tech executives who participated only occasionally as formal Demo Hour vendors
and engaged more frequently as QS members in rhetorically separating QS
"members" from commercial "vendors," and in delimiting activities that could
constitute QS as a community, this framework further solidified the imagined
borders of QS as a cultural phenomenon and the tech sector's relationship to it.
    On the whole, by separating events into the Demo Hour and the Show &
Tell, Wolf and Kelly have established a hierarchy where entrepreneurial
activity is not only visually separated but also practically marginalized and
made peripheral to individual experiences with data. The self-tracking industry
is thus often constructed as an interest yet as exterior to QS proper, and at times
even as the negative against which the feelings of community can cohere. This
distinction categorizes "members" who share personal stories of device use as
the proper constituents of the QS "community" and as the embodied representatives of the culture of personal data.
    Ultimately, the administrative arm of QS – originally titled QS Labs – has
reinscribed QS as a collective where enthusiasts and early adopters of wearable
gadgets congregate to reaffirm QS as a manifestation of cultural practices. The
original descriptions of QS Labs said so explicitly. At the time when I was

involved with the activities of the collective, QS Labs was described online as an entity that supported the Quantified Self user community worldwide by producing international meetings, conferences and expositions, community forums, web content and services, and a guide to self-tracking tools. In its rhetorical association with a clinical concept of the laboratory, QS Labs also established this connection symbolically. Much like the experimental ideas developed and tested in a laboratory setting, the term "labs" presents the "experiments" of QS participants as precursors to broader social practices. The moniker also invites comparisons between the work of the scientific laboratory and QS Labs. QS Labs putatively incubated ideas in much the same way that labs incubate bacteria. QS Labs thus implicitly gestated digital enthusiasm and rendered the "culture of personal data" as plainly visible as bacteria cultured in a Petri dish located within a scientific laboratory. It was when the forum was understood in these terms that the specific digital enthusiasts QS sought to organize could act as stand-ins for the larger imagined culture of personal data located beyond it. While thus reconstituting the parameters of membership, QS Labs also crystalized Wolf and Kelly's role in the "community." Listed as QS Labs directors, they are situated as connected to yet at an analytical and editorial distance apart from the collective at large.

Wolf and Kelly of course did not invent digital self-tracking, nor are they singularly – not even chiefly – responsible for its broader social uptake or commercial interest. However, they did more than just recognize QS as an effective name for an emerging class of digital devices, as an apt label of personal data these gadgets generated, and ultimately as a tag of a forum convening those motivated enough to use them. As experienced and well-connected media professionals skilled at gathering people and conversation, they helped to shape some of the discourse around the "culture of personal data" and its connection to digital entrepreneurialism. The latter became conditioned by their techno-utopian background, the journalistic norms through which they operated, the placemaking rhetoric that connected QS with conventional concepts of culture, and a concise format that repeatedly aligned QS with the self-monitoring efforts of motivated technophiles.

In establishing both the idea of the "quantified self" as well as the forum QS in the terms discussed throughout this chapter, the duo also set the tone for some of the ways technologists would come to relate to it. The manner in which Wolf and Kelly invited others to recognize QS as a concept and as a community mapped well onto some of the key expectations and performances animating the self-tracking arena. The framing they developed reflected, substantiated, and at times sustained how those developing self-tracking technologies promoted their devices, conceptualized and configured data, understood their consumers, as well as maintained their own professional identities. Through their gentle monitoring, censoring, and probing, Wolf and Kelly likewise didn't simply ensure that the main QS activities remained focused on private experiences rather than business ventures. As we'll see throughout the book, this narrative structure allowed, and in many ways facilitated, the necessary reframing of formal business pitches into personal terms, which was crucial not just for participation in QS but in the self-tracking market itself. The binary QS framework and the attendant transfigurations of tech executives into private digital enthusiasts additionally made it possible for me to interact both with the explicit promotional messages of digital specialists and with technologists' alternative experiences within the self-tracking industry, all in one space. Evaluating how technologists discussed self-tracking and personal data as they variously situated themselves in relationship to the "quantified self" and QS as vendors and members, and examining the intersection of these ideas with the broader technological imaginations, dilemmas, and practices shaping digital work ultimately offered unique visibility into the organizing dynamics of the tech sector, not just QS. It is from this end that the forthcoming chapters approach QS as a key interface to the narrative frames, business practices, and professional exigencies that animate the self-tracking market.

2

Seeing Double in Digital Entrepreneurialism

In the years since Gary Wolf and Kevin Kelly introduced the expression "quantified self" into the public domain, the phrase has retained its multivalent meaning. It continues to be mobilized as the name of a user group of proficient technophiles, as a classificatory handle for a set of gadgets and applications that facilitate self-monitoring, and as a term that categorizes what practitioners at times refer to as one's "digital double" produced by tech-assisted self-monitoring. This stereotyped triad rehearses a familiar positivist technological imaginary where the person, the digital gadget, and the data it collects stand in a direct, unmediated, and airtight relationship with one another. This was certainly the way Dan, a wearables entrepreneur, used the expression during a promotional speech he gave at a small function for makers of such tools in New York City. "We don't need to drown in data, we need to embrace our inner quantified self," he announced as he clicked to a slide in his PowerPoint deck showing a suited figure peppered with red flecks.[1] These hotspots represented the digital regalia, the commercially available wearable technology such as sensor-enabled rings, watches, bracelets, and patches, that collect a widening range of biometric and environmental data about their wearer that Dan had summarized as one's "inner quantified self" (Figure 2.1).

Dan's fifteen-minute TED-style talk, which was hosted in a fashionably furnished and spacious atrium of a WeWork co-working office in New York City, was one of many similar presentations delivered by engineers, designers, and developers of wearable technology in cities around the United States. As he made the case for wearable technology, some of the people renting office space in the building – likely consultants, freelancers, and startup owners – traced the perimeter of the crescent formed by the ten or so rows of chairs arranged for the occasion.

They stopped intermittently to listen to what he had to say as they walked to refill their coffee mugs from pots located in large communal areas or headed

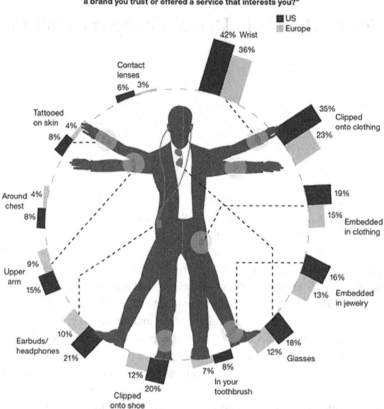

"How interested would you be in wearing/using a sensor device, assuming it was from a brand you trust or offered a service that interests you?"

- US
- Europe

42% Wrist
36%

Contact lenses
6% 3%

Tattooed on skin 4%
8%

Around 4%
chest
8%

Upper 9%
arm
15%

Earbuds/ 10%
headphones
21%

12%
20%
Clipped onto shoe

7% 8%
In your toothbrush

18%
12% Glasses

13% Embedded in jewelry

16%

19%
15% Embedded in clothing

35% Clipped onto clothing
23%

Base: 4,556 US online adults (ages 18+); 11,647 EU online adults (ages 18+)
(multiple responses accepted)

Source: Forrester's North American Consumer Technographics® Consumer Technology Survey, 2014, and Forrester's European Consumer Technographics Consumer Technology Survey, 2014

Figure 2.1 The Data Digest: Five Urgent Truths about Wearables. Forrester Research (2014).

toward the elevator banks to leave for the day. Dan's main business audience was likely not in the room, but his "pitch" to us was a practice run. He was there to rehearse his argument, one that he may soon deliver to larger crowds at a national technology conference or in the offices of an interested corporate buyer, potential business partner, or private equity investor.

While I have not met Dan or ever heard his product pitch before, I certainly recognized both the reference to the "quantified self" and the image that he used to illustrate it as tech industry staples. The graphic, first developed by the marketing research firm Forrester in 2014, or its facsimile, often accompanies corporate discussions of digitization – conversations where the expression "quantified self" has become a common trope of digital identity, and where the Quantified Self (QS) occasionally figures as an example of a forum that convenes those who most heartily embrace it.

On its face, the illustration, much like Dan's passing reference to the inner quantified self, seems ready-made for a familiar social critique of the positivist tendencies of digital professionals. It would be easy, even tempting, to write off this manner of speaking as proof that technologists remain tightly wedded to narrow ideas of digitization and corporeality. And there is certainly some irony in the fact that Dan endorses his device as an antidote to drowning in data even though it is likely to produce even more data. Meanwhile, the illustrated "quantified self," with its many gadget-toting arms and legs spread out in every direction on the model of Leonardo da Vinci's *Vitruvian Man*, conveys the idea that the data thus derived ultimately refer back to the person at the center of it all, and to him (and in the corporate imaginations, it often is a him) alone. The visual creates an overall impression of a solitary figure, of a singularized "quantified self" cocooned in an information bubble devoid of internal friction or contradictions. This image does not only invoke the idealized possibilities of wearable gadgets but draws up someone who has earnestly embraced the narrow calculative logics enthusiastically peddled by contemporary tech entrepreneurs.

Yet, such analysis would risk too hastily dismissing industry actors as epistemic naifs whose unsophisticated views of digital technology contrast sharply with the more nuanced perspectives of academic contributors. Dan's use of the concept of the quantified self and Forrester's visual as oversimplified mnemonics for the personal data generated by commercial wearables does appear reductive. However, it comprises only one way in which technologists relate to data. I call this manner of speaking the *public face of data*. These claims often circulate in media statements, conference presentations, marketing materials, or official company documents. The reference to the "quantified self" in such instances functions both as a shorthand and a screen. It certainly operates as an interface. However, without further context, what it allows one to see is only the tech sector's outward veneer. Taking these perspectives strictly at face value can create the impression that product makers' views of digitization are isomorphic with these public positions.

This chapter instead looks behind the mask, behind the public face of data. Despite appearances, my on-the-ground ethnographic engagement with the app and device developers I met at QS functions and beyond indicates that the assumptions contemporary makers of wearables hold about personal data, and how they see their own roles in generating them, are not so easy to stabilize and need further rethinking. The surface impression that they guilelessly atomize these metrics has to be weighed against the diverse ways in which they in fact approach these processes in their professional lives.

Taking a broader view, this chapter explores how tech executives work to extract legal and fiscal benefits from producing varying and at times competing accounts of data-driven bodies, that is, from presenting data as both malleable and concrete. It's an arena where practitioners are expected to purposely pursue both objectivity and ambiguity as a corporate strategy. This double talk, masked at times by singularized tropes such as "the quantified self," among others, obscures how digital selfhoods reflected in device platforms – consistent, coherent, cumulative – tend to contrast with the more multiple and flexible relationship between people, technology, and data that platform designers themselves establish. Dan's uptake of the term "quantified self" and his use of Forrester's visual to show it offers an entry point to discussing the fluctuating ways in which practitioners speak about data. It provides less of a definitive expression of technologists' limited understanding of digital representation and more of a marker of only one end of the polarities between which makers of commercial wearables and self-tracking applications tend to operate.

Data as Travel

Even though in public settings digital professionals such as Dan tend to default to promotional talk that presents personal data in simplistic terms, as an unproblematic collection of discrete digital points, these technological aspirations are routinely undercut by the practical realities of digital work. Dan may have confidently used the expression "quantified self" as a marketing tactic. Technologists I met in forums such as QS, however, often complicated this assured professional posture and made it possible to sneak a peek behind the scenes of some of these ambitious assertions. A discussion I participated in during one QS event, the 2016 Quantified Self Public Health Symposium, helped make some of these issues visible. This one-day session ostensibly constituted part of a new "community" outreach – an event intended to bring QS self-trackers and tool makers into conversation with public health scientists. Framed by an idea of QS as a gathering of digital acolytes, the meeting's impetus was facilitating researcher "access to data" produced by the prolific and motivated device users while providing the QS community better access to bespoke insights (Wolf, 2016).

With digital "access" as a central theme, participants debated its possibilities and challenges. These conversations, however, yielded more frank and nuanced discussions on interior industry dynamics. In one activity, for example, attendees were asked to explore problems of "aligning" diverse datasets with the goal of coming to some terms about how to resolve them. Following a brief discussion in small groups, where my team discussed such issues as "normalizing" datasets and accounting for differences in the way information is labeled and stored, we reconvened in the main auditorium and placed our thoughts, written down on large pads of paper, onto easels set up on the main stage. As everyone returned to their seats, Susannah Fox, an executive with the Pew Research Center's Internet Project and the session host, took on the tricky task of quickly summarizing key topics that emerged from the notes. Although there were many ideas to go through, only moments later Fox announced "data flow" as a central dilemma and theme. "Data flow was any card that had anything to do with interoperability," she hastily explained.[2]

Rachel Kalmar, a data scientist and organizer of the Bay Area Meetup "Sensored" that convened people around emerging trends in sensor-enabled tools, quickly intervened. "Flow is a metaphor that makes us think of data as water, which makes it seem that data is easy to move. I'd like to suggest that we see data as travel. It takes effort to move and it comes with its own baggage," she cautioned Fox and the audience from her seat.[3] The room erupted with excited murmurs and a flurry of approving comments on Twitter later flagged her observations for further public circulation.

For Kalmar and other technologists in the room, "baggage" was anything that weighed down data and restricted their capacity to easily connect and to flow. This included bureaucratic red tape or corporate "silos" that made it difficult to move personal data between institutions, individuals, or competing providers. The divergent standards and definitions used by companies and institutions also made it challenging to add or bring diverse datasets together into the aspirational comprehensive wholes.[4] The metaphor of "travel" ultimately spoke to the issues, the baggage, that turn the process of reconciling and "aligning" these discrepancies into a cumbersome if not practically impossible task. Kalmar thus turned the conversation to the politics of digitization, reminding the group to view data interoperability as a social, not just as a strictly technological, activity.

Kalmar's retort echoes with the writing of theorists who, though in a different vein, have also problematized effortless mobility as a default modern condition. If, as pundits often claim, the last two hundred years have been shaped by technological innovation (the train, the car, the airplane) that has enhanced the speed and efficacy with which people are able to move about the globe, scholars such as Talal Asad (1993) reassert that we cannot speak about a general form of mobility as though in the abstract. Mobility, Asad highlights, remains politically mediated and unevenly experienced (see also Joyce, 2003).[5] Condemning the "cheerfulness" of these assertions, Asad emphasizes that innovation has not simply shrunk the world as it has sped up movement. Mobility remains socially striated, as is palpable in the divergent experiences of the "expatriate" and the "migrant." Movement, Asad stresses, is mediated by the politics of recognition that reveal mobility "not merely an event in itself, but a moment in the subsumption of one act by another" (1993, p. 10). Mobility, in other words, is not just subject to technological advancements but also configured by power. Indeed, Asad highlights that "power realizes itself through the very discourse on mobility" (p. 10). In focusing on the baggage that weighs data down and makes them difficult to move, Kalmar likewise turned the room's attention to the politics, rather than technologies, that necessarily affect digitization. Seamless datasets that appear to flow together without friction between bodies, devices, and interested parties are not produced by innovative devices alone. Chiefly, they are both a product and a sign of the power dynamics that continue to shape digital circulation (Starosielski, 2015).

Kalmer is of course not alone in her more sober appraisal of digital mobility. Despite the ambitious promotional rhetoric premised on unproblematic data dynamism, technologists are often candid about challenges in achieving it, even in settings that may appear least conditioned to show these difficulties. A conversation with a sales rep for the company Scanadu, whom I came across at another QS function, the QS Conference and Expo in San Francisco in 2015, exemplifies the pragmatic and self-aware, if not necessarily always critical, posture, while adding another dimension to Kalmer's challenge.

As one of the "vendors" formally sponsoring QS15, Scanadu had erected an immodest display on the main conference floor that, on first blush, presented the possibilities of personal data in ways that were not much different from the cliche manner in which Dan, the executive whose commentary opened this chapter, used the expression "quantified self." This was evident, for instance, in the product name, which explicitly connected the digital tracker – a gadget designed to collect a range of biometric data with one fluid swipe – with a code scanner at a store checkout counter. The correlation, I later learned when researching the brand online, was of course intentional as the makers of Scanadu claimed inspiration from a fictional medical scanner called the tricorder first conceived for the sci-fi series *Star Trek*. The firm appeared to be in good company. That year, Scanadu was a top ten entrant in the X-Prize competition sponsored by the tech firm Qualcomm, with aims to bring the tricorder from the TV screen to real life.

The accompanying product display seemed only to reinforce a simplistic message of effortless digital transactions. Oversized TV monitors affixed to the wall, for instance, kept a running tally of the "9 billion and 355,789,002" (and

Figure 2.2 Scanadu display at QS15. Photo by author.

counting) data points already collected by the company (Figure 2.2). Meanwhile, slogans written on a large banner pledged to deliver digitized clarity as they announced Scanadu's mission to ensure that "we are the last generation to know so little about our health."

The magnitude of this sum and promise was bolstered by the fact that "billion" was written out as a word, not as a number, presumably to ensure that conference goers briskly walking by would not overlook its scope. This figure sourced additional authority from the site of its articulation: a TV screen adjacent to a second monitor displaying a world map. This juxtaposition at once signaled the brand's widespread global appeal and linked the device with Western innovation and science by highlighting the North American, European, and Australian regions where Scanadu had already entered into use.

As I paused at the display table, took in the firm's signage, and skimmed through its promotional leaflets, a sales associate approached me to warmly emphasize the company's message. She patiently showed me, for instance, how the gadget – white, slick, and round as a hockey puck – smoothly glides across the forehead, scanning temperature, blood pressure, and heart rate with one brisk move. As I gingerly rolled the device around in my hand, I listened to her practiced talk about the major artery that runs along the forehead, which, she noted, made Scanadu's unique swiping gesture the ideal motion with which to take these measurements. After the rep concluded her sales pitch, I wondered what made Scanadu different from the other applications that already collected these metrics in spades. Abandoning the script for just a moment, the salesperson threw a knowing look around the room, motioning to the adjacent displays of companies promoting wearable bracelets, by far the most popular "form factor" in the self-tracking market. "The wrist has become busy real estate," she shrugged. "We had to invent a new gesture."[6]

Since then, I have heard executives remark that "the wrist has become busy real estate" repeatedly, a phrase largely used as a call to arms for device makers to "differentiate" their products in an entrepreneurial environment increasingly stiffened by competition. "Differentiation" is marketing speak for the imperative to create differences among otherwise similar commodities so that identical products may appear novel and unique. Companies can differentiate, as Scanadu did, by inventing new gestures, by finding new applications for familiar things, and especially through distinct branding and packaging.

Thinking of the body as real estate over which wearable technology makers compete likewise highlights how data remain mediated by power and that their stability is continuously reaffirmed as well as undermined by social, political, and economic imperatives. The expression, after all, makes it clear that companies that make wearables do not just sell connected devices; they make claims on people's bodies. In representing limbs and arms as real estate, technologists explicitly equate body parts – and personal data – with territory, something Scanadu had inadvertently marked by including a global map in its marketing material. The language of real estate plainly reveals mobility of personal data as a byproduct of corporate boundary making and position taking rather than as a consequence of perpetual elimination of barriers to digitization. This too is part of the baggage with which data travel. "The wrist as real estate" thus exposes the politics of personal data gathering that the public discourse of data interoperability and neatly aggregable "quantified selves" otherwise disguises. Despite Scanadu's promotional rhetoric of expansive, connected, and infinitely expanding digital datasets that promise to alter how a global "we" approaches its health, the company's business strategy premised on contriving "new gestures" confounds a corporate view of data as substances that endlessly flow and accrete. Especially so given that Scanadu's own data quickly ran into a dead end even as the company promised to bring forth an era of continuous digital enlightenment. After raising a total of $49.7 million in funding, the company ultimately failed to secure the anticipated Food and Drug Administration (FDA) approval. In 2016 Scanadu announced that it was ending its "trial" and would subsequently stop providing technical support for its existing devices.

Emotional Sweat

My ethnographic engagement with a group working on a mechanized wearable device purported to detect emotion, a team led by a cognitive psychologist and designer who – for the purposes of this chapter – I will call Anne, offers additional ways to understand how and why digital professionals' view of digitization practically exceeds the narrow promotional parameters of Dan's illustrated "quantified self." I first met Anne in New York City after I heard her speak on a panel focused on the future of wearable technology. I have since accompanied her to other venues where she has spoken about her device and the data it produces, such as a lecture at a local college class, as well as to conversations with potential funders and early user-experience testing. Following Anne from place to place made visible some of the shifting ways in which she framed the work of her device and the data it collects, as well as the varied causes and implications of these equivocations, as she spoke about the technology she was developing in different settings and with different audiences.

Much like the tech executives I came across at QS events, it was evident from the beginning that Anne spoke of her wearable and the data it collects in at least two competing ways. When discussing its mechanics in formal settings, such as the public event where we first met, she presents the gadget as something very scientific and precise, characteristically situating the impassioned subjects that it tracks within the dispassionate framework of scientific discourse. In these venues, Anne typically explains that her device works by detecting trace amounts of "galvanic skin response," otherwise known as "skin conductance," a subtle bodily emission that dips or rises as the body enters fight-or-flight response. She often adds that she prefers this biometric to other modes of tracking affect because it produces what she calls a "cleaner" signal. While many commercial gadgets use heart rate monitoring as a barometer of emotion, heart rate can spike easily in response to both physical and psychological exertion. By contrast, skin conductance remains unaffected by physical activity. And so, while Anne's fondness for skin conductance appears connected to its steadfast nature, her treatment of this biometric as the cleaner signal also seems related to the fact that it can only be detected by technological means. Unlike changes in heart rate, which can be sensed through self-awareness, skin conductance is difficult for an individual to detect without mechanical assistance. Anne thus frequently speaks about skin conductance, in addition to her device's ability to place it, in the mode of "mechanical objectivity" (Daston and Galison, 2007) as the biometric she prefers precisely because it remains uncontaminated by human mediation.

While Anne thus publicly galvanizes the wearable as something that detects a cleaner signal, the clarity of data it produces blurs when she translates the specialized terminology into more familiar and idiomatic vocabulary. For example, when I or other colleagues struggled to understand what the term really meant, she improvised that we should think of skin conductance as "emotional sweating." At other times, she conflated skin conductance with straightforward emotional monitoring or explained that the device simply monitored "mood."

At a glance – and in line with her training – Anne's adaptations portray emotions only as substances that show up in the body as though affect were indeed a concrete biological secretion as palpable as human sweat. The latter view was tangible even when, in between user testing, Anne summoned me and a few other colleagues to take a look at how her gadget had captured the "pleasure" she had experienced while eating an apple. She explained that she was eating the fruit while wearing the device but that, during this time, she had not paid her snacking any special attention. When she looked at the data later, she was surprised to see that the wearable had inadvertently captured the satisfaction she had felt while consuming the fruit. We huddled around her as she pulled her laptop open to let us see the spiky graph running across the computer screen. As we gazed at the meandering lines that appeared to have surreptitiously documented Anne's pleasurable gastronomic experience, she guided us through the peaks and valleys that pointed to the "intense sensation of me eating an apple." Emotions, in this exchange, appeared singular, sensible, and amenable to precise detection. This conversation also suggested that Anne saw digital knowledge making largely as a process of patient distillation, of methodically eliminating the dirt to reveal the pure – clean – sentiment itself.

It is not enough to reject Anne's framing as an expression of her cognitivist bias and to reveal that what may seem to her as a straightforward biological factuality is also an ambiguous and socially contingent reality. Her casual movement between skin conductance and emotional sweating is worth examining further. While this shift at first appears only to confirm her positivist views, a closer reading provides alternative explanations. Namely, the back and forth between skin conductance and emotional sweat indicates that for developers of commercial wearables such as Anne, data and human bodies never take on the stability and the singularity they publicly ascribe to them.

To start with, it is notable that although "emotional sweat" is a neologism coined by Anne, this turn of phrase joins a cascading set of metaphors that pundits and data professionals have already widely employed to characterize data. These include expressions that variously compare data to bodies of water or to substances such as pollution, oil, exhaust, and toxic waste.[7] Much of the scholarship on data metaphors has examined these terms alongside metaphor theorists such as Lakoff and Johnson (1980, 1999) (also see Puschmann and Burgress, 2014; Hwang and Levy, 2015; Watson, 2015). These scholars have argued that such metaphors are used to naturalize data as an organic substance. They have also highlighted that this type of language allows digital profes- sionals to represent data as a single mass and as matter that is composed of discrete, divisible particles.

While metaphors sourced from nature provide coherence, this vocabulary also registers the difficulty of simply adding data up. When practitioners describe data as as ethereal as gas, as precious as oil, or as polluted as waste, these conflicting interpretations undermine the possibility of any easy digital commensuration. Indeed, simply taking stock of the growing quantities of data metaphors without even attending to their different semantic qualities can "provoke a sense of vagueness" rather than "certainty," as anthropologist Dawn Nafus (2014) observed in a related context. Given this endemic instabil- ity, and "baggage," as Kalmar had also earlier articulated, it is indeed a wonder that "indicators become part of calculative infrastructures at all" (Nafus, 2014, p. 208).

My point about the variable ways in which those working in the commercial sphere relate to data is connected to Nafus's observation about data's epistemic vagueness. I additionally note that data and their qualifiers often serve different masters in commercial settings. If data metaphors such as "emotional sweat" can be understood as motivated metaphors – expressions, as comparatist Dennis Tenen explains, that help transfer "a number of concepts from one domain . . . into another domain to produce insight" (2017, p. 32) – it is important to recognize that in the wearables industry, the domains into which these expressions extend are numerous and often conflicting. Among other applications, Anne uses the qualifier both as an imperfect proxy for skin conductance and as a fitting synonym for it. She thus constructs data both as building blocks of firm calculative infrastructures and as nebulous approxima- tions that create unsteady edifices. The data her device produces emerge as palpable and elusive, as clear and ambiguous, all at the same time.

To view Anne's substitution only as a metaphor for "clean data" would be to overlook, for example, the many ways she displays deep awareness of the limitations of her device. In private conversations that took place away from the presenter's stage, she spoke candidly about skin conductance as an imper- fect metric, one that was itself hindered by the practical variability of devices and bodies. When I asked her about some of the challenges associated with collecting sentiment data, we discussed how skin conductance fluctuates with age, individual physiology, and even environmental factors. More anxious people have higher skin conductivity, she noted. And while low arousal typically correlates with feelings of sadness, the biometric is less reliable as an indicator of joy and anger as these contrasting emotional states are both marked by high skin conductivity. As we spoke, the challenges associated with skin conductance slowly accrued. Age impacts the numbers: older people tend to experience lower skin conductivity compared to younger people. The temperature in the environment matters too: if it is too cold, skin conductivity may be low; if the setting is too hot, the measure may likewise become skewed. At one point, Anne even joked about the limitations of her device, laughing about the LED light that she added to her wearable to indicate whether skin conductivity was high or low, saying that "on a cold day, only young people will glow."[8] Responding in kind, Rachel, another participant in this project, kidded that to test how this device performs, we would need to be highly selective about the conditions of our experiments and so may just not be able to "embarrass people on a hot day."[9] Technological certainty and objective rationality dissolved in moments like these, and all that remained was a finicky gadget whose sensitivity the technologists needed to grapple with before the device could contend with the sentiments of others.

Anne and her team, moreover, were not alone in their appreciation of the limitations of biometric tools. The various technological, environmental, and social challenges remain present for those involved in the wearables field. When I spoke to other product makers, for example, I routinely heard similar responses. "Steps are easy; it's walking that's hard," one engineer pithily summarized for me when I wondered if at least measuring walking compared to monitoring emotion was a technical problem that was relatively straightforward.[10] Segmenting the various movements of individual bodies from irrelevant jerks and twitches into a pattern of readable "steps" to produce an accurate account of walking remained, for product makers, a formidable task complicated by weight, height, age, body type, as well as social factors such as manners of walking associated with gender types.

In this unsteady engineering context, one way to understand "emotional sweat" is as a proto-boundary object rather than as a straightforward synonym for "clean" data. As Star and Griesemer emphasized in their analysis of natural history museums, "scientific work is heterogeneous" (1989, p. 387). On any given day, it requires the collaboration of people with vastly different scientific, political, and economic commitments. Only through the creation of boundary objects such as natural specimens that are "simultaneously concrete and abstract, specific and general" (p. 409) can cross-disciplinary partners work toward a common goal. Boundary objects produce what, in a related context, historian of science Peter Galison called the "trading zone," a term characterizing a "set of linguistic and procedural practices" whose key role is to bind a diverse set of scientific approaches under a common frame (1997, p. 808). As they supply a mutual purpose and shared language, vernacular alternatives such as "emotional sweat" create just such a trading zone for interdisciplinary wearables development work. As Anne collaborates with a diverse set of colleagues, including data scientists, designers, marketers, as well as anthropologists, she frequently employs this vocabulary to maintain productive dialogue and move the development of her device forward despite the ongoing technological challenges or interpretative differences recognized by these actors.

Thinking about emotional sweat (and indeed the contrasts between Dan's cliche deployment of the term "quantified self" in a promotional speech and technologists' more pragmatic assessments of digitization echoed in QS conversation) as a boundary object or as a trading zone rather than as a direct equivalent of skin conductance or as a de facto correlate of emotions highlights some of the skepticism with which practitioners such as Anne actually accept biometrics such as skin conductance as proxies for sentiment, thus complicating their public assessment of these data as clean signals. In fact, the capaciousness of boundary objects and the connective tissues of the trading zone only betray their own fragility. As they promote cooperation and coherence, they mark the field as inherently contested and unsettled. The rhetorical bridges they erect allow participants to suspend as much as to sustain their differences. And so, even as Anne appears to deploy skin conductance and emotional sweat as unproblematic substitutes, our conversations reveal that she and her colleagues remain keenly aware of the difficulties of translating affect into data and that they do not take for granted that neither skin conductance nor emotional sweat represent emotions tout court.

Comparing and contrasting the ways Anne discusses the work of her device in public conferences and private conversations with colleagues offers one way to appreciate the layered view of wearable technology and digital data shared by product makers. While Anne publicly endorses her device and the data it produces as exacting and precise, doing so contrasts with the more careful ways she characterizes her data in other professional settings. On industry panels, her presentation of skin conductance as clean emotional signals still aligns neatly with a classic positivist posture. In dialogue with her teammates, the transfiguration of skin conductance into emotional sweat takes on a different tone. Here, "emotional sweat" points to a milder professional stance on data, one that dilutes some of the concentrated certainty of her public expressions.

Anne's equation of "clean" biodata with what is effectively dirty emotional sweat unwittingly registers such divergent aims. While the comparison may at first appear unwieldy, given that sweat is the very thing that clean bodies lack, it is all the more fitting for the contradictions it implies. This seemingly paradoxical construction readily suggests that for makers of commercial wearables such as Anne, data do not only move linearly from a state of dirty to a state of clean; they remain both dirty and clean, depending on their context. In the right promotional environment, skin conductance can still read as "clean" data. Yet, when taken out of this framework, the same indices become "matter out of place" (Douglas, 1966, p. 50). The expression "emotional sweat" only further registers data's murkier entrepreneurial reality, muddling the view that developers of wearable computing see data only as clean biomatter distilled from messy bodies.[11]

Vaporware

Looking at how device makers negotiate the investor environment through their use of poetic speech opens another window onto wearables entrepreneurs' more complicated relationship to data. This is especially so given that the role figurative language plays in these settings contrasts with its function in cross-disciplinary work. Whereas expressions such as "emotional sweat" help register the limitations of wearable devices when deployed as boundary objects or trading zones, in discussions with financial backers, these types of phrases instead help companies compensate for their products' deficiencies in order to dramatize technological capabilities. Even as entrepreneurs continue to publicly endorse their tools as objective devices that produce clear knowledge, the use of "emotional sweat" as an investor-oriented hyperbole offers another way to appreciate product makers' more pluralized view of data and bodies.

A robust body of literature on advertising has already revealed businesspeople as charismatic and highly metaphorical admen for whom inflated and figurative speech is a routine part of doing business. Anna Tsing refers to elements of business grounded in hyperbole as the "economy of appearances" (2005, p. 57) to highlight how positive economic performance often hinges on little more than its dramatic rhetorical counterpart. Where a theatrical rehearsal of investment possibilities helps to bring about desired financial results, the making of spectacle is revealed as a crucial component of fiscal success. Kaushik Sunder Rajan (2006) similarly argues that contemporary high-tech capitalism increasingly calls for a more expansive understanding of productivity, one grounded in the ability to generate both things and spectacular scenes. In the commercial sphere, the crafty manipulations associated with the swift gestures of a magician who is "able to pull rabbits out of hats" (p. 114), making much ado about nothing, are as valuable as the generative capacities of laboring limbs creating commodities.

Timothy Malefyt (2018) has taken up the figure of the magician as a more explicit analytical category to examine the beliefs and practices of those working in fields such as advertising. He found that for advertising executives, particularly for the advertising "creatives," business and art remain complementary rather than contradictory.[12] These professionals readily view advertising as a mode of transformation, a process by which skilled practitioners take "feeble" concepts and turn them into grand ideas, converting "ordinary commercial products" into "extraordinary campaigns" (Malefyt, 2018, p. 173). Similar to the work of the magician, the transfiguration of products from ordinary to extraordinary is brought about through specialized rhetoric as well as a carefully orchestrated social performance, rather than just cleverly crafted advertising messages. The latter include over-the-top business pitches, industry award ceremonies, and the wholesale cultural valorization and fetishization of advertising "creative" labor itself. In the end, like the magician, advertising executives are able to captivate their audiences through accruing power in the hands of the few and keeping that power "mysterious, ambiguous, and elusive" (Malefyt, 2018, p. 164).

By examining advertising professionals alongside magicians, Malefyt (2018) underscores that admen-cum-modern-day magicians operate "within, as opposed to against, modern rationality" (p. 176). This duality is even replicated at the structural level, as the industry's creative function exists hand in glove with its business arm. The subjects of this chapter are also salespeople for whom objectivity and fanciful metaphor alike are persuasive. The different ways in which they frame data in varying commercial settings only further highlight that the clean biometric signals and objective technologies they publicly promise continue to be shaped by messy business realities.

The coincidence of business artistry and scientific rationality is particularly pronounced in the context of investor relations, in which entrepreneurs are routinely cautioned against producing "vaporware" and simultaneously encouraged to create inflated promises. Vaporware is a derisive term that distinguishes device makers committed to function and accuracy from those who manufacture airy hype. When stories about businesses that produce vaporware flare up in industry news, they are quickly snuffed out as radical singularities. Theranos, a company that alleged to have developed a device that could diagnose countless diseases on the spot from a single drop of blood, has been the poster child for such scorned practices since 2015. At its height, Theranos managed to collect as much as $700 million in venture capital. By 2015, however, the company had experienced a dramatic fall from grace after John Carreyrou, an investigative journalist writing for the *Wall Street*

Journal, revealed that the claims its founders made were nothing more than exaggerated assertions.

The news coverage that followed largely interpreted the firm's early gains through a gendered lens, often attributing the company's explosive financial success to the hypnotizing appeal of its then nineteen-year-old female founder Elizabeth Holmes. Reportage emphasized Holmes's youth and beguiling charisma – which some said even outmatched that of her adopted hero, Steve Jobs – as well as her unusually deep voice. Holmes was routinely presented both as a masculinized figure – a female Steve Jobs – and as a hyperfeminized, modern-day siren (Bilton, 2016; Hartmans and Leskin, 2020). In a book about the company, *Bad Blood: Secrets and Lies in a Silicon Valley Startup* (2018), Carreyrou counts these qualities as among the factors that enabled Holmes to lure high-profile backers such as Rupert Murdoch, the Walton family, and the Devos family as well as to secure the endorsement of large corporations like Walgreens.

Framed as a false prophet who peddled empty promises, Holmes has become an industry outcast whose success appears exceptional, maybe especially so given her ambiguous gender identity. The accusations leveled against her have shattered her credibility, but they also unwittingly bolstered the reputation of the commercial wearables industry. Those denouncing Holmes implicitly place vaporware and inflated speech outside of the industry's legitimate limits. In doing so, they reinforce an invisible line that separates her unstable gadget, suspect data, and hyperbolic promotional style from the stable devices, clean data, and sober scientific rhetoric located within the parameters of the field proper.

Yet, the favor Holmes's bloated claims curried with investors is perhaps less anomalous than it is representative of routine dynamics in the wearables industry. After all, inventors of wearable technology (WT) are also regularly counseled to inflate the capacities of their tools in order to inflate investor confidence. For example, at one workshop hosted by Microsoft for wearables startups that I attended in New York City, a venture capitalist speaking on a featured panel advised the room full of entrepreneurs to work on developing dramatic effect alongside their technologies. Explaining that financial backers are "people too," he admitted that "investors want it [a new product] to look big because if it looks big, there is a chance that it will be big."[13] At an event for industry entrants and future "insiders," this panelist was blunt about the fact that performing success is an important part of creating success because businesses that appear established are better able to attract venture capital that will help them to actually thrive.

Today, there exist myriad ways, both familiar and new, of staging business success before fully achieving it. In addition to glossy marketing materials, this process now frequently entails continued self-promotion and self-branding (Marwick, 2013; Gershon, 2017; see also Chapter 4). Ambitious and exciting claims about the ways wearable devices will function likewise help product makers to stoke investor confidence.

Bloated promises – something that one of my interlocutors aptly called "pitch theater" – are particularly common for products in prototype such as the one that Anne had created, a stage of development that is typically referred to in the technology field as an MVP. MVP is not an initialism for "most valuable player," as in sports, but rather for "minimally viable product," and the contrast between the two MVPs is telling. In sports, the MVP represents the most accomplished member of a league. The MVP in the context of digital innovation often represents the opposite – not the best iteration but the one that meets the bare minimum standard of usability. An MVP is not the final version but only a "proof of concept." It is a model that conjures a world for investors where, given proper funding, the product may work as imagined.

As a model, the MVP plays both an explanatory and a speculative function; it anticipates and does not simply assume its future form. A successful MVP demonstrates how a product may work and puts on airs in order to secure the resources necessary to one day become a fraction of what its makers fathom. This is where the two forms of MVP converge. Entrepreneurial bluster helps to represent the minimally viable product as the most valuable player in the making and to implicitly reframe an apparent contradiction in terms as a meaningful product trajectory. In contrast to the self-conscious and modest deployment of emotional sweat as a boundary object or as a trading zone, in this digital economy of appearances, Anne's conversion of skin conductance to emotional sweat translates the work of her device for potential investors. And so, the expression is purposefully affected; it is strategically bombastic. The MVP, as much as Anne's translation, speaks both in the present and the future tense. Reflecting the entrepreneurial imperative to model size, to act big before becoming big, Anne's device and her transfiguration of skin conductance into emotional sweat represent a working model and a flight of fancy that daringly expresses what the device may become once it is properly funded and developed.

The entrepreneurial doublespeak expected of product developers makes it difficult to evaluate wearable devices and their outputs as knowledge forms that exist in any binary relationship to falsehoods, echoing Rajan's (2006) observations related to the biotech field. Speaking of documents such as corporate forward-looking statements in which biotech entrepreneurs characteristically express bold claims, Rajan notes that what is at stake in these forms is "credibility" rather than calculability – the sincere desire to make plausible rather than the practical ability to make possible. If the assertions entrepreneurs make in a forward-looking statement eventually do not materialize, they have not lied "because the future it promises is precisely *incalculable*" (2006, p. 133, emphasis in the original). Hype, as scholars of speculative bioscience have likewise noted, produces "promissory capitalism" (Helmreich, 2009, p. 143; see also Fortune, 2008[14]) that has taken scientific work from a domain marked by "regimes of truth" grounded in existing scientific evidence to one marked by "regimes of hope" grounded in future-oriented expectations and uncertainty (Brown, 2005). Regimes of hope represent the life sciences in terms of their potential – an idiom that describes something that is at once inevitable and plastic. Potentiality in this context connotes both a "hidden force" with "its future built into it" as well as the flexibility of futures that can "transmute into something completely different" (Taussig, Hoeyer, and Helmreich, 2013, p. S4). In the framework of wearables entrepreneurship, hyped-up MVPs are objects that are similarly fixed and elastic. As a simulation filled with potential, an MVP does not determine reality (Baudrillard, 1994) but posits it. It conjures desirable futures but keeps their outcomes flexible. As Anne's transfiguration forwards her sincere intentions to bring skin conductance in closer alignment with sentiment, the ambitious claims she makes articulate her promises as convincing but necessarily unstable goal posts that could lead to success as well as to failure.

The inflated promissory claims characteristic of the early MVP stage indicate that vaporware is the equivalent of the entrepreneurial MVP, not its antithesis. Derisive comments about vaporware distance hype from sober product design. The two-sided MVP, on the other hand, exposes hype as a routine feature of entrepreneurial performance. It shows that hype is the flip side of sensible toolmaking rather than its opposite. Transforming meager skin conductance into emotional sweat helps Anne to make her product and investor futures look big so that, with investors' support, she will be able to take her turn at converting a feeble MVP into an extraordinary product poised for commercial success.

The connection between vaporware and the entrepreneurial MVP is not only expressed in investor expectations but also encoded in tools such as the Gartner Hype Cycle for Emerging Technologies that steward entrepreneurial imaginations. "Have you heard of the Hype Cycle?" my interlocutors repeatedly wanted to know, because it was central in their own experience within the tech sector. The Hype Cycle for Emerging Technologies is a map of sorts that tracks the progress of "emerging" technologies. Updated yearly, it has five stages: Innovation Trigger, Peak of Inflated Expectations, Trough of Disillusionment, Slope of Enlightenment, and Plateau of Productivity

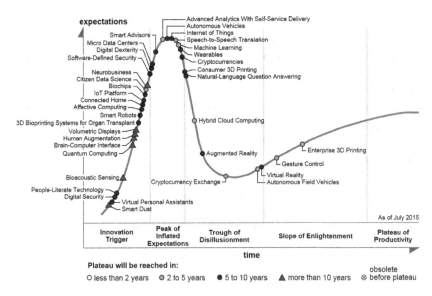

Figure 2.3 2015 Gartner Hype Cycle for Emerging Technologies.
Source: Gartner (2015). GARTNER and HYPE CYCLE are trademarks of Gartner Inc. and/or its affiliates.

(Figure 2.3). The dramatic, even poetic, terminology notwithstanding, the Hype Cycle is meant to plot new technological trends across time. The first two phases are marked, according to Gartner, by heavy competition but successful products must survive the steep drop-off at the Trough of Disillusionment.

When the Hype Cycle is understood as a linear and meritocratic progression of innovation, as many entrepreneurs in fact view it, the chart can be seen to map the separation of the wheat from the chaff, of effervescent vaporware from the solid MVP. As hype dies down, only those products whose exuberance coats a solid technological core will make it down into the Slope of Enlightenment. This reading casts successful investors and inventors as visionaries. They are people who – like the venerated Silicon Valley hero Steve Jobs – have a knack for spotting technologies that will "get ahead of the curve" early on and a gift of foresight that allows them to confidently surf the rising tide of innovation to stable ground.

My engagement with product makers indicates that hype in this configuration is not just empty boasting that marks the early, undisciplined euphoria of entrepreneurial speculation, which dissipates as vaporware evaporates into thin air, leaving behind only the genuine MVPs. Hype is also mobilized as an important mechanism of entrepreneurial endurance, one that helps product makers to stay above ground long enough to make it past the steep and crushing Peak of Inflated Expectations. Little wonder that some of the most breathless claims are typically issued by companies perched atop this precarious graphical height. Read in this way, the 2015 Hype Cycle for Emerging Technologies also indicates that the comfortable descent of entrepreneurs into the Slope of Enlightenment is not predicated on their prognosticating powers alone but on their capacities to make promises that generate the funds necessary to spirit forth the very future of innovation they conjure. Only in hindsight will inventors and investors turn out to be clairvoyant visionaries and each other's mirrors.

Hype as a mode of entrepreneurial endurance does not just fill products with hot air, air that disperses when the idea runs out of steam and the technology is revealed to have been little more than vaporware. For product makers such as Anne, developing hype qua vaporware, that is, emotional sweat and not just clean data, is one way they stay the course so that their inventions may eventually be lifted to new heights. It is how most inventions build up steam, working up the energy and the financial resources necessary to realize some version of the products that they make up. Considered from this perspective, Elizabeth Holmes' actions may also be read as more conventional than unusual, with the large sums of money she raised as an outcome of commonplace industry practices taken to their extreme and not just the product of cunning machinations performed by a deviant personality.

Thinking about the modalities of hype that expose the entrepreneurial MVP and vaporware as counterparts rather than as opposites offers additional ways to appreciate the wearables industry's more complicated relationship with knowledge making. In part, it shows what science and technology studies scholars have long argued: truth claims result from political and not only scientific work (Latour, 2005). Digital entrepreneurs are not naive to this reality. On the contrary, especially as they pursue financing, they routinely find that rhetorical acumen and not technological sophistication alone creates the conditions for digital knowledge making. Often enough, their ability to produce digital truths qua data primarily hinges on their aptitude for enticing tales, on their facility to make things look big before becoming big. When skin conductance becomes emotional sweat by sleight of hand as well as by industry demand, and when the MVP and vaporware are thus revealed as opposite sides of the same coin, they indicate that in the entrepreneurial environment of WT, there is not even one truth claim to stabilize or to forestall. Far from exclusively operating from a place of scientific rigidity, the vacillation between scientifically narrow skin conductance and more inflated ideas such as emotional sweat that digital entrepreneurs mobilize as they seek financial support show that digital practitioners invest deeply in producing analytic plasticity.

Digital Equivocations

The competing ways that wearables developers frame the outputs of their devices to the purchasing public can further challenge the perception that device makers credulously endorse their tools only as objective gadgets. These tactics continue to indicate how corporate denial of digital objectivity can be as vital to the commercial success of WT as its defense. They also indicate that practitioners both contest and revel in the constructed nature of digital knowledge.

Anne's take on data that I have evaluated throughout this chapter makes yet another turn here. On the one hand, her use of the phrase "emotional sweating" – particularly when mobilized to translate between expert developers and nonspecialist wearables customers – fits neatly within a wider history of metaphorical language in computing. Media scholars and historians have examined how symbolic language and iconography have long played a key role in helping to accommodate the personal computer for use by a lay public. The electronic mouse developed by Douglas C. Engelbart in 1964 was one early innovation that gave the neophyte control of computer functions. Amateur computer use was likewise bolstered by what Tenen (2017) calls a shift from "dialogical" to "direct" models of computer interaction. The direct model substituted simple graphics for the specialized commands that had to be entered on the keyboard to activate computer processes as recently as the 1980s. The now-familiar icons such as trash bins, document folders, and windows emerged as explanatory mechanisms that made complex technical functions accessible to ordinary users. Anne's occasional use of emotional sweating, in conversation with future users, echoes some of these designs.

Since 2013, when Edward Snowden released the details of the surveillance program conducted by the National Security Agency (NSA) and thus elevated to public consciousness the uses to which corporate and government bodies may put the personal data of ordinary citizens, corporate deployment of computer metaphors has acquired additional political appeal. This shift has been particularly visible in the changes made to privacy policies of digital companies, whose former arcane vocabulary has become emblematic of the larger ways that technology firms operate as informatic "black boxes" (Pasquale, 2015). To mediate these concerns, many companies have begun making concerted efforts to convert some of the more inscrutable legal terminology used in privacy policies into everyday terms. This use of vernacular responds to an implicit critique of official language as well as its associated differential in power and social status (Labov, 1966, 1972; Baudrillard, 1994; Barbrook and Cameron, 1996; Asif and Wortham, 2005; Agha, 2006).

Commonplace design specifications such as "make it so simple that a child or my grandmother can understand it" reflect similar aims. Despite their patent paternalism and sexism, these statements indicate an industry imperative for technical mastery and domain expertise to be increasingly displayed in ways that are accessible rather than alienating to the general public. Anne's rewording of skin conductance as emotional sweat can be viewed along the same lines. In other words, such an idiomatic construction does not simply resonate as an explanatory mechanism that grants nonexperts access to specialized tools. It can additionally be viewed as an instrument of unmasking. By transforming unintelligible scientific vocabulary into plain speech, Anne's colloquialism evokes the linguistic adaptations technology companies have started to make in order to appear transparent and open to public scrutiny.

On the other hand, Anne's transformation of skin conductance into emotional sweat aligns equally well with corporate uses of vernacular and metaphor intended to challenge rather than to enhance consumer comprehension. Consider, for example, some of the following ways that companies such as Fitbit and Oura characterize their wearables on the home pages of their respective websites. Fitbit describes its wrist-worn step tracker as a device that "puts the world of health and fitness in your hands" and as a gadget that carries the "innovative features you need for a healthier life" before calling on would-be customers to "get motivated to move with inspiration and guidance in a slim form factor." For its part, Oura claims that its ring-shaped sleep tracker "makes accurate health information personal and accessible to everyone" and that it yields "critical insights to help you build good habits and harness your body's potential every day."

Fitbit's and Oura's use of plain speech expressions such as "the world of health" and "your body's potential" to describe the indications of their devices or their qualifications of digital outputs as "insight" and "guidance" may, on first pass, appear to be of a similar kind to vernacular strategies employed by technology companies aimed at elevating public understanding and trust. Yet, these expressions can also be read as double entendres that enable businesses to make claims to customers that differ from those that they make to federal regulators. Notably, the therapeutically resonant marketing copy places these devices squarely in the realm of healthcare and medical science. Meanwhile, references to "innovative features" and "accurate health information" confirm the technical soundness of these tools. These descriptions, however, stop just short of announcing the gadgets *as* medical or diagnostic devices, connotations that are further softened by assertions that their data offer only "inspiration," "motivation," "insight," and "guidance." In Fitbit's case, the "slim form factor" of the band, which the company can safely deliver, acts as an added stand-in for the health and fitness ambitions of the firm's customers, the results of which Fitbit cannot guarantee.

Such equivocations are byproducts of federal limits set on non-FDA-approved wearable devices. For example, only those companies that have federal authorization are allowed to use terms such as "medical device" or "diagnosis" in their marketing. Obtaining FDA approval, however, often poses a significant business challenge. It can take years and cost a fortune – two things that entrepreneurs characteristically lack – to develop a device that surmounts regulatory hurdles. Even given these resources, authorization remains out of reach of most commercially available wearable tools. The Apple Watch Series 4, for example, made news in 2018 when its electrocardiogram (EKG) and the irregular rhythm notification functions became among the few direct-to-consumer wearable applications to receive FDA clearance. But even these features fell short of full FDA approval – the current gold standard for wearable tools (Chen, 2018). And yet, given that FDA approval or clearance remains an optional process for commercial wearables, the absence of federal authorization need not be a decisive roadblock for savvy marketers. Companies whose devices do not or would not meet federal guidelines can continue to inflate consumer confidence through their marketing by substituting protected words with allied terminology. By exercising the flexibility of language, product makers thus work to relieve regulatory tension on corporate resources and stretch the limits of rigid law.

Strategic wordplay, in these instances, does not only ensure legal compliance; it produces a usefully doubled effect. As distinct expressions, phrases such as "insight" and "guidance" help product makers to sharpen the differences between their own tools and federally sanctioned technology. Yet, as concepts linguistically related to terms such as "diagnosis," they help to prime customers to recognize the imputed similarities between FDA-backed and nonauthorized wearable devices.[15] Ultimately, these equivocations help companies to convey to customers that their wearables are credible and high-performing gadgets while reassuring regulators that the same tools are fallible guides meant only to motivate and inspire. In Anne's case, the substitution of emotional sweat for skin conductance is still uttered casually rather than strategically. It is these seemingly natural slippages, however, ones that appear as spontaneous exchanges, mere translations, that allow product makers to both represent their tools as science-backed and federally sanctioned devices as well as distance themselves from the regulatory oversight that governs their production. Corporate use of figurative speech and everyday language such as this offers one more example of the way wearables companies take recourse in interpretative differences of symbolic speech to simultaneously produce the

semblance of objectivity and digital clarity at the same time as they manifac-
ture opacity and carefully placed doubt. These rhetorical strategies also reveal
that it is not only social scientists and literary scholars who appreciate that
translation remains mediated by power (Asad, 1993) or that computer metaphors can only ever create partial commensuration (Tenen, 2017).

   Such marketing doublespeak also casts new light on entrepreneurial cri-
tiques of regulation. Product makers I have met tend to vociferously object
to regulation, often claiming to do so on philosophical grounds. Some caution
that excessive federal control hampers innovation, which they believe outpaces
law. Others worry that regulation stifles entrepreneurial competition, which
they see as a self-regulating force in its own right akin to the invisible hand of
the free market. The promotional equivocations that companies engage in,
however, highlight that their dismissal of regulation has as much to do with
the business advantages reaped from a soft regulatory environment as with
philosophical differences between inventors and federal agencies. These rhetorical strategies also reveal that product makers who flout regulation do not
simply hope to liberate engineering ingenuity; they help to incubate a commercial environment that favors digital ambiguity. More, while device makers
focus on ways innovation outpaces law, their plastic vocabulary suggests that
it is marketing that outpaces both innovation and law.

   Corporate maneuvers such as these likewise complicate the academic view of
bias in computing. Scholarly discourse on algorithmic bias often pivots on two
related sets of debates. Bias is either viewed as something to be recognized in
order to be rectified (Eubanks, 2015; Noble, 2018) or as that which is constitutive of knowledge more generally (Clifford, 1986; Dumit, 2004; Dumit and
Nafus, 2018). In the latter view, acknowledging bias necessarily entails
accepting that it is also impossible to completely remove it. My ethnographic
research with makers of wearables adds to these debates by highlighting that
device makers remain neither completely oblivious of digital biases nor fully
forthcoming about data's social variability. Corporate use of vernacular and
metaphor as instruments of disclosure run parallel to their use as shields that
promote closure. As makers of WT cannily take advantage of interpretive
slippages, they actively create unstable forms of knowledge by design, capitalizing both on the presumptions of scientific objectivity and on the ambiguities
inherent to digital knowing. In the end, precisely what their devices may tell
becomes not simply dangerously skewed or narrowly conceptualized but purposely difficult to establish. In a neoliberal frame, the responsibility falls to the
purchasing public to do the research to tell the difference.

   So, what does one make of expert technocrats who straddle both business
and science, who use the language of science and even the methods of science

in service of business art? The rhetorical maneuvers described in earlier sections – the entrepreneurial acceptance of emotional sweat as a fitting approximation of skin conductance or even the corporate uses of hyperbolic speech leveraged for dramatic effect in financial negotiations – do place pressure on the supposition that product makers view data in exclusively positivist terms. However, these fluctuations still seem qualitatively different from the explicit misrepresentations made with the express aim of destabilizing public opinion and trust. This disparity narrows when the advantages product makers reap from both widening and collapsing interpretive differences in their promotional materials, as this section has explored, are also added to the equation. In particular, when examined as a set of rhetorical vacillations poised to disclose as much as to obscure the workings of their devices from the purchasing public, the corporate substitutions of "insight" for "diagnosis" or of "innovative features" for "medical device," just like Anne's swift shift from "skin conductance" to "emotional sweat," highlight how product makers selectively open and close the margins of the plausible to produce decisively dissembling effects. While amplifying nostalgia for the real in public-facing pronouncements, wearables entrepreneurs approach the search for truth in data as a fiction and often exploit both the simulation of the real and its breakdown for profit.

***

On the surface, the "inner quantified self" illustrated by the digital *Vitruvian Man* that opened this chapter suggests little but the analytic rigidity of wearables developers such as Dan. However, the shifting digital talk I encountered at QS events and in my wider interactions with practitioners like Anne troubles this narrow view. The vacillating perspectives of technologists on data speak to the equally varied significance data take on in a range of business settings. Executives may continue to endorse uncomplicated perspectives on data in public venues. Broadening the lens beyond the promotional context, however, reveals that digital executives display a keener awareness of the politics of digital representation. They recognize that data do not just accrue without issues, as if they were figurative streams spouting from bodies and channeled directly into myriad digital gadgets. Data come with baggage that necessarily weighs down the rhetorical effortlessness of digital circulation. This baggage constrains and determines the type of information technologists can aspire to collect. Data thus emerge as always already multiple, variously packaged by a broad range of professional obligations. In this context, Anne's metaphor for biodata as emotional sweat, just like the concept of the "quantified self" itself, has to be seen as a loaded but unstable signifier. This expression works as an explanatory metaphor for skin conductance that fits with her cognitive understanding of emotions and as an imperfect proxy for sentiment in the context of collegial product development. It can also be understood as a flatly bloated hyperbole in the framework of investor relations or as a conveniently unstable referent in a regulatory environment.

Technologists, in other words, approach digitization as something that is both clear and murky, as steady and changeable. The discursive dexterity defines a professional environment in which contradiction, obfuscation, and hyperbole emerge as meaningful business strategies alongside product makers' more public commitments to scientific rationality. As these digital professionals respond to commercial pressures, balance entrepreneurial anxieties, and manage social expectations related to WT, they deliberately advance multifaceted and even competing notions of personal data. It's this rhetorical volatility, rather than straightforward entrepreneurial certainty, that makes wearable devices and self-tracking applications commercially viable and safe from liability.

From this end, we can appreciate the digital Vitruvian Man that opened this chapter, as an unlikely symbol of the analytic dexterity of WT that I encountered in QS forums and beyond, rather than its opposite. Certainly, on its face, the flat and idealized movement of data visualized therein appear to block a broader appreciation of the way technologists also dart between multiple concepts of data, knowingly representing data as enduring and plastic. By refocusing attention on the duality expressed within this image, however, we can see how it also inadvertently contains within it its own critique. Despite initial appearances, the multiple, spread-out limbs and arms of the digital Vitruvian Man indicate that the data wearable devices collect is similarly always already multivalent.

3

Acting Like Members, Thinking Like Vendors

Moving beyond the label and analyzing some of the role Quantified Self has played within the digital economy offers additional ways to understand the work and lives of digitals professionals, especially in the early to mid-2010s. That is because this forum has come of age in a business climate shaped by twin forces: the growing importance of consumer-centric principles within the tech industry, and the expanding neoliberalization of the workplace marked by flexible conditions of employment. Executives in this climate are variously pressured to channel desire for technological innovation toward business ends. Another way to understand QS as an interface to the dynamics powering digital entrepreneurialism, then, is to examine it both as a product and as an instrument of these business tendencies.

The way executives exercise passion for digital technology in settings such as QS typifies some of the ways digital fetishism has come to shape the self-tracking arena. Especially so as these interactions highlight how those employed in the tech sector increasingly work as *extracurricular entrepreneurs*, as I call technologists who now take on a range of affective work as a matter of standard operating procedure. These executives recognize that fostering and stoking desire has emerged as necessary labor that sustains the digital economy. Theorists of critical data often highlight what feminist Marxist scholar Silvia Federici (1975) has called "affective labor" and what sociologist Maurizio Lazzarato (1996) named "immaterial" investments of low-wage workers who toil in the shadows of algorithmic processes to emphasize how eager workers laboring in the margins of automated systems help maintain them and forestall their collapse (see also Irani, 2015; Gray and Suri, 2019).[1] This analysis supplements earlier articulations of fan labor (De Kosnik, 2013), social media commenting (Andrejevic, 2013), or more general extracurricular online engagement (Terranova, 2000; Zuboff, 2019) as free labor. As the next two chapters explore, those engaged in the making of contemporary self-tracking devices and applications likewise routinely harness uncompensated passion toward business ends, particularly as they work to realize two figures central to digital entrepreneurship: the devoted employee and the desiring "end user" for whom the industry innovates.

The current chapter addresses how extracurricular free and "emotional labor" (Hochschild, 2012) allows technologists to recognize the aspirational covetous consumer. More specifically, we will see how Wolf and Kelly's polarized view of QS as a cultural found object (see Chapter 1) has supplied some of the affective register necessary for technologists to apprehend the "needs and wants" of prospective customers and to perceive these predilections as discoverable in accords with humanistic and voyeuristic principles of user-centric marketing and design. Chapter 4 will examine the importance of passion in projects of professional self-making, the role QS has played within them, and how this cultivated enthusiasm ultimately feeds back into the social imaginary surrounding the popular response to digital innovation.

Examining how digital executives have situated themselves and their work in relationship to QS also exposes the more circuitous ways in which extracurricular entrepreneurs now work to capitalize on desire. While user-centric tech professionals are typically trained to place themselves in a binary and extractive relationship with their customers, in practice this separation is often realized through a productive mingling of identities. This chapter thus analyzes QS as among the contemporary devices that allow digital executives to convert their own interventions into indicators of preexisting consumer demand. Examining the significantly more entangled role digital professionals play in formulating user preferences, and some of the part that QS has played within these dynamics, reverses the linear business trajectory suggested by industry common sense. It additionally reveals QS less as an ensemble of passionate self-trackers that spells the future of digital possibilities and more immediately as a collective that exemplifies some of the novel forms of entrepreneurial sociality that increasingly underpin contemporary technological production.

Investigating QS as a mechanism that equips technologists with the means to instrumentalize passion so as to meet the demands of the tech market also highlights some of the new ways community has become incorporated into cycles of innovation. It shows how digital technology does not simply support the formation of community[2] but how community building developed through the extracurricular labor of digital professionals has been transformed into an essential feature of digital work. Ultimately, this chapter approaches QS as an interface that connects wearables entrepreneurialism with acts of invention – of culture, community, and forms of desire to be absorbed by tech capitalism – in ways that extend executives' creative capacities beyond new technology.

Acting Like Creators, Thinking Like Marketers

As a stating point, its worth considering that Wolf and Kelly's formulation of QS as a cultural found object acquires some of its meaning and purpose within a business world focused on consumer centricity. Device makers tend to see themselves as participants of a dynamic and ever-changing field where they actively engage in building new possibilities and futures. This work, however, remains shaped by rigid business conventions such as the notion of buyers as fixed others that companies must seek to discover.

Phillip Kotler and Gary Armstrong, authors of a leading introductory marketing textbook, *Principles of Marketing*, articulate some of the basic parameters of this business philosophy as they guide students to recognize that the work of marketing involves more than product development and selling to an indiscriminate pool of shoppers. "Blasting out messages to the masses" is business building in the "old sense," the authors explain as they caution readers against such "myopic" thinking (Armstrong and Kotler, 2018). They clarify further:

> Many sellers make the mistake of paying more attention to the specific products they offer than to the benefits and experiences produced by these products. These sellers suffer from marketing myopia. They are so taken with their product that they focus only on existing wants and lose sight of underlying customer needs. They forget that a product is only a tool to solve a consumer problem. A manufacturer of quarter-inch drill bits may think that the customer needs a drill bit. But what the customer *really* needs is a quarter-inch hole. (p. 31, emphasis in the original)

Unlike shortsighted, "inside-out" sales tactics that focus on "customer conquest" and on selling "what the company makes rather than . . . what the market wants," contemporary businesspeople are advised to start with an "outside-in perspective," that is, to ground their work in a thorough under-standing of the "needs and wants" of prospective buyers. In contrast to the "make-and-sell philosophy," the outside-in perspective articulates a "cus-tomer-centric sense-and-response" as the gold standard of contemporary busi-ness thinking (Armstrong and Kotler, 2018, p. 36).

As the marketers explain, executives committed to such approaches do not begin with the development of a product that can then be matched with a receptive buyer. Instead, business professionals are routinely advised to start with a comprehensive assessment of "the market," which the authors define as "the set of actual and potential buyers of a product or service" (Armstrong and Kotler, 2018, p. 33). This initial audit also includes a careful cataloguing of consumer preferences from which executives can identify the "particular need or want that can be satisfied through exchange relationships" (p. 33). Only following this rigorous process of classifying and sorting, one where managers compile and review studies that carve up the market – conceived as a singular whole – into "distinct groups of buyers" known as consumer "segments," can executives begin to "identify the parts of the market they can serve best" (p. 212).

Even though such descriptions present "the market" and the "needs and wants" of prospective buyers as reified abstractions, businesspeople frequently embrace these schemas as humanistic improvements over even more rigid models of consumption. Principally, unlike product-focused and blunt selling tactics of business past, contemporary consumer-centric approaches guide executives to recognize their buyers as desiring humans and to see their primary task as rooted in deep, even empathetic, listening and relationship building.

This framing endorses interpersonal intimacy as a new model for business. In the same way that Branislaw Malinowski (2014 [1922]) once established the importance of understanding the "native's point of view" for anthropologists, marketers who support customer-centric approaches aim to prioritize the consumer's point of view. Admen like David Ogilvy continue to be remembered for introducing this sentiment to business thinking. After founding the eponymous advertising agency in the 1950s, Ogilvy routinely admonished his copywriters and ad executives to remember that "the consumer is not a moron, she's your wife" (1976). This statement is clearly steeped in the paternalism and sexism of the era. However, like Malinowski, who encouraged his colleagues to accept the rationality and humanity of indigenous people, Ogilvy issued this directive to encourage his admen to see customers for whom they were developing promotional campaigns as real as the people they may know in their own lives rather than as distant business caricatures.

Today, executives who sing paeans to consumer-centric strategies see a focus on the "needs and wants" of potential buyers not just as a less myopic but as a more ethical and humane way of doing business. Businesspeople thus frequently describe an attunement to consumer preferences as the very means by which they work to understand the inherent humanity of their customers and connect with prospective shoppers as "real people" rather than as numbers. One advertising executive echoed this sentiment in a message he shared with his colleagues on LinkedIn, the social media platform used mainly by business professionals. The adman posed the following, seemingly open question to his online followers: "But, what does the consumer think?" In his role as a brand strategist at an advertising agency, he is charged with answering this very question for a range of "clients" – the companies that are responsible for developing both the product and its promotional campaigns, and who contract with advertising agencies and brand strategists to learn about and respond to their consumers' desires. The question, it turned out, was a segue to a confession as this executive used the probe to announce his own struggle with the answer. The difficulty, he quickly clarified, lay in categories such as "the consumer" rather than in any challenge he may have with interpreting human behavior. He explained why he continues to find the question difficult to answer, as follows:

> But, what does the consumer think? I'm not sure how to answer. I don't think I've met one in all of my years in strategy or market research. But I have met lots of moms and dads. Sons and daughters. Some fans of Charlie Tuna and people who always wanted to adopt . . . Who are people. That live in the world. And sometimes buy things that help.[3]

While the query first echoed as a rebuff of the profession, the comment received a high number of approving "likes" and reposts by colleagues who shared his commitment to recognizing the fundamental humanity of the people that they design and produce for.

An understanding of consumers as "people who sometimes buy things that help" is meant to curb grandiose business thinking by guiding executives to recognize the significantly more modest role most consumer goods play in people's lives. Nevertheless, executives are frequently advised that a keener focus on buyers' preferences and habits can also positively benefit the bottom line, if not help these executives to "reimagine capitalism" altogether (Henderson, 2020). For this reason, Kotler and Armstrong endorse consumer-centric approaches as the more sensible, not just the more humane and ethical, way of doing business. While "aggressive selling . . . carries high risks," the marketers write, consumer-centric approaches help companies to build "relationships with the right customers" that are both long-lasting and profitable (2018, p. 36). More, the authors discuss compassionate and active listening as practices that endow executives with near-telepathic awareness of the "latent" needs of the market (p. 36). A marketing manager from 3M quoted in the textbook put the matter even more directly: "Our goal is to lead customers where they want to go before *they* know where they want to go" (p. 36, emphasis in the original). Kotler and Armstrong thus conclude that it is by focusing on customers' needs (e.g. their need for a quarter-inch hole) that companies will be able to accomplish more of what they actually want, such as selling more drill bits.

It is fitting that these authors introduce an instrument such as the drill as a prototypical example to make their point in a contemporary business textbook. While companies producing consumer-packaged goods (CPGs) have long accepted the premise that corporations must respond to the preferences of their customers, the technology sector has largely remained "product-focused" in its approach. By the mid 2000s, consumer-centric ideas have filtered down to the technology sector as well, aided by popular methodologies like "design thinking" established by innovation consulting firms such as IDEO and design programs like the Sandford D-School.

These days, as executives have become increasingly aware that people see advertising as bothersome, consumer-centric approaches promise to open new horizons for consumer–company interactions, such as the means by which to make the mediating work of commercial interests disappear from (buyers') purview. The social media company TikTok articulated this position when it announced a new set of features for its advertisers in 2021. "When brands join TikTok, we tell them to think like marketers and act like creators,"[4] the company's press release advised as it advertised the platform as a forum where executives could encounter their customers (TikTok, 2021). In this framing, marketers who "act like creators" are not just looking to deceive would-be platform users. In the same way that authors such as Kotler and Armstrong encourage companies to walk in the shoes of their buyers by learning about their needs and wants, the corporate counsel for marketers to don creators' clothes articulates a view of marketing as a reflective mirror. There is another implied business advantage as well. This corporate invocation also accords with Martin Heidegger's concept of "ready-to-hand" (Dreyfus, 1990). According to Heidegger, our world remains "ready-to-hand" so long as the tools we use escape our attention. To make his point, he often used the example of simple technology, such as the doorknob, which enters people's consciousness only when it jams. Business executives likewise seek to make their work as "ready-to-hand" as Heidegger's doorknob. Indeed, executives frequently speak of consumer-centric approaches as the very means by which promotional tactics and consumer–company exchanges can be made as invisible as a well-oiled doorknob that has become "seamlessly" incorporated into the currents of life.

QS and Consumer Centricity

As an interface, QS plays a dual role in this professional context. It allows technologists to register and formulate some of the parameters of consumer desire in accords with consumer-centric business principles. As it reflects industry reliance on reified notions of the consumer, it also acts as an engine that produces and reproduces that consumer in a way that abstracts the corporate impact on these interactions.

That technologists perceived QS, particularly when the forum is understood primarily as a user community, as a site for undercover consumer engagement and discovery surfaced most clearly in moments of denial. In particular, it echoed in the repeated refutations I heard whenever I invited participants to interview with me about their involvement with QS. "I'm happy to talk with you, but I'm not a real self-tracker," I was frequently told. Early on in my research, I would wince a little at this response, feeling slightly embarrassed of my mistake. And yet, as I continued to engage in QS affairs, as I interviewed "members," "vendors," and QS meetup organizers, this hesitation turned into a familiar pattern. Many of the people I encountered repeatedly qualified their willingness to speak with me about their interest in data and QS with a familiar though unsolicited retort: "I'm happy to talk with you, but I'm not a real self-tracker."

As used by my interlocutors, the expression "self-tracker" conflates self-tracking devices with the people using them. The consistent rejection of this label at first felt surprising given that the forum ostensibly organized those with an explicit interest in self-tracking practices. With time, I came to realize that the renunciation of this moniker did not simply indicate a research blunder. Nor was it just uttered out of modesty to cover for participants' more casual interest in these tools in the same way a second-language learner might claim that they do not speak the language to conceal their insecurity over still humble linguistic abilities. In refusing this title, those I spoke with often revealed themselves as tech sector executives who were acting in accords with user-centric principles. Some attended at QS events as corporate researchers investigating grassroots practices, others as digital executives conducting their own due diligence on the self-tracking market, and still others attended as device developers in search of relevant "use cases" for a broad range of wearable and self-tracking devices.

From the perspective of executives mindful of user-centric business mandates, it was neither surprising nor dishonest to relate to QS as putative "members," and these executives often readily accommodated Wolf's request for leading group interactions and presentations with their personal interest in self-tracking tools. By disguising, or at least by decentering, their professional roles in forum activities, they mingled in QS precisely in the terms suggested by Kotler and Armstrong and translated into a corporate solicitation by companies such as TikTok: as consumer-centric businesspeople who were acting as creators, or in this case as self-trackers all the while thinking as executives.

Admittedly, I likewise initially looked to group activities in these terms: as a forum where real self-trackers came to put their passion for digital metrics and wearable gadgets on display. Indeed, I was originally attracted to QS as an ethnographic field site that could help me reconcile the tech-driven rhetoric on wearable technology (WT) with people's lived experiences of such tools. To be sure, I was not engaging in this mission alone. Academics were such a common fixture at QS meetups that I occasionally heard those studying QS remark, sometimes with emphasis and at other times with consternation, that there was a "social scientist in every group." These researchers generally mirrored the bifurcated posture of digital professionals when engaging in QS activities. Social scientists just like my interlocutors in the digital arena approached QS and the site of the "real self-tracker" to be discovered by humanistic researchers (see Introduction). If technologists I came across did not always see themselves as the legitimate foci of an anthropologist's attention, it was because they saw our involvement with QS as of a kind. Putatively, we were both at QS to witness the real self-tracker. The denial invoked us both as participant observers, as outsiders who were looking in on the community rather than as constitutive members of the cast. It also placed us in the position of visitors who engaged with QS as a space that materialized "in here" the consumer needs and wants representative of a broader "culture of personal data" (Wolf, 2008) located "out there."

Still, even as QS was widely patronized by social scientists, among others, as a community it found an especially eager audience in the tech sector shaped by the consumer-centric imaginary. The premise that QS represented a "real community, with real people all over the world ... talking about themselves using data," as Wolf (2016) once described it (see Chapter 1), prompted technologists to turn to the forum as though it were a distinct ethnographic miniature. The narration of QS as a stable community allowed practitioners to place themselves at an observational distance from it. This framework played a legitimizing and authenticating function. It empowered technologists to act as if from under the cover of membership, and therefore to turn to QS as one type of user community, that is, as a delimited field site that made the needs and wants of digital enthusiasts manifest. When accepted in these terms, QS aligned with the aspirational linear trajectory of user-centric discovery. This formulation promised to connect technologists with concrete beliefs and practices that could be witnessed and described as if they were experiences slowly incubated for "the market" at large. They could then be mobilized as one more means by which technologists could "sense and respond" to consumer demand.

Certainly, not everyone in the tech sector saw QS in such generative and providential terms. Many of the executives working on self-tracking applications that I connected with outside of QS gatherings often dismissed the group for its particularity. They described QS participants in more restrained ways than their advocates to explain why they were not interested in following the forum's activities. Primarily, they saw QS as a space that brought together only extreme and expert users, people, in other words, whose informed and passionate devotion to data and self-tracking technology did not represent, in their view, the desires of the mainstream technology neophytes these executives typically identified as their core customers. "Those are not my users," I would often hear executives in the tech sector remark in reference to QS, echoing the refrain Donna Flynn (2010) had faced in her work as a user-researcher at Microsoft.[5] Many firms, I learned, simply didn't see QS members as their "target market" even though representatives of wearables companies at times continued to participate as visitors, some to support the community, others to keep their fingers on the pulse of developing cultural trends.

This more removed and disinterested posture nevertheless conformed to industry conventions. Even as these executives rejected QS "members" as representatives of their specific consumer targets, and identified QS as a "niche" community, they only reaffirmed QS as a self-evident user "segment." Therefore, even as they discounted the forum as a site worthy of their own attention, these practitioners continued to respond to QS as a collective to be discovered by tech capitalism. Indeed, the moniker "Quantified Self" readily aligned with business practices where executives endeavor to first divide all conceivable users into manageable and relevant-for-business groupings and then assign these sets a catchy title. In this context, the journalistic practice of generating a prospective headline for a story that first led QS founders to come up with the catchphrase "quantified self" neatly maps onto established marketing practices. QS effectively shortcuts some of the work associated with consumer segmentation as it presents digital executives with an apparently ready-made assemblage and label.

Reconciling Wolf and Kelly's construction of QS as a user community with the demands of consumer-centric business reveals how QS has supported some of the mechanisms that make the business of self-tracking work. The removed way businesspeople are generally taught to see their customers is well accommodated by the conceit that forums such as QS are a site where specific consumer practices can be witnessed and observed. Forums such as QS enable technologists to place themselves into a binary relationship with would-be buyers in ways that best align with the expectations of consumer-centric business. At the same time, this symbiotic relationship between curious companies and apparently self-organizing consumer communities already points to the creative functions of business where industry conventions anticipate and even necessitate the construction of QS-type forums as a technophile phenomenon.

Corporate Camouflage and Its Discontents

The refutation "I'm not the real self-tracker" that I often heard at QS events also speaks to some of the more circuitous dynamics of recognitions that shape consumer-centric principles as much as it offers further insight into the relationship between the tech sector and forums such as QS. Consumer centricity may exist today as a business ideal. Nevertheless, it remains difficult to fully realize in practice. Contrary to the linear and extractive imaginary established by these business dictums, executives camouflaging as self-trackers at forums such as QS operate in a world where the posture of curiosity and distance dictated by this corporate ideology contrasts with market realities. Technologists primarily work in professional settings open about the leading role executives must take in molding consumer desires. The repeated disavowal I heard in QS registers this entrepreneurial duality as it indexes QS as a forum that supplies the ends and means of this familiar corporate abstraction. It also indicates that QS offers companies functioning in the tension between the seeming certainty of humanistic business principles and their practical absence in the workplace alternative mechanisms for refashioning corporate interventions as modes of discovery.

Anthropologists and sociologists of work have of course long recognized that business professionals, like those mingling at forums such as QS, exert influence on social and commercial imaginaries through their work. Consumer-centric principles may conjure executives as both humanists and as intrepid explorers. These researchers instead highlight the critical role businesspeople play in configuring the subjects of their commercial efforts. Those who have studied executives in fields such as advertising and finance, for example, have explored standard business tactics such as segmentation, targeting, and consumer profiling as acts of invention (Kemper, 2001) that reflect the company's own corporate structure (Flynn, 2010), the cultural imaginations of managers (Mazzarella, 2003) and financiers (Tsing, 2005), the "algorithmic configurations," that is, the "the calculative device created by experts of marketing and stock" (Callon and Muniesa, 2005, p. 1239), as well as the conspiratorial relationship of marketers and their vendors (Malefyt, 2003), rather than any lived reality of would-be buyers. The logic and the language of this corporate infrastructure produce a territory of "total survivability" much like maps and charts did in Benedict Anderson's study of colonial rule of India, argues anthropologist Timothy Malefyte (2003, p. 152). They impose a semblance of order and certainty onto an otherwise mutable set of interactions and relationships, as they organize disorderly social experiences into "manageable collections" (p. 152). Prospective shoppers thus falsely emerge as "subjects of pursuit . . . [and] become reified as objects of desire to be captured and contained" (p. 157), as groups of people that exist in a sphere of activity situated outside of the business when, in fact, they are brought into a relationship with business only through executives' own labor. As consumer-centric approaches empower executives to reframe the central dilemmas of business around humanistic ideals, such scholarship suggests that these corporate principles instead produce an adversarial relationship between buyers and sellers as it continues to articulate the work of business building as a form of heroic conquest that holds people out as distant others to be subjugated and managed. Even as they prepare executives to understand the marketplace as made up of people who live in the world and sometimes buy things that help, the free-range sociality they invoke in fact remains structured by corporate ambitions and business frameworks.

Scholars of science and technology have likewise challenged the stability of so-called virtual communities where corporations often believe they can engage in what executives at times refer to as unfiltered "social listening." Tiziana Terranova (2000), for example, was among the early digital critics who encouraged analysis of online communities, the kind that are at the heart of voyeuristic imaginations of consumer-centric marketing and product design, as those that are "voluntarily channeled and controversially structured within capitalist business practices" (p. 39). Her analysis challenged the para-capitalist notion of community then still ardently endorsed by a chorus of technology pundits and scholars, including futurists such as Kevin Kelly, who saw community as a self-contained field of action that is vulnerable or perhaps simply available to appropriation by the "bad boys of capital" (p. 38). Terranova upends this linear trajectory. If tech capitalism continues to co-opt community, "this incorporation," she insists, "is not about capital descending on authentic culture but a more immanent process of channeling collective labor (even as cultural labor) into monetary flows and its structuration within capitalist business practices" (p. 39). While the former view of community "freezes the subject, just like a substance within the chemical periodical table" (p. 40), Terranova calls for a more dynamic view of the role and impact of collective action on capitalist modes of production. Companies such as TikTok may continue to invite advertisers to act as creators while engaging with platform users as marketers. There is growing critical awareness, however, that this performance only disguises how the consumers that these companies aim to encounter online are generally already presorted into advertisers' own categories.[6] Such acts of corporate making also recall the work of scholars of "audit cultures" that have explored the more longstanding creative function of seemingly objective and neutral taxonomic projects.[7]

The digital professionals I've encountered throughout the course of my research, including in venues such as QS, certainly do take consumer-centric principles to heart. Yet, such scholarly critique also overstates the degree to which corporate actors remain unaware of their influence on market dynamics. As consumer-centric approaches encourage executives to reframe the central dilemmas of business around humanistic ideals, digital professionals remain cognizant – indeed they indicate that they are often painfully aware – of the fact that business realities challenge any neat divisions between executives and their customers. Venture capitalists even at times provocatively reveal the linear trajectory of consumer centricity as an industry fiction by bluntly requiring device makers to generate rather than to simply uncover consumer desire. "Investors are social creatures," announced one venture capital executive at an informational event for tech startup founders. "If you want investors to pay attention, you have to first engineer interest," he stated frankly.[8] The interest to which this statement refers speaks both to the enthusiasm felt by private equity firms and consumers of self-tracking applications. In other words, device makers are expected to actively stoke so as to demonstrate the popular appeal of such tools in order to attract the attention of venture capital. These remarks echo both as candid reflections on the raw nature of tech entrepreneurialism and as observations meant to briskly disabuse young developers of any textbook notions of straightforward consumer discovery that are otherwise socialized as the bedrock of sound business strategy.

As executives strive to work within the humanistic confines of these business principles, they therefore remain aware that they can never fully obscure their own world-making function. In fact, contrary to the removed posture conceptualized by consumer-centric ideology, there exist relatively few means by which professionals can unproblematically enact the desired company–buyer relationship. I locate QS at the nexus of these corporate strategies and as a novel node within them. Forums such as QS can be seen as of a kind with entrenched professional devices like conference showcases and consumer research that allow companies to perform the ideals of consumer-centric business. They are also more than additional means by which technologists strive to self-consciously "engineer interest." By drawing on technologists' own extracurricular and affective labor, they offer digital professionals a new way to more effectively insert themselves into corporate narratives, that is, to act as creators who continue to think like marketers, while simultaneously bracketing their contributions to them. Examining QS as an extension and as a mutation of these corporate mechanisms therefore supplies additional ways to appreciate some of the dynamics shaping digital innovation in the self-tracking arena, and to understand QS as an interface between them.

Among the instruments currently available to business executives for these forms of professional transfiguration, industry conferences play an important function. In my research, I also found that these settings made the tension between the goals of user discovery and the practical realities of corporate meddling especially pronounced and visible. Tech executives may aspire to work in a way that accords with consumer-centric business and eagerly represent their goods as keen responses to social interest. Nonetheless, their roles as creators of narrative and user imaginaries are only ever thinly cloaked in these venues.

The fact that industry conferences act as sites of active corporate intervention in consumer imaginaries is largely unambiguous to digital professionals. Not least because companies generally secure conference display space as well as speaking slots by acting as official paid sponsors, rather than through a merit-based selection process. Sponsored corporate exhibits and speeches are explicitly designed to attract media attention, and vis-à-vis this reportage, to capture the interest of corporate buyers scouring exhibit halls as well as the technological imaginations of the wider purchasing public located beyond them.

Backstage conference chatter always brings these competing objectives to the fore. When the stage lights are on, tech executives dutifully illuminate windowless meeting rooms with bright forecasts of digital futures fueled by "hockey sticks," meaning upward-directed, projections of consumer demand. Midday, however, typically puts these paid, electrified performances on pause as both speakers and spectators shuffle out to atriums for refreshments and coffee. As tired bodies slump over warm beverages in these interim moments, the flashy talk temporarily dims just as the projectors do in the rapidly abandoned meeting rooms. Then, one can hear colleagues set aside the consumer-centric framework that guides their professional representations and worry candidly that the gadgets they are promoting are still mostly "solutions looking for a problem." These off-stage conference comments serve as fitting examples of the doubled corporate negotiations of technological possibilities. As they reverse the marketing dictum that responding to people's problems is a corporate responsibility, such back-room conference griping disrupts the confident, masculinized posture of consumer discovery even as it reaffirms corporate desire for it.

Throughout my research, the dueling realities of corporate performance were particularly well marked at major industry summits such as the Consumer Electronics Show (CES) – the technology industry's most esteemed and newsworthy annual event orchestrated specifically to produce a media spectacle that helps to engineer consumer desire. In the years since Forbes declared CES 2013 "the year of the Quantified Self" (Clay, 2013), wearables have taken on an especially visible presence in this industry gathering. By the time I attended CES in 2015 and 2016, wearable tech dominated the conversation. Both in response to and as fuel for these discussions, CES has dedicated a new, vast, and centrally located exhibition area to showcase the more than 700 wearables companies in each of those years.

On the main exhibit floor of The Sands conference center, colossal corporate sets appeared to radiate the emerging consumer interest for wearable tools as well as the industry's confidence in them. For example, to promote a device measuring jump height, one company constructed a full-size basketball court (Figure 3.1). Taking advantage of the breadth and ceiling height of the massive exhibition hall, a firm selling a fitness wearable built a two-story display filled with rooms one could walk through. Many others constructed oversized showrooms filled with celebrities and glitzy add-ons, spending thousands of dollars to endorse as yet fledgling technologies as long-lasting manifestations of inherent consumer desires. In addition to the sublime quality of such displays, Natasha Dow Schüll (2016) has noted the outsized predictions that

Figure 3.1 Displays set up at CES. Photo by author.

3. Acting Like Members, Thinking Like Vendors

energize conference goers in curated sessions of supporting events such as the Digital Health Summit.[9] These tactics are part and parcel of the inflated promises executives make as they work to move their products from market concepts to financial success stories, that is, as they strive to "look big" in order to "be big" (see Chapter 2).

When set against the critical tone of casual conversations, these corporate displays of market enthusiasm can register as compensatory efforts intended to project confidence in an uncertain market. The contrast between the seemingly assured conference performances and the anxious coffee-hour chatter also suggests that digital professionals and device makers recognize their work as involving acts of creation beyond technology. Even if professional identities and ambitions remain wrapped up in upholding and producing humanistic marketing abstractions, this difference routinely breaks corporate illusion to reveal device developers as fabricators of narrative and consumer demand, introducing friction into otherwise slick digital imaginaries. These brief exchanges thus serve as rough patches that occasionally slow down smooth sales talk for further analysis.

At events such as CES, industry media likewise remain a key and visible partner in reconstructing corporate ambitions into "solutions" made to address specific consumer "problems." As I walked the exhibit floor and circled the spectacular displays set up by wearables and self-tracking companies, I often jostled for space with journalists with press credentials strung around their necks. Their part in the theater of digital enthusiasm was undisguised. Reporters covering the event often billed as the "biggest technology event of the year" (Turrentine, 2014) conducted interviews with tech executives in full view of the visiting professional public, broadcasting "top ten" countdowns through pithy articles and blog posts or through videotaped segments filmed on lights-flooded mock sets erected in the heart and around the periphery of the showcase floor. As they circulated countless lists tabulating conference winners and losers, they used corporate sets and eager professional crowds both as props and as symbols of looming consumer demand. As the fantastical displays rehearsed idealized user scenarios, journalists stood at the ready to rebroadcast corporate dramatizations and carefully crafted (and, for those who could afford it, cleared by hired PR firms) speaking points often shared with press contacts in advance, as expressions of organic consumer interest. When practitioners at conferences worried that the gadgets they were making were still solutions in search of problems, the press covering conferences such as CES helped to reengineer corporate desires as signs of emerging ground-level social passions.

Companies working to understand would-be buyers in accords with humanistic dictates of consumer-centric business also reluctantly recognize that marketing research often works to manufacture rather than simply manifest consumer desire. This more complex industry position may not always be obvious at the outset. Indeed, textbook examples assembled by authors such as Kotler and Armstrong (2018) make it appear plain that businesspeople engage marketing research, and increasingly methodologies like ethnographic research, as instruments of "consumer discovery" (p. 130). While ethnographic studies once held a subordinate position in marketing formally dominated by focus groups and survey work, marketing textbooks now often identify these approaches as the premier means of "observational" research (p. 134).

In describing ethnographic research as primarily "observational" and in highlighting the "fresh customer and market insights that people are [other-wise] unwilling or unable to provide" (p. 134) as the principal advantages of such methodologies, Armstrong and Kotler (2018) express the commonplace consumer-centric business position that marketing research more generally, and ethnographic methods specifically, are rooted in distanced witnessing. The research these authors offer as examples of industry ethnography supplies additional evidence of such corporate positions. One study the marketers describe is a project commissioned by the makers of Coors beer. Readers learn that Coors sent ethnographic researchers to visit "bars and other locations in a top-secret small-town location" that they saw as sites that functioned as a "a real-life lab" (p. 133). Analysts spent time in these locations, "hob-knob-bing anonymously with bar patrons, supermarket shoppers, restaurant diners, convenience store clerks, and other townspeople, to gain authentic insights into how middle American consumers buy, drink, dine, and socialize around Coors and competing beer brands" (p. 133). A study conducted by the branding firm Landor supplied another example. The company has set up a multi-year ethnographic project with selected families that researchers visit two times a year. "There is no better way to understand people than to ~~talk~~ observe them in real life," reads a promotional flier. The word "talk" has been crossed out and replaced with "observe" to further stress unobstructed obser-vation as the central advantage of ethnographic research. Armstrong and Kotler reinforce the promises of this methodology, assuring readers that ethnography "provides a window into customers' unconscious actions and unexpressed needs and feelings" (2018, p. 134).

Characterizing ethnographic research in these terms at once restrains and grounds the field of analysis. The "real" accessed through this approach is conjured as a site outside of corporate mediation, one where consumer "needs and feelings" can be made as plainly visible as looking through a window in a geographically fixed "real-life lab." This description also serves to sharpen the contrast that businesspeople are taught to perceive between makers and users of products. In these textbook examples, the small-scale, the traditional, and the local set corporations apart from the social world their customers inhabit. The difference in scale juxtaposes the location-specific particularity of Coors customers with the invoked generality, ubiquity, and cosmopolitanism of the company who commissions such investigations. Furthermore, the small town qua "lab" on which researchers from Coors descend acts as a prototypical symbol of the simple life, as a social miniature that can make plain in scaled-down form the social complexities that may exist elsewhere.[10] So separated and cut down to size, research conceived as a window or as a laboratory helps to authenticate ethnographic discoveries as well as to authorize ethnography as a premier methodology that negotiates corporate access to real life. Ensconced in such a "natural environment," the "real people" that companies engage can appear finite, fixed, and knowable. Indeed, it is through these modes of ethnographic consumer discovery that people's needs, wants, and desires are perceived as accessible to the corporate gaze, all the more so because their experiences are framed as remote, miniaturized, and self-contained.

Notably, the concept of culture that operates in such corporate configurations often remains equally limited in scope. Business executives tend to approach culture as "the invisible glue that holds together the unexplainable behavior of consumers," as Malefyt and Moeran (2020 [2003]) note in their introduction to the edited volume *Advertising Cultures* (p. 9). The concept of culture that is mobilized in such corporate ethnographic imaginaries continues to act as an "explanatory concept" (Trouillot, 2003, p. 102), and as a distinct "variable" (Ortlieb, 2010, p. 189) that companies can adjust for. What is avoided here," Mazzarella (2003) warns, "is any consideration of the multiple mediations – advertising and marketing among them – that serve to rework and reproduce what we think of as culture and cultural difference" (p. 63).

Not surprisingly, just such a circumscribed concept of culture echoes in Kotler and Armstrong's broad understanding of consumer "wants and needs." In defining the meaning of "wants and needs" for their readers, the authors explain:

> Wants are the form human needs take as they are shaped by culture and individual personality. An American *needs* food but *wants* a Big Mac, fries, and a soft drink. A person in Papua New Guinea *needs* food but *wants* taro, rice, yams, and pork. Wants are shaped by one's society and are described in terms of objects that will satisfy those needs. (2018, p. 30, emphasis mine)

So articulated, these marketers express a business view of culture as an abstract yet distinct force that shapes the contrasting eating patterns of Americans and Papua New Guineans. Indeed, the geographic distance of these fictional characters stands in for their invoked cultural difference. The stereotyped eating habits of Americans as Big Mac lovers, moreover, find their exotic foil in the preference for taro, rice, yams, and pork of Papua New Guineans. In either case, the intangible but distinct American culture, rather than, say, the historical influence of American corporations on the eating patterns of low-income Americans, is invoked as that which cultivates local preferences for Big Macs just as sharply and distinctly as nebulous culture shapes the eating patterns of Papua New Guineans.

Today, as advanced analytics reorient businesses toward an even greater focus on metrics, corporate interest in the concept of culture as an explanatory mechanism and as a distinct variable companies can isolate has only intensified. Metrics, executives now increasingly note, help companies to learn about *what* people do. They turn to the cloistered concept of culture as the means of answering the bigger question of *why*. So long as companies narrate culture as the social sphere they make, manifest, support, or penetrate – much like the venues where QS events take place – rather than co-inhabit or construct, corporations can continue to act as creators even as they think like marketers while systematically abstracting their influence on the social possibilities they help to generate from their interpretations of consumer experience.

It's not a coincidence that executives trained to see themselves as students rather than as purveyors of social life mirror the pretensions of participant observers for whom the boundaries between the self and the field they are studying remain clear. Indeed, as anthropologist William Mazzarella (2003) discovered while studying advertising executives in India, marketers who are taught that they "do not invent or impose consumer preferences; rather they track pre-existing and objective empirical consumer information by means of research" often see common cause with anthropologists. These executives, he notes, view anthropologists and businesspeople as "really doing the same thing: that is, discovering an underlying and already existing cultural order" (p. 62).

And yet, even as the view of the (ethnographic) researcher as an "outside-observer-of-everyday-action" (Sunderland and Denny, 2007, p. 44) continues to dominate the business imaginary, the supposedly clandestine nature of observational research described by Kotler and Armstrong indexes ongoing corporate anxieties about the mediating influence of the corporate eyewitness. After all, it's especially telling that Kotler and Armstrong present Coors and the Landor Families studies as though they were hidden locations. In practice, ethnographic research conducted by corporations, much like marketing research more broadly, is anything but secret. It primarily takes place through prearranged encounters where participants are not only (rightfully) informed of their role in the research process but are also typically compensated for their contributions. Characterizing such research as covert says more about marketers' aspirations than their business realities. In the same way that business executives often speak about the corporate need to "tap into the culture" of their customers, the staging of ethnography as an undercover methodology speaks to corporate ambitions to perceive people's actions as though from without and to mystify purchasing decisions as direct manifestations of innate and already extant cultural tendencies and personal passions. "Clandestine" ethnographic research that abstracts the mediating role of the corporate researcher as a pure fly on the wall similarly represents an idealized rather than a realized industry perspective. It construes what business people recognize as an as yet fictional world where companies can unproblematically perceive customers living in the "real world" as disconnected from the social realm that corporate executives themselves inhabit. Indeed, TikTok's reminder to its advertisers to act as creators while thinking like marketers seems issued to just such a self-aware professional audience, one that knowingly constructs both intimacy and distance between themselves and TikTok "creators."

While forums such as QS have been comparatively overlooked by scholars studying the role of corporations in shaping consumer identities and preferences, I argue that they should also be examined as self-made arrows in the quivers of tech marketers eager to operate within the feel-good constraints of consumer-centric business. Particularly so as technology executives have taken on a large share of the work associated with community building in forums such as QS, whether they fully recognize their contributions to this collective labor or not.

As a forum that, in many ways, is a product of technologists' own making, QS offers an effective lens through which to observe the additional dimensions of the technologists' creative function at work. Especially so as QS's public image as an enthusiast community, and particularly the informal structure for membership set up by its original founders, offered technologists a new mechanism for constructing customers as distant others that businesses can discover and therefore as a novel means by which companies can "engineer" both consumer interest and customer "problems" in need of solutions. As the mediating work of business professionals remains difficult to fully abstract in corporate activities such as tech conferences and marketing research, QS extended and amended the spectacle-building work of the former and the idealized observational stance of the latter.

Mingling Members with Vendors

Technologists produced the self-tracker they wanted to find at forums such as QS while distancing themselves from this creative process as mere observers through at least two types of extracurricular labor. They did so by directly engaging as speakers, spectators, or organizers of local QS meetups. They also did so through more passive modes of participation – for instance, through the mere act of registering for QS events online. In this work, the forum's public image as an enthusiast community and especially the terms set by Wolf and Kelly for recognizing "members" of QS provided some of the means by which technologists could enact the self-trackers they were often in attendance at QS to encounter.

As discussed in Chapter 1, the bifurcation between members and vendors established by the forum founders tactically designated a display of individual passion for digital self-monitoring as the constitutive element of group belonging. In group interactions, participants were therefore explicitly asked to center their personal rather than professional interest in self-tracking tools. Even though contributing digital professionals occasionally crossed this soft boundary by delivering talks that were barely veiled product pitches, to the chagrin of QS organizers, the demarcation generally helped to visually keep the personal apart from the professional so as to maintain a perceptible distance between self-tracking enthusiasts and tech sector opportunists.

And yet, the large number of technologists who engaged with QS by producing content, delivering talks, and discussing their personal interest in self-tracking mechanisms in the mode of QS "members" inadvertently played an active role in engineering the very community they putatively aimed to witness or understand. As they vocally embraced self-tracking applications and attended QS under the cover of membership, they helped to model the consumer excitement that the tech sector sought to uncover in the market at large. By relating to QS as a community that technologists qua members were visiting rather than actively co-creating by translating their professional interests into the language of digital enthusiasm, they also unwittingly reaffirmed QS as a reified abstraction. It is vis-à-vis these interactions that technologists attending as members helped to confirm the "real self-tracker" as a figure of curiosity and interest that ratified QS as a space that can bring practitioners like themselves into closer proximity with emerging forms of technological desire.

Not everyone of course took on a leadership or a speaking role in these forums. These people, however, contributed to the narrative that QS was one setting where popular interest in self-tracking tools found its early expression in other ways. Here, website mechanics of platforms such as meetup.com, which forum organizers generally used to coordinate meeting logistics, and the security protocols of office buildings, where QS events were largely held, were among the additional elements that helped technologists to translate their more complicated and professionally motivated contributions to QS into markers of unfiltered consumer demand.

These more passive modes of participation let tech professionals enact the real self-tracker and looming digital zeal in ways that were both particular and abstract. On the one hand, because QS hosts typically used meetup.com to circulate announcements regarding upcoming activities, those interested in learning the address of local functions or even just in receiving updates about forthcoming events had to first register with the group's meetup web page. Due to the fact that these events were often held in corporate offices, building security protocols also routinely required that people signed up for QS meetups using their full names to pass an ID check at the building door. By registering for group events in this way, technologists enhanced the narrative-building work of QS attendees, presenters, and organizers by further transforming digital passion from an abstract phenomenon to one situated in the experience and interests of concrete persons, many of whom, thanks to meetup.com automatically generated and publicized digital records, could be directly identified by name.

On the other hand, meetup.com's data aggregation methods helped to depersonalize and generalize these contributions. Just like the terminology used by Wolf and Kelly to define group belonging, the platform does not meaningfully nuance group participants. It classifies anyone signing up to events through its website as a "member" by default. By leaving the professional motivations of registrants invisible at the level of website metrics, the virtual membership worked as an additional mechanism of corporate abstraction that visually separated even as it practically mingled the difference between vendors and members. As a result, the many digital professionals, venture capitalists, professional trend spotters, and others registering under the label of membership remained undifferentiated at the level of QS and meetup mechanics.

By structurally bracketing the varied business commitments of participants, meetup.com also helped to reduce the humanistic QS narrative to a story of numbers. Indeed, it was the growing numbers of these seemingly concrete yet abstract contributors, particularly as they have become tallied by web platforms such as meetup.com, that helped to support the often-referenced group and media narrative that QS represented a ground swell, even a "movement," of grassroots digital excitement that was growing from the bottom up. By virtually adding themselves to the ranks of QS participants, those indiscriminately registering as "members" thus effectively bolstered the view that QS was a budding subcultural community whose expanding numbers recommended it as an authentic, developing phenomenon. Due to this lax system of accounting, my participation in QS also counted toward the sum total of those who represented the imputed expanding numbers of QS participants. It was this numbers-driven narrative that allowed technologists to relate to QS in the terms that tech executives were taught to recognize: as a "real community" with "real people" that could be quantified and apprehended by technology firms seeking to detect and connect with emerging "needs and wants" of potential buyers.

In mediating the parameters of group belonging, the category "member" effectively provided technologists with a useful shield. The designated framework interpellated digital professionals as ordinary contributors, all the while leaving their doubled position within the "community" as vendors usefully undefined. It enabled practitioners to interact with QS as though they were digital hobbyists even as they privately emphasized that they were not real self-trackers. Because the structure of QS belonging prioritized centering methodological enthusiasm, technologists mingling as members played a part in conjuring QS as a site that made consumer desire for self-tracking tools manifest without necessarily accounting for the ways their own participation contributed to this narrative. This formulation supported technologists in converting their ulterior professional motivations into uncomplicated indicators of interest in digital self-monitoring as it empowered executives to relate to QS in the manner of Coors's "real-life lab" – and all the more so by virtue of QS's administrative arm actually titled QS Lab (see Chapter 1) – as a delimited field site that made the needs and wants of digital enthusiasts manifest.

The narrow boundaries of memberships enabled those engaging in QS more passively to similarly decenter and repackage their own professional motivations in QS as hallmarks of a preexisting enthusiasm for digital tools. The process that sorted technologists as members as it obscured their roles as vendors provided digital professionals with additional means of contributing to QS while setting themselves apart from it, that is, to understand themselves as vendors acting as members rather than as the forum's main conveners and participants.

This is not the result of entrepreneurial ignorance or of willful deception. Rather, it is a logical consequence of the interface of the public QS narrative with business common sense. While related corporate mechanisms, such as tech conferences and consumer research, make it difficult for professionals to fully screen out their own contributions, forums like QS supply technologists with both familiar and alternative tactics for enacting the relationship between themselves and their users in ways that more readily align with observational goals of consumer-centric business.

It is from this end that QS can be understood as an interface that allows us to witness and analyze some of the elements at play in digital entrepreneurialism. By serving as a mechanism for operating in accords with accepted business conventions, it not only facilitates the production of desired abstractions but also brings these industry dynamics into focus. QS thus supplies one more way for technologists to rebalance entrepreneurial terms of engagement as it makes it possible to see how industry transfigurations mediated by forums such as QS enable tech executives to recognize user communities as thing-like and the passion its participants place on display as clearly observable and open to commodification. Analyzing the active and passive ways QS has helped technologists to locate themselves as the "bad boys of capital" poised to co-opt QS and the real self-trackers as though from without, even as these practitioners effectively worked to produce these figures from the inside out, offers insight into the activities that structure the work of digital professionals. Analyzing QS as a figurative lab where technologists working under the cover of membership cultivate interest in self-tracking devices as though in vitro helps to make visible some of the processes that make this work possible.

QS as a Consumer "Trend"

The loop that cuts digital professionals off from QS and the figure of the real self-tracker is finally closed by industry trend reporting that companies routinely turn to for accessible, "off-the-shelf" customer insights. This reportage frequently operates through a circular logic similar to the one this chapter has analyzed so far. It uses popular media coverage and commentary issued by technology companies as evidence of the very social trends of interest to technologists. In doing so, it produces an editorial distance that more firmly disconnects technologists from being recognized as the selfsame architects of consumer preferences.

A study titled "The Future of Wearable Tech: Key Trends Driving the Forms and Function of Personal Devices" published in 2014 by the market research consultancy PSFK offers one example of this type of circuitous analysis. In business circles, PSFK is a respected source known for timely reporting on emerging social phenomena. Companies routinely incorporate information presented in documents produced by firms such as PSFK to substantiate their own assessments of the market as well as to make the case for their business strategy to a range of industry stakeholders that span the gamut from managers looking to rationalize their promotional choices before their superiors to private equity firms investigating the validity of their investments.

A notable feature of this report is the specificity of its sources. To start with, PSFK's assertions about "the future of wearables" are made on the borrowed authority of iQ by Intel – an entity that the introductory pages of the document describe as a "news site that narrates the impact of technology on our lives" (Fawkes, 2014) maintained by the technology company Intel. iQ by Intel, PSFK explains, has "kindly underwritten" the study as an "independent report." The relationship of iQ by Intel to its parent company already complicates the invoked impartiality of the news organization as it suggestively and not so subtly blends corporate research with self-promotion. In this instance, however, iQ by Intel's status as an "independent" contributor to the document, as well as its imputed position as the subject matter expert by virtue of its association with Intel, reinscribes PSFK as a neutral arbiter of dependable content.

In a manner similar to press coverage of technology conferences, this document makes claims about digital futures by largely rehashing the promotional claims of wearables startups and their founders. For example, echoing the enthusiastic predictions typically publicized by such firms, Piers Fawkes, the founder and president of PSFK, makes the following confident predictions about the impending digital future in the report's Foreword address: "By 2018, bio-integrated computing will have moved from the fringes, where it's at today, to a place where early adopters will widely experiment with it. For those of us who may not be ready for the scalpel, wearables that we can still take on and off will still change the way we work, live and play" (2014). Fawkes appears to take for granted the already dated belief that "bio-integrated computing" will quickly move away "from the fringes" to a place where "early adopters" will enthusiastically embrace a binary choice: implantables or wearables. Meanwhile, the executive summary emphasizes that this outcome will come as a result of burgeoning social desires to which contemporary companies are actively responding, rather than as a consequence of the future digital companies are vigorously promoting, noting that it will come as a function of "user-centric technologies" that are "beginning to adapt their form and function to align with our unique set of needs" (2014). Guided by the commentary offered by technology sector insiders cited in this project, including people such as Kevin Kelly and Steve Dean who are, notably, identified as Senior Maverick at *Wired* and as Designer at Prehype, respectively, the report thematizes the wearables future as a hurried answer to evolving social practices, concluding ultimately that "technology features and designs are evolving alongside our behaviors to take on a more essential role in our daily lives" (2014).

By squarely situating WT as a reaction to emerging social desires, the document speaks with the "user-centric" vocabulary familiar to business executives. The omissions the report makes, however, are also instructive. While it highlights the professional positions of contributors such as Dean and Kelly, it glosses over their additional roles as organizers of the New York City and Bay Area QS meetups, respectively. The exclusion subtly demonstrates how documents such as this help to situate wearables as things that develop alongside "human behavior" in ways that accord with a "user-centric" model of business. This responsive position can only be sustained, however, by publicly disconnecting the social uptake of these devices and trends from the explicit influence of industry advocates and insiders such as Kelly and Dean.

By contrast, when an organizer of QS is identified in the report, the reference is mobilized solely as a voice that speaks on behalf of emerging consumers. For example, it is with the caveat that popular interest in wearable computing remains on the "fringe" but with the expectation that this situation will change quickly as "user-centric technology" continues to adapt to the "needs" of its users that PSFK includes commentary from people such as Ernesto Ramirez, then one of the leaders of the QS meetup in San Diego. "These [wearable] trackers make it easier to understand ourselves, our world and the interaction between the two. Ten to fifteen years ago, you were stuck with paper and pencil. Now, you can wear a device that syncs to an application," Ramirez is quoted as saying (Fawkes, 2014). This citation carries its own evidentiary and authenticating quality. By virtue of his role as a QS coordinator, Ramirez's commentary is incorporated as a putative spokesperson of motivated technology users who are eagerly replacing pen and paper techniques with wearable devices. And, crucially, by reemphasizing people's interest in incorporating WT into their journeys of self-discovery, Ramirez's remarks usefully echo the perspectives of technologists interviewed for this project. His observations thus serve to reconfirm the paradoxical teleology of the digital future mapped by PSFK, one where emerging user-centric technologies herald new possibilities as they articulate with the already present social needs.

Even though PSFK broadly recycles a pseudo-promotional narrative as sound research, the document carries its own authoritative weight. As Trouillot has theorized of the historical archive, these types of recitations help to naturalize a story that the technology industry often recounts about itself by submitting the narrative to repeated rounds of circulation and "retrieval" (1995, p. 26). To paraphrase Trouillot's thoughts on history, then, what QS is, in the end, matters less than how QS works. The narrative process that has solidified QS as a user community has also shaped the nature of its influence in the technology sector and beyond it.

Similarly, what Michael Foucault (1990) has said of sexuality may well be applied to QS and digital self-tracking practices. Contrary to the framing of the forum's founders, the name "Quantified Self" does not simply usher a sub-merged practice into fuller view that now "knowledge tries gradually to uncover." It is a "name that can be given to a historical construct; not a furtive reality that is difficult to grasp, but a great surface network . . . which is linked, in accordance with a few major strategies of knowledge and power" (p. 106). Indeed, QS and "the real self-trackers" are not only furtive realities that reports such as PSFK help to diligently unveil. They are constructs composed through an interplay of corporate desires, business conventions, and emerging forms of entrepreneurial sociality. In the end, QS functions just like the gloves described by philosopher Ian Hacking, where "the category and the people in it emerged hand-in-hand" (Hacking, 1998, p. 165).

Through the mediating role of reports such as the PSFK one, the gap between what QS represents and the professional creators of this image grows. The distance empowers marketers and makers of WT to stand even further away from the phenomena they help to engineer so as to become reinscribed as distant observers, removed all the more from the act. Little wonder, then, that even as commercial imperatives transformed the "real self-tracker" into a hunted figure, I found it to be a haunted one as well – a ghostly entity whose simultaneous presence and absence have become particularly well marked in forums such as QS. In the course of my research, the "real self-tracker" seemed to be present everywhere: in talks delivered by QS participants, in casual chatter with technologists, and in industry reportage. In practice, however, the real self-tracker was always situated just one more encounter away. This perpetual displacement rendered the real self-tracker both proximate and distant, both palpable and difficult to grasp. In the end, though the notion that QS represented an enthusiast community put forth the passionate self-tracker as a figure that was enduring and real, the real self-tracker's repeated absence from forum activities also rendered it fleeting and fragile.

Scholars and technology pundits have largely interpreted QS in the terms first offered by its authors and sustained by its participants: as a community of motivated technophiles (see Introduction and Chapter 1). This techno-imaginary, as the current chapter has addressed, also remains buttressed by a linear and extractive view of business, one premised on a unidirectional mining of consumer "needs and wants." In this environment, QS – when narrativized as a self-organizing collective of motivated technophiles – pro-vides digital practitioners with something more than a pseudo-obscured perch for consumer surveillance. Forums such as QS offer new positions from which to realize these aspirational business goals in ways that enhance existing mechanisms of professional transfigurations, like industry conferences, marketing research, or trend reporting. The creative executive labor that goes into drawing up buyer preferences and "engineering interest" remains conspicuous in latter channels. Contrary to the ambitions of consumer-centric business, these sites never fully obscure the mediating role of (competing) corporate interests on people's lives. The organizing structure and identity of QS as a forum anchored primarily in enthusiasm for self-monitoring mechanisms, however, introduces distance between technologists and their desired buyers. By virtue of the ad hoc and free labor performed by extracurricular entrepreneurs acting like self-trackers while thinking like tech executives, the contributions of professionals charged with engineering interest become further obscured. And so, the forum more thoroughly disguises these industry practitioners as originators of the preferences they are expected to uncover. Collectives such as QS thus offer not just an additional but in some ways a better means of representing motivated corporate intervention as an unmediated encounter.

It's in these ways that forums such as QS act as novel instruments that help technologists maintain digital innovation as anchored in the act of daring masculinized discovery that remains the cornerstone of an entrepreneurial ideal.[11] When framed as a collective of engaged self-trackers, QS facilitates vital forms of professional abstraction by means of which digital practitioners can continue to locate themselves as on the outside of the "community" looking in rather than as constitutive members of the cast in ways that accord with the voyeuristic and humanistic principles of consumer-centric work. As technologists worry that gadgets they make remain solutions without clear problems, forums such as QS offer digital practitioners alternative means of converting ongoing commercial uncertainty into entrepreneurial hubris.

The challenge I faced in locating the real self-tracker in forums such as QS, however, reveals one more tech sector reality: the heroics of entrepreneurial discovery can be sustained only by bracketing out the creative task of community building, one performed by the largely unwaged and much less formally recognized extracurricular work of contributing technologists themselves. As the next chapter further explores, the desired heroic entrepreneurial posture uncomfortably contrasts with the feminized forms of affective labor technologists are increasingly called to perform through participation in forums such as QS.

4

Hustling with a Passion

The affective labor technologists carry out in forums such as the Quantified Self (QS) transcends the demands of user-centric business. In a turbulent job market defined by high degrees of flexibility, QS also acts as a vector for achieving professional security through extracurricular work. This chapter situates QS in this broad employment environment to examine it as another element of Silicon Valley-style neoliberal digital entrepreneurialism and as an interface that demonstrates the expanding connections between community, desire, and the tech sector.

Some of the associations between recreation and digital labor I discuss in this chapter were already visible in a brief presentation that Anna, a stylish twenty-something data scientist, gave at a QS New York City Show & Tell, where she subtly linked her personal interest in self-tracking with her work as a data scientist. From a distance, this presentation looked no different than any number of the tech talks I attended throughout my fieldwork. In the style of such gatherings, Anna spoke on a weekday and at an event hosted after work hours in a spacious Manhattan office. Indeed, the gathering, where a group of thirty or so youthful-looking executives first mingled cordially over cheese, chips, and wine, could have been mistaken for a corporate affair. Even more so when everyone settled into chairs arranged in rows before a large screen to listen to a presentation mediated by a set of PowerPoint slides. And yet, despite the formal aesthetics of this event, those in attendance did not assemble for a business meeting but, ostensibly, to find community with people like Anna who welcomed digital self-tracking into their lives.

When everyone was seated, lights dimmed and Anna began:

> Hi, my name is Anna. I'm a data scientist and I crunch a lot of numbers for work. And I thought, why don't I crunch my personal numbers? I wanted to make my Annual Report at the end of the year and I wanted to see all of my data in one place.

[Pointing to the projector screen behind her] This was my attempt number one. It was in 2013. I basically armed myself with Jawbone, and all of the quantified tracking apps, and I wanted to see how my year went. I could see where I go in New York and what I read, and how much I sleep, and how many steps I make.

What did I learn in the end? It was so hard to get my numbers back. So, all of these apps that would show me their diagrams won't give me my data so I had to build a lot of scrapers, I had to connect to a lot of APIs [application programming interfaces] just to get it back. Defining what to track was really difficult. I thought, once I have my Jawbone, it's going to show me everything. Actually, that was not the case. It was also a lot of self-discipline. Logging in, making sure that I record everything, was very difficult.

This year, I'm smarter. I prepared in the very beginning of the year that I'm going to get all of my data back. So, I connected all of my apps to IFTT (If This then That), so it automatically backs up all of my data to Google or Dropbox. I have it all safely; everything is organized. I wanted to share the project I did this year.

[Turning to the screen again and flicking to the next slide using a clicker] This is my location data. This is me moving through the city. This is my geo-location across the US. And when I visualized it, it was really funny. This line across the US was when I took the StartupBus. It's a bus that was leaving from New York to Austin and you build an app. So, seeing it on a map was really great. It was also awesome to see let's see, I went to Montreal to visit my sister. And then I could see all of Montreal immediately here. So, that was great.

This year, I also tracked books, just to see how I did in terms of reading. My friends recommended to me RescueTime. And it's the best app I've ever had because it just runs in the background of my computer and captures everything, how I work. Low productivity this week was my summer vacation so seeing it was really good.

So, what I learned this year is that perceptions are really deceiving. I thought my 2014 was awesome – I was so productive. But when I looked at it, my gym check-ins were 10 percent down, the books that I read decreased mostly by 20 percent. So, everything I think in my head, when I look at the numbers, it's actually not true. Then, the second point, I don't know what habits I'm developing because I'm not measuring by habits, but Quantified Self is definitely a habit. Every time I get to a place, my first thing is to check in. A lot of my friends are irritated with it. But I do think that I have a Quantified Self habit right now.

If the intimate nature of the night first seemed out of place in a professional setting, Anna's talk and choice of subject matter quickly brought the two together. That evening, she walked us through the joys and challenges of gathering her personal data, which she scrupulously organized in a private inventory she then called her Annual Report.[1] "Annual Report" was a conspicuous nod to Nicholas Felton – a graphic designer who first attracted the attention of the tech and advertising industry in 2005 with his meticulously crafted and beautifully rendered personal digital records (Figure 4.1). For the next nine years, Felton had organized the details of his life in the style of a corporate chronicle, charting his experiences through graphs, maps, and metrics and sharing this analysis online.

Certainly, in assembling these data-rich archives, both Felton and Anna enacted a disciplined digital subject who embraced calculative digital logics. However, the personal records did not only serve as a vehicle for data-driven self-reflection. As the term "Annual Report" already not so subtly suggests, these private chronicles indicated that both executives approached themselves in neoliberal terms, that is, as a business to be organized and managed.[2] Fittingly, Felton's personal Annual Reports played an explicit professional function. He had used these documents as a place to experiment with data visualization techniques that he could later channel into his day job as a product designer for companies such as Facebook (Gerdau, 2014). He also deployed these records as an instrument of self-promotion. They recommended Felton as a skilled digital professional whose work became viewed as a masterclass on data visualization. As importantly, they also endorsed Felton as a dedicated tech executive for whom vocation and passion intertwined.

The Annual Report that Anna shared with us was likewise notable for the way it toggled between the personal and the professional. Like Felton, Anna used these documents as an experimental medium to practice technical approaches. They also styled her as someone for whom data analysis was not only something she does for a living but also a personal "Quantified Self habit" that she cheerfully cultivates in her spare time. Her records reflect these ambitions, where travel mixes business (building an app) with pleasure (visiting Austin), and where her private preoccupations (checking in, collecting data, and tinkering with technology, to the apparent chagrin of her friends) feed back into her work as a data scientist.

This chapter examines QS as a further expression of the entrepreneurial dynamics that compel technologists such as Anna to mix private storytelling with business aesthetics. I discuss QS as a safe-for-work hobby and as a narrative template that has supplied digital professionals with additional tools for enacting the type of self that allows them to find success within the confines of a capricious workplace. For extracurricular entrepreneurs called to reconcile their work with private commitments (see also Chapter 3), QS functioned as a mechanism for drawing on the feelings of desire, enthusiasm, and forms of

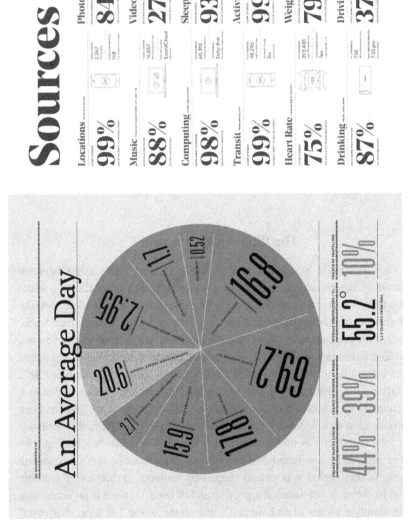

Figure 4.1 Feltron Annual Report 2014. Nicholas Felton. http://feltron.com/.

97

sociality necessary to construct a more salient and marketable professional image – not just a more salient consumer target as discussed in the previous chapter. As the forum supported technologists in both honing and brandishing their personal interest in digital self-monitoring, it furnished some of the means by which they could put their passions to work. QS thus offers a fitting lens onto the additional value and logic of desire in the digital economy as it reflects, responds to, and shapes these dynamics of employment. It also offers an additional way to appreciate how technologists' extracurricular labor has stoked some of the digital enthusiasm professionals seek to find reflected in the marketplace.

As a conduit and as a gateway to such practices, QS likewise acts as an apt portal to the problematic role of passion in the neoliberal workplace. The part QS has played in helping technologists to enact an expert identity marked by desire accounts for some of the early popularity and success of forums such as QS among data scientists like Anna. As we will see, however, there is growing irony in this position as QS inadvertently contributed to some of the very problems it has also helped to address. As it tempted technologists with a ready-made framework that promised to elevate their professional stature while helping to reduce their emotional labor, it only further amplified these affective demands.

Hustling with a Passion

QS only functions as an interface to the enhanced relationship between community, desire, and the tech sector if understood in the context of a wider social-technical framework that has pressed enthusiasm and worker sociality into service of consumer capitalism. The devoted professional like Anna, whose work commitments shape their personal life and vice versa, is of course a familiar figure in social thought, antecedents of which Max Weber had traced in the influential text *The Protestant Ethic and the Spirit of Capitalism* (2012 [1905]) over a century ago. The late nineteenth century, Weber had noted, was marked by a total reversal of people's relationship to work. Where work was once seen as a necessary evil, Weber's contemporaries started to embrace their jobs as ardently as though performing it were a religious "calling" (p. 18). Weber ultimately concluded that the devout attachment to one's occupation notable in this period was indeed shaped by religious principles. If working today, he wrote, is "considered a good in and of itself ... what is preached here is not simply a means of making one's way in the world, but a peculiar ethic"

(p. 17). It is this ethic, what he classified as a specifically "Protestant ethic," that characterized the "spirit" of capitalism.

By identifying religious origins of the modern attitude toward work, Weber highlighted a contradiction. He recognized that the pious occupational posture had become so ingrained in society that it no longer needed a religious system to support it. The result was that working emerged as its own religion, as "an absolute end in itself" (2012 [1905], p. 24). Weber condemned this commitment as empty, even "irrational" (p. 32). When professional striving became decoupled from religious salvation, the modern vocational attachment seemed to him to be meaningless.

Weber's analysis is also punctuated by a doubled notion of "spirit." The concept of "spirit" points to the religious underpinnings of the work ethic that powers modern capitalism. It also speaks to a force that is at once pervasive and ephemeral, fickle and strong. On the one hand, Weber reveals the spirit of capitalism as contingent and thus potentially fleeting. In historicizing the devotional vocational attitude and recognizing it as a product of "a long and continuous process of education and socialization" (2012 [1905], p. 24), Weber aims to denaturalize and thus to break the spell capitalism exerts over people's lives. On the other hand, "spirit" names a force that is diffuse and insidious, one that spreads into life's every nook and cranny as extensively as dispersed gas. While Weber thus recognized capitalism as a system sustained by effervescent beliefs, he also saw it as a "steel-hard casing" that constrained one's actions as firmly as an iron cage (p. 124).

These days, paeans to extended work hours issued by technorati such as Elon Musk indicate that Weber's original thesis may well have reached its logical extreme in the technology sector. In November of 2018, for example, Musk drew equal parts admiration and ire from his online followers when he paired an announcement on his personal Twitter page advertising several job openings at his many firms with advice that prepared applicants to work sixty to one hundred hours per week. The pain, he declared with a noticeable hint of pride, "increases exponentially above 80" (Musk, 2018). He followed it up with an ambiguous promise that so do the rewards.

These proclamations reveal the degree to which the contemporary tech sector remains shaped by a Protestant work ethic where pervasive striving is still lauded as a professional ideal. And it continues to fuel the disregard of male industry figureheads like Elon Musk for structural impediments such as the absence of meaningful childcare, family leave, or access to healthcare as among the barriers that prevent people, often women, from committing this many hours to their jobs (Wajcman, 2015; Gregg, 2018; see also Chapter 5).

This rhetoric likewise obscures the economic and social changes that, in recent decades, have pushed these tendencies to the extreme.

The unmitigated surrender to work that Musk advocates also unfolds today in a neoliberalized tech arena where Zygmun Bauman's (2000) concept of liquidity and Emily Martin's (1994) notion of flexibility have reached maturity. Bauman and Martin have examined liquidity and flexibility as central organizing metaphors of the late twentieth century. In the book *Liquid Modernity*, Bauman draws on ideas developed in literature and philosophy to conceptualize post-modernity as a period marked by an epistemic shift toward fluidity and flexibility. Martin primarily focuses on medical records to examine flexibility as a concept that has shifted Western understanding of the body from a static fortress to something more elastic. Both of these authors, however, connect notions of liquidity and flexibility with the workplace that has become altered by a progressive dissolution of the corporation as a durable form of employment. Martin in particular highlights that flexibility in the workplace remains a double-edged sword. On the one hand, it implies a greater degree of autonomy and agency for the workers, where individuals may "set goals as they see fit for the organization." On the other, it speaks to the expanding capacities of organizations to "hire or fire workers at will" (1994, p. 145).

If flexibility today acts as an organizing principle of the workplace, its origins can also be traced back to the 1970s, when rapid de-unionization led to wide-scale erosion of worker protections. Since that period, corporations have gained more and more control over the office, slowly instituting both longer hours and greater employment insecurity. People today work significantly more hours for lower returns, and sociologist Jamie K. McCallum (2020) highlights that this shift has changed the work lives of middle-class knowledge workers the most. In an average year, the latter now log as many as 660 hours more at the office than their 1970s counterparts.

Anthropologist Karen Ho (2009) has additionally examined the specific impact of the financial sector on these altered professional realities. In the book *Liquidated: An Ethnography of Wall Street*, she argues that the financial machinations of investment bankers in the 1990s facilitated both steep market ebbs and flows and high levels of turnover within investment banking itself. The swinging pendulum style of work that shaped the professional experiences and investment strategies of bankers eventually brought cost cutting and consolidation to industries beyond the financial sector. These tactics ultimately rendered the lithe and liquid worker both as a more routine contemporary reality and a symbolic standard-bearer of the workplace where the adaptive mobility of well-heeled bankers, who modeled their flexibility on the liquidity of money their offices managed, had become paradigmatic of hard work. This mode of work has created what Emily Martin (2009) has relatedly called, using a medical idiom, "bipolar" markets that correspond to "manic" forms of employment.

By all accounts, the tech industry now embodies and helps to advance this intense and erratic form of work, a trend evident even in the speed with which people in this sector switch jobs. Research conducted by the social media company LinkedIn indicates, for example, that tech companies now experience the highest rates of turnover of any public or private institution (Lewis, 2022). Popular industry aphorisms bear this out as well. After all, this is a field that continues to celebrate principles of "disruption" and, in the now (in)famous words of Mark Zuckerberg, founder and CEO of Facebook (now Meta), routinely calls upon app and product developers to "move fast and break things" (Zuckerberg, 2012).

Tech journalist Erin Griffin (2019) has described the contemporary employment environment marked by perpetual, anxious striving in which many technologists work as "hustle culture." Hustle culture still orients people to cultivate a pious attitude toward their jobs in ways that are similar to the affinities observed by Weber. Under the spell of hustle culture, Griffin writes, "not only does one never stop hustling – one never exits a kind of work rapture." Indeed, in a professional arena where the conventional sales role has become retooled as "Tech Evangelist" (Priestley, 2015), the religious tonality of this work is often rendered literal. This is also a social context where the expression "Rise and Grind" has become a ubiquitous call to arms of the work-obsessed – a motto seen on the covers of books by leading entrepreneurs as in advertising slogans of popular brands (Griffin, 2019).[3] Yet, "hustle culture" underscores how the tech sector infuses a zealous attitude toward work with a contemporary sense of urgency. Although job precarity has long defined the experiences of low-wage workers (McCallum, 2020), the tech industry's imperative to hustle now registers the routine fretfulness and volatility that defines the professional experiences of elite knowledge workers as well.

Success in this context is not defined by a stoic endurance of professional precarity alone. Technologists who constitute a vital part of the "creative class" (Florida, 2002)[4] are additionally enjoined to *hustle with a passion*, as I call it. Hustling with a passion requires an occupational commitment that goes beyond grit and stamina to ride out vocational turbulence. In part, as legal scholar Daniel Markovits (2019) has noted in a related context, hustling with a passion is marked by a "capacity to bear these hours gracefully" in ways that personalize both success and failure, and de-emphasize the financial and social capital necessary to sustain professional commitments. Markovits quotes one executive interviewed by Arlie Russell Hochschild for her 1997 book

The Time Bind who describes the ability to effortlessly confront the arduous demands of one's job as a central characteristic of success in the rise and grind economy. "Some people flame out, get weird because they work all the time . . . The people at the top are very smart, work like crazy, and don't flame out. They're still able to maintain a good mental set, and keep their family life together. They win the race." These comments highlight that people hustling with a passion are called to remain resilient in the face of mounting stressors. Such imperatives place the burden of maintaining physical and psychological composure amid escalating professional demands on the eager employee, rather than on the structural conditions that may help cultivate a sustainable working life.

Technologists who hustle with a passion are also prototypical extracurricular entrepreneurs. Hustling with a passion calls on these professionals to actively recode their labor around affective, not just material, rewards. For this group, work and personal hobbies ideally overlap. Steve Jobs may well have expressed this attitude when he advised the Stanford class of 2005 to "find what you love . . . love what you do," as Carolyn Chen (2022) notes in the book *Work Pray Code: When Work Becomes Religion in Silicon Valley*, where she analyzes the insidious effects of this vocational aspiration. This expectation is especially well pronounced in fields such as computer programming where the figure of the child prodigy who has coded since childhood remains a prominent archetype. Hiring managers for IT departments continue to idealize candidates who have grown up playing around with code. The attraction of such applicants goes beyond the pragmatic orientation of Michel Foucault's (2008) "homo economicus," an expression that describes someone whose entire life has been oriented around activities that maximize their wage-earning potential. Inherent in the figure of the child coder is also the idea that pre-professional tinkering testifies to intrinsic enthusiasm, not just meticulously cultivated ability. The pubescent extracurricular eagerness supplements formal experience. It also precedes and shapes vocational passion.

The imperative to relate to work as an expression and extension of private interests configures the professional identities of tech executives more broadly. It echoes in now routine business practices, such as corporate mission or vision statements where companies articulate higher-order ideals powering their work. It is also notable in the way people are oriented to frame their business aspirations as byproducts of personal hobbies, as a realization of private longings, or even as a fulfillment of deep-seated desires. This tactic is clearly marked in the business pitches delivered by participants on TV programs such as *Shark Tank*, where entrepreneurs typically bolster their credentials with tributes to what librarian Fobazi Ettarh has called, in a related context, "vocational awe" (2018) that both softens the transactional nature of these business presentations as well reinforces the speakers' organic ardor for their work. It is equally standard in the expected self-presentation of job seekers for whom talking to the intersection of personal interests and their business aspirations has become an important element of executive stagecraft.[5] Vocational awe, therefore, is not only something one increasingly advertises but also commoditizes. Work focused around a personal mission has become both a badge of honor and a selling point that testifies to the depth and sincerity of one's professional commitments.

Paradoxically, even though demands of the neoliberal workplace thus reveal sociability as a distraction, where people long to be relieved of personal commitments, or, as Melissa Gregg writes, for the "opportunity to remove themselves from the demands of the social," in order to be free to work (2018, p. 96), hustling with a passion also promotes a specific type of sociability. Certainly, a relentless focus on work presupposes a person capable of suspending or outsourcing private obligations and responsibilities – friendships, household duties, organizational labor. Impassioned hustling nevertheless involves both the commodification of social interactions, where nonwork experiences are increasingly sought out as business opportunities, and the promotion of oneself as a social self whose interests are intertwined at the same time as they exceed – or at least appear to – any utilitarian commitments. Hustling with a passion thus marks sociability and extracurricular interests as key components of employability rooted in a well-rounded selfhood. That person must display an unyielding commitment to their profession at the same time as they must appear to want to do more than just work.

Contemporary forms of communication such as social media render the professional image centered on performative sociality especially visible and necessary. Alice Marwick (2013) develops this point in the book *Status Update: Celebrity, Publicity, and Branding in the Social Media Age*, where she tracks the emergence of social media as a premier mechanism that helps people cultivate what she calls the "safe-for-work self" (p. 163). A safe-for-work self is a curated online persona that is crafted to appeal to potential employers. Broadly speaking, producing this professional image involves "thinking about the self as a sellable commodity" (p. 166) and then leveraging the branding tactics of marketing to promote oneself. The specific parameters of this practice are often rendered nebulous by its proponents. However, pundits profiled in her book, such as wine critic-turned-digital marketer and social media "micro-celebrity" Gary Vaynerchuk, often maintain that this image building hinges on articulating passion for one's work and then using social media to incessantly "broadcast about it" (p. 172).

Vaynerchuk reveals online tools such as social media as both the means and the cause of this professional self-realization. He also articulates the construction of an impassioned safe-for-work self as a relentless project. In his widely read self-branding guides such as the *New York Times* bestseller *Crush It! Why NOW Is the Time to Cash In on Your Passion* (2009), Vaynerchuk makes the intensity of the commitment necessary to sustain this public image explicit. Comparing the requisite effort to home maintenance, he emphasizes its ceaseless quality as well as the perils that come with its neglect: "No matter how successful you get, you cannot slack off or the grass is going to grow, the paint is going to peel, and the roads will start to crumble. Stop hustling, and everything you learn here will be useless" (cited in Marwick, 2013, p. 174).

Vaynerchuk's own accomplishments as a businessman and author, which he attributes to his inexorable regimes of online self-promotion, may well be anomalous. Nevertheless, success stories like his have rendered online impression management in the personalized terms that he advocates a commonplace and even a compulsory feature of the contemporary job market. In this way, as Marwick notes, the language of passion normalizes the development of one's safe-for-work self in Vaynerchuck's image as it renders the labor required to sustain this marketable public persona both inevitable and invisible. Even as Vaynerchuk exhorts job seekers and entrepreneurs to follow their passions and his lead in realizing them, his fretfulness highlights the volatility and insecurity of the employment context that renders this work necessary, arduous, and continuous.

The difficulty of maintaining what Ilana Gershon relatedly calls a "hirable identity" (2014) is not only associated with the intensity of effort involved in sustaining it. Gershon stresses that knowledge workers today must not just relentlessly render themselves visible to potential employers online. They must do so while reconciling the demands of a neoliberal self that is managed as a business with the entrenched Enlightenment notion of selfhood as singular and coherent. On the one hand, neoliberal selfhood requires perpetual attunement to change. One's online persona therefore has to be regularly updated and adjusted to the shifting demands of contemporary business. This is one reason why Vaynerchuk prepares his readers to approach this online performance as a never-ending task. For those in the tech industry, the high rates of turnover and the attendant search for the next job means that this work never stops. On the other hand, applicants seeking employment in places such as the United States remain shaped by liberal models of selfhood where the self is understood to be a stable entity. Maintaining the steadiness of a liberal self is particularly taxing online, where applicants managing a multiplicity of online profiles on a diverse set of media platforms must "appear coherent across media platforms"

(Gershon, 2014, p. 282). Doing so requires continuous coordination of one's online activities on a range of digital channels, each with its own audiences, applications, and affordances, in a way that "ideally demonstrates that one is a recognizable, consistent, and employable self" (p. 282). While candidates are thus expected to remain "distinctive" (p. 287) from other applicants and to demonstrate their ongoing versatility and adaptiveness, they are also required to maintain an online identity that appears enduring and steady. More, as philosopher and cultural theorist Michel Feher (2009) notes, the neoliberal job seekers must work to plot an upward trajectory, to present and to produce an identity that appreciates in value over time.

The Safe-for-Work Hobby

QS provides further visibility into some of these dynamics as it serves as an additional vector for channeling passion into work. For extracurricular entre-preneurs hustling with a passion, the forum effectively serves as a safe-for-work hobby – one of the building blocks and extensions of Marwick's safe-for-work and Gershon's hirable self, although the forum's utility and impact also transcends digital reputation management. I define the safe-for-work hobby as a pastime that technologists can effectively use in projects of professional self-making. I argue that digital executives adopted QS as a safe-for-work hobby and thus readily engaged with the forum as spirited technophiles not only because they enjoyed discussing shared interests with like-minded folks (although some surely did) or because they were engaging with QS in the terms prescribed by the dictums of consumer-centric business (as Chapter 3 explores), but because it offered them simple means by which to channel personal commitments toward business ends.

Anna, whose QS talk opened this chapter, exemplifies some of the ways technologists subtly mobilized QS and self-tracking as a safe-for-work hobby in their own professional self-representations. From the start, Anna introduced herself as someone for whom self-tracking is an organic extension of her work, not just a hobby. "I'm a data scientist and I crunch a lot of numbers for work. And I thought, why don't I crunch my personal numbers?" she announced to the seated crowd at the top of her talk. The subject matter – the Annual Report that she built based on her lifestyle data – further indicated the degree to which her professional goals have shaped her private pursuits down to the types of metrics that she chose to track.

For example, we learned that productivity, or "hours spend (sic) in front of aluminum block with a bright monitor," as Anna playfully reframed time spent

Registrar of Other Numbers

Different random statistics to quantify the success of 2014.

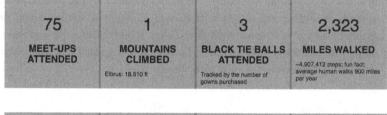

75	1	3	2,323
MEET-UPS ATTENDED	**MOUNTAINS CLIMBED**	**BLACK TIE BALLS ATTENDED**	**MILES WALKED**
	Elbrus: 18,510 ft	Tracked by the number of gowns purchased	~4,907,412 steps; fun fact: average human walks 900 miles per year

154	17	763	6.30
GYM VISITS	**CITIES VISITED**	**PHOTOS POSTED**	**AVERAGE HOURS OF SLEEP PER DAY**
Outdoor runs are not taken in account due to inconsistent tracking	Long Term trips out of NYC requiring public transportation (trains/planes/busses)		

Figure 4.2 Excerpt of Anna's Annual Report. https://quantifiedself.com/blog/ anna-nican-year-numbers/.

at the computer, was among the key data points that she had collected using applications such as RescueTime. Productivity for her was a more expansive concept, however, as revealed through other metrics she gathered. In addition to RescueTime statistics that tabulated the number of hours she logged on her laptop, she also calculated that she spent "370 hours on Software Development, 334 hours on communication and scheduling, and 104 hours on social networking." She also recorded the number of meetups she attended: 75; mountains climbed: 1; Black Tie balls attended: 3; miles walked: 2,323; gym visits: 154; cities visited: 17; photos posted: 763; and average hours of sleep per day: 6.30 (Figure 4.2).

Though Anna downplays the value of productivity by recasting these metrics in lighthearted and self-deprecating tones while complaining that collecting these data points took "a lot of self-discipline," her high scores speak for themselves. Beyond demonstrating the personal appeal of numbers to Anna, this project highlights her as a motivated professional capable of self-control on and off the job. Her data likewise indicated that she is an entrepreneurial thinker who continues to invest in her skills – taking a StartupBus, tinkering with the latest technology, and experimenting with data visualization techniques. The personal story of her trials and tribulations with self-tracking, itself a multi-year process, additionally testifies to Anna's ability to experiment, iterate, learn, and improve. Most notably, Anna's presentation articulates work-related tasks – building apps, toying with technology, presenting in public forms such as QS – as activities she enjoys in her spare time. Ultimately, the type of "self" that emerges through the numbers highlight Anna as an energetic, fit, well-traveled, and well-networked professional who leaves little time for sleep. So, even though she frets that 2014, according to her data, has been a less productive year than the one before, these metrics continue to endorse her as someone who cheerfully and carefully arranges her life around the demands of work.

In this context, QS does not only operate as a space for Anna to connect with other tech geeks for whom tracking is a private passion and not just an occupation. It also acts as a stage on which to enact this image. It's one of the platforms that enables Anna to perform the committed technologist and then to recoup her hobbies as meaningful building blocks of a professional narrative. While her presentation at forums such as QS thus helps to reframe these efforts – and the work involved in monitoring them – as joyful pastimes, the lengths she has gone to to collect and then to publicly promote her self-tracking projects also speak to the increasingly taxing affective extracurricular investments demanded of digital professionals to reveal themselves as devoted and well-rounded individuals for whom life and work, as it were, seamlessly overlap.

This interaction, and the role that QS plays within her professional self-representation, is further visible on her personal website where she incorporates QS into a larger narrative of an impassioned executive (Nicanorova, n.d.). The contents of the website may on the surface seem desultory. On the home page, one is greeted with a lineup of options that, initially, appear to bare little connection to one another. For example, the first category, titled "9–5," archives some of Anna's professional achievements, including mentions she has received in the press from respected industry publications such as Adage and CNBC (Consumer News and Business Channel). Meanwhile, the second category, titled "Projects," catalogues her personal hobbies and extracurricular activities that variously mix the personal with the professional. This category compiles a mixed bag of initiatives ranging from the irreverent (Anna was an organizer of a meetup for book and whiskey lovers) to the studious (she spent time "solving important life problems with Linear Programming"). The same toggling between hobbies and work-related commitments repeats in subsequent sections. While the third category documents her involvement in mountaineering and opens onto detailed visual essays of her adventurous climbs, the adjacent field, "Talks & Accolades," offers up a list of tech talks Anna has delivered in professional venues. Though this page itemizes the speeches she's made at a range of technology conferences, it also includes a link to the presentation that she gave at QS. QS is additionally broken out as a separate category, one that adapts the expression as a general handle for her self-tracking projects. It's here that she catalogues the Annual Reports she's discussed in her QS talk.

These topics may at first seem incongruous and their audience might appear unclear. On closer analysis, however, this arrangement makes plain that it closely follows the edicts of extracurricular entrepreneurs hustling with a passion. On the one hand, it presents Anna as a dedicated professional who never stops hustling, not even when she is off from work. When she is not at her desk, she keeps busy organizing or attending relevant meetups, delivering speeches, or toying around with technology she may filter back into her office job. On the other hand, the website creates an equivalence between her professional and personal pursuits. By arranging her work-related accomplishments (tech talks, awards, press mentions) alongside her private interests (writing, reading, mountain climbing, self-tracking), the website helps Anna articulate an orientation toward work as on par with, and even as an extension of, her private preoccupations. The overall effect is of a woman who approaches her hobbies with the seriousness of her work and her work with the eagerness of her hobbies.

Such miscellaneous mentions, which have additionally become a common resume feature, endorse the candidate as an accomplished individual with interests beyond the narrow confines of their job and so, implicitly, as the type of colleague with whom one can enjoy spending the better part of their day. These conglomerations also assist knowledge workers in integrating seemingly unrelated aspects of their personal and professional experiences into a cohesive and marketable self. Here, extracurricular pursuits no longer exist as non sequiturs. Instead, they are woven into the fabric of a stable professional identify.

QS is mobilized here as a vital instrument of this professional self-fashioning. Along with mountain climbing and reading, QS helps Anna round out an image of someone who is an informed and tech-savvy risk taker with her finger on the pulse of cutting-edge adventures as much as of the latest technological trends. Moreover, the fact that QS plays a twofold role here, archived both as a professional talk and as a hobby category, itself points to the double function QS occupies in the safe-for-work personal narratives of technologists such as Anna. The elision between QS as a pastime and as a business function subtly reveals how QS helps digital professionals hustling with a passion to stage private interests as conduits of professional self-realization. All the more so given that she lists her QS talk as the first in what is now a substantial set of professional engagements and media mentions. QS, here, serves a double legitimizing function: a hobby that testifies to her intimate interest in data analysis, as well as a stepping stone to more formal industry recognition.

Anna is not alone in leveraging QS for business, not just for personal, ends. Other digital executives I met in QS likewise routinely framed their engagement with the forum in this dual way. Like Anna, these technologists often described their professional roles as extensions of their private passions in self-tracking, ones that they nurture in forums such as QS. Our conversations also highlighted how their involvement with QS was shaped by the varied demands of their jobs. Individual pastimes became articulated here as evidence or as early prototypes of maturing professional commitments.

Laila Zemrani, co-founder and CEO of Fitnescity, for example, connected her personal data-driven business with an interest in self-tracking and QS to bolster her professional image. Like Anna, she recruited QS as a central feature of her corporate and personal profile. "Laila is an early adopter and advocate of personalized wellness, self-collected data and the Quantified Self," her website bio reads (Zemrani, n.d.). She also referenced the talk that she delivered at a QS function as the first of her professional presentations. These mentions did not just testify to Laila's private interests. In the same way as they did for Anna, they served to enhance her business stature. In the startup world, where an impassioned persona has become de rigueur, these references perform additional work. They at once signal early consumer enthusiasm – that is, they show that there is real desire out there; just look at me! – and reassure potential business partners and clients that the venture stems from Laila's own long-term commitments. Although the digital monitoring company Laila had founded was new, her experiments with self-tracking and with QS supplemented her work; they pointed to a much broader history with digitization. Moreover, by indicating that self-monitoring was her lifelong passion, not just a passing preoccupation, these private pursuits justified her dedication to what was still a fledgling business.

Other participants spoke of the business value of forums such as QS even more explicitly. Sharon, for example, stressed that her curiosity in QS and therefore personal data bled directly into her professional life as a product manager for a data company:

> It's helpful for me on the personal side but also now on the professional side too because I understand the process of cleaning up data and using the tools we actually are developing actively and offering feedback back to the developer. So, it's almost been this marriage of my personal and professional life. To the extent that it's part of my job to play with. (Sharon, 2015)

When I interviewed Ben, an engineer working for a large IT company, he explained his interest in QS this way:

> [At work] they have what they call a "white space" program where you can kind of go off and work on your own thing – either for professional development or to experiment with new products that may help the company. And there are a few of us here that are experimenting with how self-tracking applies to small business, which is one of our key customer segments. And how that tracking can improve their business – a lot of Internet of Things (IoT)-type stuff. But because most small businesses are sole proprietorships, the business is the self. So, we think about how it [IoT] can help improve efficiency or make a small business more effective. (Ben, 2015)

QS helped Ben satisfy his company's "white space program" where employees are expected to cultivate personal projects and hobbies that may meaningfully contribute to the company's bottom line. QS, in this sense, was an ideal pastime. Beyond entertainment, it offered him a place from which he could source inspiration and business ideas to incorporate back into his job. Not surprisingly, at QS15, the conference we both attended in San Francisco in 2015, he was most impressed with stories of self-tracking projects and experiments that turned into actual businesses.

While Mark generally found discussions in the forum interesting and was additionally relieved to find "down to earth types," not just data "fanatics," at QS15, like Ben, he was mainly motivated by seeing "how people were trying to commercialize and have money-making businesses in this space" (Mark, 2015). At the conference, he kept an eye out for potential partnerships that could enable the software company where he worked, which mostly focused on the business sector, to enter the data-driven consumer market. On several occasions I also noticed that technologists included their engagement with QS in their professional LinkedIn or Twitter profiles, and, like Anna, shared videos of their talks online.

These participants all indicate that they do not attend QS events simply because tinkering with technology has become an occupational hazard. They take on the unpaid and often time-consuming work of organizing local meetings, of delivering presentations at events, or of attending these functions in their spare time in order to expand their professional credentials in an environment where reconciling personal interests with work commitments and assuming this labor have become a crucial strategy of establishing one's professional credibility and value. It's therefore not counterintuitive to see technologists engage in QS activities as technophiles. If practitioners embraced the personal language of QS even as they engaged with the forum in order to pursue business ends, doing so already constituted a familiar part of hustling with a passion. The first-person narrative around which QS has built its identity as a "community" mirrors the expectation that technologists articulate their work in intimate terms as well as demonstrably reconcile their jobs with private commitments.

In all of these examples, QS forums were places to practice as well as to enact the self-motivated business posture. Indeed, it's the collective's staging as a lens onto the private self-tracking experiments of app and wearables users that has enabled professionals to effectively translate their business-driven engagements with the group into hallmarks of intimate passions. These efforts ultimately reconnect the labor of extracurricular entrepreneurs hustling with a passion in forums such as QS with the work of tech executives mingling in QS as members while continuing to think as vendors, as discussed in the previous chapter. The restaging of professional obligations as expressions of personal interests in both instances produces (and responds to the need to produce) some of the digital social enthusiasm that tech executives are eager to see in the market at large.

From "Obsolete Tech Guy" to "Most Quantified Man"

Technologists such as Chris Dancy offer an extreme example of the way an impassioned personal narrative can intersect with the framework and the "imaginative haze" (Hepp, 2020, p. 934) produced by QS to manufacture a lucrative professional image. Since 2012, Dancy has successfully parlayed these elements into a branded identity as the "most connected man on earth" (Dancy, 2017). The latter has helped him move from "an obsolete tech guy" (Finley, 2013) to a popular speaker and digital entrepreneur. His story dramatizes how technologists now instrumentalize desire and the complex relationship of forums such as QS to this type of work.

As Dancy tells it (2015), his personal and professional success in the tech arena were both organic and spontaneous. His fortunes turned around after he was unexpectedly "discovered" by a set of journalists at Amber Case's tech-themed CyborgCamp in 2012, which Case, a self-styled "cyborg anthropologist," ran as an "unconference." This meant that participants brought ideas they wanted to discuss, and talks emerged naturally out of that collection. In the early part of the event, Dancy came across someone who recognized his name from his Twitter profile where he was already sharing thoughts and results of his early self-tracking efforts, and who then prompted him to discuss these ideas with a broader group. He recalled the conversation this way:

"You are the guy that tweets about information every now and then," the man said.
"And I go 'yeah,'" Dancy responded.
"What do you do with it?" he probed further.
"I take it all and I put it into a Google calendar," Dancy briefly explained. He then pulled up the calendar on his computer, a psychedelic page filled with myriad color-coded fields and tags [Figure 4.3].
"That's your entire life?" the guy asked Dancy, apparently impressed and intrigued by the careful way in which he had cataloged his experiences.
"Yes," Dancy claimed to have answered unassumingly. (2015)

The man immediately flagged Amber Case down to see the calendar and Case encouraged Dancy to share it at the event. Telling me that he was reluctant to take the floor at first, he eventually agreed to speak. And Case penciled him in for an afternoon session at one of the unconference's open slots.

That day, reporters from *Wired* and *TechCrunch* were in attendance and they sat in on Dancy's impromptu presentation. Afterwards, they approached Dancy for an interview and each ultimately published an article detailing his self-tracking escapades (Finley, 2013; Williams, 2013). Following these encounters, things quickly took off as one media mention seemed to beget another. Dancy recalled:

I can't remember what the next big story was, but it was probably some television piece out of some foreign country. And then by the end of that year the BBC called me. And then beginning of last year [2014] the *Wall Street Journal* did a piece on me. And then after the *Wall Street Journal*, I went over to England to meet some people. I've done some real cool secret stuff. (2015)

His extreme self-tracking practice led to sustained media coverage as well as to him securing speaking slots at popular technology conferences such as South by SouthWest (SXSW). In 2014, he returned to CyborgCamp as a celebrated keynote speaker. With time, this attention opened up paid television opportunities too. The invitation to appear on the Showtime series *Dark Net*, which premiered in 2016, Dancy told me (2015), came "one day, out of the blue" when he received a phone call from an unknown number. The voice on the phone asked Dancy to do some "fact checking" and quizzed him on what had happened on a given day. "Hold on," Dancy replied, immediately starting a search on his computer where he kept an intricate calendar cataloguing the minutiae of his daily pursuits. According to Dancy, the caller was pleased by his unfazed and fast response. "Don't worry about it," he told him and booked him on the spot. In short order, a Showtime camera crew arrived to spend a week with him.

Though Dancy tends to describe this media frenzy and the resulting professional rise as unexpected, and claims that he was even reluctant to embrace the attention at first, they were not just products of a happy coincidence. They

Hi 83F
Low 58F

SLEEP:

Went to bed at 12:05am
Slept 8 hours 35 mins

ENVIRONMENT :

Hi 76.1
Low 75
NOISE:
Loudest Moment 66db 1201pm
Most quiet moment 58 db (Through out day)
Air Pressure/ quality
30.37 10:59amHigh 1805 PPM 11pm
Low 792 ppm 645am
Humidity:
High 55% 1:30pm
Low 50% 4:57pm
MOVEMENT:
Weighed 223.4 lbs
Walked 3.76 miles / 8088 steps

PURCHASES:

$34.91 Facebook ads for Mindful Cyborgs Podcast
$17.63 CHICK-FIL-A

SOCIAL MEDIA:

First Facebook "Like" at 12:55am by a friend "Shane Carlson likes your comment: "In watching it, I felt the connection..."
19 Facebook likes
First Tweet personal account(RT): 9:25 am
https://twitter.com/chrisdancy/status/36658118766742732297:17pm Last Screen Shot taken
First Tweet professional account 9:40am
https://twitter.com/ServiceSphere/status/366584907675340
800
7:40 Pinterest image pinned

TRAVEL:

1:04pm Dog Park: http://instagram.com/p/c4oMYTNTCs/
See Attached Drive to dog park
5:43 Arrived Home
Home 2013-08-11T00:00:00-06:00
transport 2013-08-11T12:26:47-06:00
walking 2013-08-11T13:02:06-06:00
Place in Cherry Creek State Park 2013-08-11T13:12:39-06:00
walking 2013-08-11T13:16:03-06:00
walking 2013-08-11T13:24:38-06:00
Place in Cherry Creek State Park 2013-08-11T13:29:08-06:00
walking 2013-08-11T13:51:09-06:00
transport 2013-08-11T14:00:40-06:00
Place in Cornerstar Shopping Center 2013-08-11T14:15:12-06:00

TOTAL EMAILS SENT: 21
First email at 12:11am from Google Alerts on "Mindfulness study out of Texas Tech"
Last email at 11:43pm on Robotics
12:25pm First Screen shot taken
13 Chatter posts read - First "BMC is a Silver Sponsor at VMWorld 2013 at the Mos" last "Tremendous amount of positive reaction from press"
11pm Meeting with UK Company on Agile ITIL using Go To meeting
11:03am first trello task created
9:27am First Evernote created from email
FILES UPDATED ON COMPUTER:
ohlife_backup_aug11.txt Comment Open in Dropbox
iTunes Library.itl by Chris Dancy Comment Open in Dropbox
iTunes Library.xml by Chris Dancy Comment Open in Dropbox
Diary stuff.doc by Chris Dancy Comment Open in Dropbox
Diary1.doc by Chris Dancy Comment Open in Dropbox
Image DB Temp 2.tmp by Chris Dancy Comment Open in Dropbox

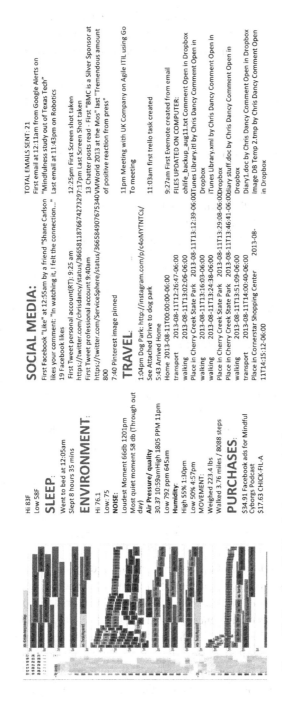

Figure 4.3 Page from Chris's calendar. www.chrisdancy.com.

were certainly shaped by his skilled cultivation of an impassioned persona and by his effective channeling of it into monetizable activities. As a prototypical example of a technologist hustling with a passion, there are several elements to his success.

Dancy's made-for-TV personality that is equal parts sincere and sensational accounts for part of his media and professional achievement. With an ear for language and an eye for theater, Dancy appears to intuitively grasp the value of a good story – a knack, he told me, he likely inherited from his mother. He addresses an audience of one or one hundred with the fervor and conviction of a pastor, his delivery rousing and engaging. Impassioned "This guy gets it!" or "I completely agree with him!" were comments I routinely heard rise up from the audience at the various conferences and meetups where he spoke. Hearing his talk at SXSW, Ernesto Ramirez, one of the co-organizers of QS in Los Angeles, approached Dancy afterwards. According to Dancy, he exclaimed, "Chris, it's like Data Church with you!" (2015).

Dancy's effective dramatization of his self-tracking interests, not just his outsized private devotion to digital tools, has played a leading role in his public narrative and business achievements as well. He routinely makes headlines for claiming to use as many as seven hundred different mechanisms to monitor his life. His excessive self-monitoring habit was one of the elements that attracted the attention of tech journalists. By now, the figure has become part of his popular appeal, regularly repeated in article after article as evidence of his incredible dedication to this beguiling passion. The number he often cites has weight, solidity, even import. It is meant both to entice and to alarm. In the press it is largely mobilized as evidence of his identity as "the most connected man on earth." When I asked Chris about it, he modified the claim, explaining that he does not actually use that many devices at any one time. Rather, he arrived at this figure after tallying up all of the devices that he estimates track his activity, online and offline. That includes the mobile applications he has purchased or installed himself, and to be sure, there are many. But the total also involves the forms of monitoring he guesses he has been exposed to through-out his life: surveillance cameras that Chris has come into contact with in stores, airports, and tollbooths, information gathered by merchants, as well as the mechanisms used by his employers, insurance companies, and doctors to track his whereabouts, performance, and health at one time or another. The art of the sale, here, is not in nuance, but in daring and delivery. Neither false nor true, the audacious statement is characteristic of the claims advertisers often make, such as "Made from the best stuff on earth" or "The best a man can get." Clearly exaggerated and not easily verifiable, the grandiose assertions carry the veneer of the plausible while avoiding the burden of proof required of more specific and easier to confirm statistics. In the business world, it is common knowledge that a company can often get away with a pompous statement without legal repercussions on the premise that something that ambitious must clearly be a hyperbole.

Dancy is additionally a self-aware subject who adroitly leverages contemporary modes of communication such as social media to construct a marketable identity. He was an early and avid user of Twitter who began using this platform to develop a more consistent and curated online image following his bout with unemployment. Ever on alert for a catchy phrase, Dancy frequently paused when we spoke to jot down a comment that he planned to use on social media later: "You don't become happy, happy becomes you." He then stopped. "I need to remember that." At one point, I said something that caught his ear – "You should Tweet that," he advised me (2015).

Moreover, ever since he was profiled in *Wired* as an "obsolete tech guy" (Finley, 2013), a description that left him disappointed, he's taken concerted steps to consolidate and take control over his public image. Like many knowledge workers now do, he has created a website to curate his public profile and to collate his press clippings. But he went farther. To standardize and elevate his online profile, he commissioned professionally rendered art and photography to distribute to media outlets and to use as a consistent template in his presentation materials and social media communication. These portraits were finely tuned to reflect popular and tech-driven dystopic and techno-utopian narratives. Their subject matter also suggested that he embraced these pursuits wholeheartedly.

One of the earlier portraits, painted with oil on canvas by artist Aaron Jasinski in 2012 (Figure 4.4) and titled *Real You*, features Dancy dressed in a crimson suit facing off a steely robot, with an arid, lifeless desert behind them while ominous clouds build up above. Each holds a mask in his hand. Dancy is holding up the mask of the robot while the robot wields a mask of Dancy's face.

The work trades on the notion of the cyborg popularized by science fiction films that sensationalize the curious origins and outcomes of human beings mixed with bionic forms. Of course, it harkens back to classics such as *The Terminator*, which still shape the visual vocabulary for self-tracking and self-quantification in social discourse. Such sci-fi aesthetics also continue to provide the "cultural backdrop" for the tech sector at large (Dourish and Bell, 2014).

The 2016 Consumer Electronics Show (CES), the largest annual technology trade show, even leveraged parallel imagery to Dancy's portrait (Figure 4.5), as it pictured two interlinked hands, one robotic, the other human (and white), magnanimously rising out of the ground like two buds of a flower whose paths

Figure 4.4 *Real You*. Painting. Aaron Jasinski.

Figure 4.5 Life-size poster greeting visitors at CES 2016. Photo by author.

have crossed but who are facing in opposite directions in a gesture of both friction and fraternity.

Jasinski's painting of Dancy the cyborg, much like the juxtaposed, extended hands of the CES marketing materials, likewise recall *The Creation of Adam*, the famous fresco painted by Italian master Michelangelo, which purports to capture the moment Adam was created by the hand of God (Figure 4.6). In the Western context, the opposing, reaching, limp arms have become a familiar visual trope of primal contact. This motion also foregrounds a spiritual change and awakening, a religious idea that continues to support the rags-to-riches

Figure 4.6 *The Creation of Adam*, Michelangelo. Wikimedia Commons.

ideology of the American Dream as well as technological enthusiasm where the encounter with technology heralds a formative transformation in the fabric of society.

Dancy's stylized portrait adroitly plays upon this popular iconography. Indeed, the theme of transformation has become central to Dancy's own narrative of data-fueled personal reinvention. In the press and in his own online image, his professional about-face is persistently attributed to his private self-tracking practice. Since he started digitally monitoring his experiences, the story goes, Dancy has reorganized his life. Thanks to the digital technology he engaged, he claims to have lost weight, shed poor habits, and ended bad relationships. In older photographs included in journalistic profiles, he is often pictured as overweight and unkempt, gazing timidly through oversized glasses, wearing an old and wrinkled T-shirt. These "before" headshots are contrasted with the sleek, trimmed physique and more finely styled hair of the "after" shots. When thus symbolically aligned with his digital collection, he is stylized as a focused man purposefully gliding into the future.

Dancy also regularly refreshes this imagery. A year after he commissioned the original artwork, he arranged a photoshoot in Japan where he was visiting to watch the screening of a film based on his tracking activity produced by a Japanese film company. This time, in a photograph called *Inner Net* taken by Kyle Thompson that has since frequently accompanied media articles featuring Dancy, he once again toyed with the cultural mystique of the cyborg identity (Figure 4.7). In the picture, he sports a black leather jacket, staring dejectedly at his raised arm. Instead of veins, wires are seen protruding from a bloodless, open gash in his wrist. A row of yellow bandages mimicking electrical tape suggestively cover additional wiring on his neck.

At a time when panicked articles about the robot takeovers were experiencing a renaissance fueled by the dystopian predictions of Silicon Valley

Figure 4.7 *Inner Net*. Photograph. Kyle Thompson.

futurists such as Ray Kurzweil (2005), the urban setting, the slashed wrist, and the black leather attire signaled this communion as risky, but therefore somehow renegade and adventurous.

At the time of our last interview in 2016, Dancy was most proud of a new set of prints, also captured by Thompson, that were taken during a follow-up sojourn to Japan in 2015 (Figure 4.8). This photographic series is completely wireless; there is not a cable in sight on any of the photographs as Chris poses against a set of natural backgrounds, a stark contrast to his dystopian industrial and lunar theme of years past. His favorite one echoes the photograph of the wire-strung arm from two years earlier. However, where wires once erupted from punctured skin, a single branch delicately sprouts as he gently, almost protectively, gazes over it in a contemplative posture. This picture also subtly gestures to the oil-on-canvas portrait from 2012. In the latest image, Dancy is once again pictured wearing a maroon jacket. This time, however, he traded in the suit for a more casual look.

The relaxed posture and pastoral landscape mark Dancy's own growing interest in Buddhism, meditation, and technology-assisted – or, as he calls it, enhanced – spirituality. But it also signals his shift in attitude toward technology. Rather than simply something external, Dancy has come to speak of technology as something he has internalized. In public forums and online, he often describes his digital self-tracking as an additional sense that he has now added to his repertoire of embodied perception.

Figure 4.8 Photograph. Kyle Thompson.

Dancy's ability to deftly couple techniques of self-promotion with his own interest in self-tracking certainly elevated his professional stature. However, the mediating framework of the "quantified self" has also played a critical role in this persona, whether he directly acknowledges this influence or not. As our discussions and his own media record make clear, his successful public image and career in the tech sector derive not only from his fined-tuned deployment of the impassioned personal narrative but also the business and media appeal of self-quantification that, at the time that he "came out of his 'data closet' in Portland" (Case, 2014), was already anchored by the public narratives of collectives such as QS.

Dancy may have told me that at CyborgCamp in 2012 he was still reluctant to really talk about QS and his broader interest in this sphere. Remembering the moment, he described to me the image he still held in his mind's eye:

I didn't want to drive too far down the Quantified Self route yet. It was still really hard to talk to people [about it]. People didn't quite understand what was happening with bodies and information . . . [But] I held the unconference, and she put it up on the television, and I started showing people days, not in calendar mode but in the agenda mode. There are thousands of pieces of information. You can just see it, this beautiful diary. And people were really surprised. The idea of self-tracking as footnotes to emotion, dog-eared pages of a life, became real. They'd never seen it. They were playing with these ideas, but they've never seen it so personified. (2016)

Nevertheless, the year Dancy was "discovered" by the media at the unconference, the construct played a central role in Case's promotional materials of the event. Although the structure of the gathering was loose, Case mapped out a set of themes, including one emphasizing the "quantified self," that she communicated to conference goers in advance: "This year's CyborgCamp will be a full day of conference and unconference sessions, fun, food and great people together to talk about the future of humans and technology. Three scheduled speakers will give talks on *biomedical engineering, cybernetic control systems and the stock market, and quantified self.* The rest of the day will be unconference sessions" (Case, 2012, emphasis mine).

In this announcement, Case clearly used the term "quantified self" generally. By 2012, however, five years had passed since Wolf and Kelly had coined the term, and three since Wolf had penned articles about QS in premier publications such as *Wired* and *The New York Times*. At this point, familiarity and buzz around the expression and group activities had begun to build, rendering the motif a reliable media and conference draw. It's evident that the idea of the "quantified self" functioned in Case's invitation both as a conference topic and as a promotional tactic.

This framing attracted both participants such as Dancy as well as members of the press who were working the "quantified self" beat. In fact, articles that were published about Dancy following his presentation at CyborgCamp 2012 explicitly linked him with the language of self-quantification and QS. "The Quantified Man: How an Obsolete Tech Guy Rebuilt Himself for the Future," *Wired* magazine introduced Dancy in the headline (Finley, 2013), and it then identified Dancy as being "on the cutting edge of the 'quantified self' movement kickstarted by *Wired*'s Gary Wolf and Kevin Kelly" in the body of the article. The expose hyperlinked "quantified self" (even though spelled in the lower case) to the forum's website. "Quantified human," echoed *TechCrunch* when describing Dancy in its own coverage (Williams, 2013).

Over time, coupled with his skilled self-promotion, the mediating thematic of the "quantified self" created attention for Dancy and enabled him to build the broader idea that he was the most "Most Quantified Self in America," as a headline of an article published by Bloomberg.com announced (Boudway, 2014). On his LinkedIn page, the work-focused social media platform popular among white-collar professionals, Dancy emphasizes his oversized persona as the "World's Most Connected Person. Seriously, just google "Most Connected." But cherry-picked media soundbites featured in his "About" section continue to center his association with the concept of the "quantified self" and the QS "movement."

"Dancy is the ultimate example of two revolutions underway in tech: the Internet of Things (smart thermostats, garage doors, toothbrushes, tennis racquets) and *quantified self* (what you learn about yourself from trackers)." (Mashable)

"You probably know someone, like Chris Dancy, but not really. Chris Dancy is arguably the most *quantified self* in America, probably the world." (Marketplace)

"Dancy's a pioneer in the *"quantified self-movement."* (NPR)

In the years since he delivered his presentation at Case's CyborgCamp, he has effectively parlayed this combination into several new tech jobs and ventures. In 2015, Chris took the stage at the QS conference in San Francisco, where he promoted himself as an avid self-tracker while also exhibiting a new self-tracking application, Compas – which he co-developed with Case – as an event sponsor. In advance of the conference, Ernesto Ramirez profiled him as a featured toolmaker on the QS website.

The story that is publicly recounted about Dancy, and the story that he himself tells about his digital pursuits, is one of personal awakening sparked by private interests in self-tracking that just happened to catch fire and lead to a rewarding career. However, it's evident that Dancy's personal and professional transformation has as much to do with the cycles of "micro-celebrity" (Marwick, 2013; Senft, 2013) that have opened him up to new revenue streams and the extracurricular demands of professionals successfully hustling with a passion as it does with the mediating framework of the "quantified self" that had spurred attention and helped drive media and business curiosity in such pursuits.

Dancy is someone who has cultivated and leveraged these elements skillfully and indefatigably. At one point, he invoked the metaphor of sewing to describe his self-tracking practice to me, but this metaphor, it seemed, was also an apt way to depict the nonstop labor of this extracurricular entrepreneur hustling with a passion. "I'm like a seamstress fixing up a dress," he said to me once over coffee, commenting on his carefully curated online settings and preferences that he updates constantly in accordance with miniscule shifts in his life (Dancy, 2016). Then, he grabbed the end of the tablecloth laid on the table we were sharing and pretended to repair the seams of an imagined tattered edge. "A stray thread here, a stray thread there," he said, miming a needle pulling through the cloth. "Or if there is a loose bead . . ." he trailed off as he delicately tucked a fictional crystal back into place. Just as likely, though, he could have been speaking about the skill, work, money, and time involved in stitching together this patchwork professional identity. It's these efforts that have elevated Dancy both as a tech visionary and as a specimen on the tech media and conference circuit.

Of course, the lengths to which Dancy has gone to cultivate his professional profile – and the supporting role that QS has played in this (self-)construction – are not typical. Yet, his story is exemplary, even if extreme, of the extracurricular investments demanded of technologists hustling with a passion. Dancy's experience channeling his private self-tracking interests and his association with groups such as QS into a professional persona of some significance dramatizes how intricately technologists hustling with a passion must lace the personal with the professional. It also provides a small window onto the legitimizing and supporting frame that forums such as QS have offered in these pursuits. Once again, therefore, QS can be understood as a product, as a mechanism, and as an interface to these industry realities. In some measure, it's these professional demands, too, rather than organic cultural enthusiasm for said practices, that have raised the social profile and entrepreneurial uptake of digital self-tracking and of QS itself.

QS as a Template

Like Dancy, digital professionals are navigating an uncertain and unstable employment environment where they are called to act as seamstresses tasked with patching up loose ends of their own identities in order to sew together a vibrant and quilt-like personal narrative that reveals the professional as closely tied with the personal. Most, however, are not able to invest in their self-construction to the same degree as Dancy for lack of money, skill, and time. This challenge, as Gershon points out, exposes the irony of the expectation that job seekers relate to themselves as a business. Unlike a corporation, the resources any one person has at their disposal to manage the process of professional image making are relatively few. Therefore, as Gershon highlights, job seekers face a key dilemma: "how to animate a self that can evince corporate personhood when one does not have the person-hours or labor that a corporation can draw upon" (2014, p. 292).

A wide set of web tools has of course now emerged to support job seekers in this task even as these platforms simultaneously help turn such labor into a professional prerequisite. These include mechanisms such as social media or website development tools that reduce some of the work involved in managing and representing oneself as a business. These platforms help technologists enhance their professional credentials as they work to further harness social interactions for business ends.

These mechanisms also include a crop of digital event-organizing platforms, such as meetup.com – the company used by QS organizers to convene events.

Meetup was started by Scott Heiferman in 2002 as an attempt to revive what he then saw, following political scientist Robert D. Putnam, as a declining sense of community in American cities (Fairbanks, 2008). Still, the role that the platform has played in professional organizing cannot be reduced to what Sherry Turkle (2015), in a related context, has called the alienating nature of online communication. Companies such as meetup.com have emerged as vital tools for extracurricular entrepreneurs tasked with hustling with a passion. Organizing meetups around a range of tech topics has become a routine strategy for demonstrating leadership and professional eagerness, not just as a mechanism to assuage loneliness. Meetup.com supports these efforts by providing hosts with scripts and formats that automate the process of managing event logistics. This platform also supplies a prefabricated web environment that makes archiving materials associated with each event and serializing such functions appear both simple and necessary. Finally, it fulfills a promotional role. It helps organizers to advertise events to a broader audience.

Still, even though content moderation tools and event-organizing platforms provide logistical support, they offer little in terms of substance. Developing original material and hosting an event that consistently draws an audience and contributes to participants' reputations remain formidable tasks. They require creativity, spare time, and status in order to establish credibility, attention, and professional value. This is one of the reasons why many of the meetups I've attended throughout my fieldwork have been relatively short-run affairs. The extended tenure of QS, which at the time my research wrapped up in 2018 was nearly ten years old, stands out against these numbers as an uncommon success story.

For extracurricular entrepreneurs hustling with a passion, then, QS supplied both an effective narrative frame and a ready-made rubric for a meetup that worked. While still demanding, contributing to QS required relatively less effort. That is because both conveners and participants of QS events could leverage the reputations, media experience, and promotional efforts of the group's original founders. QS hosts and participants alike also benefited from Wolf and Kelly's skill as writers and content creators, which produced continuity and a sense of scale for QS through well-curated articles, videos, and commentary on group activities featured on quantifiedself.com in between meetups.

Technologists could additionally benefit from the original founders' experience as journalists and media professionals who applied their expertise to construct a consistent and an easy-to-replicate format for QS meetups and conferences centered around the Show & Tell. This framework created a strong "hook" that attracted interest in addition to lending group activities narrative uniformity. The outline speakers were given when asked to formulate their self-tracking stories not only in the first person but as a response to the questions "What did I do?" and "What did I learn?" provided further structure. This story scaffolding visually and thematically brought together otherwise disconnected gatherings into a unified social happening. The pithy arrangement reflects the media savvy of the QS founders who surely recognized that a simple and repetitive structure was necessary to sustain the attentions of an increasingly overburdened and distracted audience.

Finally, the stylized elements that supplied the forum with a distinctive "look and feel" and elevated it from a local gathering to a recognizable brand that the founders applied to QS communications raised the public profile and the visual appeal of this forum. These elements included a logo, an "unofficial" tagline ("Knowledge through Numbers"), as well as a consistent presentation template that could be replicated across a range of media "touch-points," as marketers might phrase it, such as the website, the presentation deck, or media mentions.

With time, these efforts have rendered QS a familiar forum and a catchphrase that has entered the general lexicon. These elements also equipped busy professionals hustling with a passion with a consistent, skillfully rendered, and easy-to-use framework that alleviated some of the practical challenges of organizing such events. Those meeting under the banner of QS were therefore able to leverage the expertise and relationships of the group founders for themselves. For extracurricular entrepreneurs hustling with a passion who were already spread thin, affiliating with a well-socialized and well-structured forum such as QS extended contributors' professional footprints as it helped them to enfold their participation in QS into projects of professional self-making.

The Home Office Conundrum

As a templated, well-curated, and well-branded safe-for-work hobby, QS responds to the paradoxical imperative extracurricular entrepreneurs hustling with a passion face to professionalize the personal as they personalize the professional. The forum has played a double role here. It has supplied some of means for meeting these requirements and in doing so, has served as an effective interface to the standards that power the tech sector.

However, QS, and namely the corporate locations where many of the meetups were held, highlight another curious aspect of the self-tracking market: the way the business persona centered on performative passion that technologists today are called to embody has developed alongside organizational changes such as the dissolution of the corporate office as a fixed place of employment and the concurrent rise of amenities-filled offices that aestheticize the workplace as a space of comfort and leisure. Examining these institutional shifts further offers one more way to understand the key drivers of the contemporary need knowledge professionals experience to hustle with a passion, as well as how QS has interfaced with them.

In the tech sector, well-designed and stylish offices that suggestively mix work with pleasure were first popularized by companies such as Google in the early 2000s. By the mid-2010s, this setup was already a tech industry hallmark. Technology companies now increasingly aim to operate beautifully furnished, airy, and snack-filled offices that help to socialize and care for their employees. Some even infuse elements of entertainment into their office setup, putatively offering overtaxed professionals a place for relaxation and mingling over yoga or a game of ping-pong.

From the corporate point of view, these refurbished and reimagined environments were often explicitly offered as contrasts to autocratic and uninspiring office settings, the type memorialized in the popular late-1990s film *Office Space*, whose plot revolved around disgruntled computer scientists who rejected endless rows of generic cubicles that endorsed conformity in favor of passion projects and hobbies that could be comfortably completed from home. Companies now employ design to entice young professionals looking for a better work–life balance by ostensibly restaging work as an organic extension of personal life. Such accommodations explicitly frame the office as a vital social space rather than as a site of pure obligation (Hochschild, 1997).

Because many knowledge workers contemporaneously find themselves located outside of the corporate gated communities modeled on the creature comforts of home, a growing crop of co-working firms that rent office space to individuals and startups has also emerged to fill this corporate void. Since 2008, when companies such as WeWork opened their doors, co-working facilities have energetically imported the design choices and messaging of tech giants along with their progressively unmoored tech force. Taking after the promises of the refurbished tech headquarters, WeWork, for example, claims to promote "human-centric" forms of work (Pietra and Rowell, 2019). The de-corporatized sentiments likewise echo in signs that greet those renting offices at co-working company Spaces, which address businesspeople in New York City with messages such as "Welcome Home" emblazoned on their front doors.

Like the imperative to hustle with a passion, the domesticated office is both aspirational and ironic. By offering the office as a space of comfort and entertainment, the arrangement helps to assuage and accommodate those who are progressively working longer hours in flexible and unstable corporate settings. However, an avowed commitment to employee "wellness" is surely an inadequate solution to vocational realities that compel knowledge workers to spend more time both on procuring and performing their jobs. Especially so as reimagining the workplace in the symbolic terms of home subtly devalues labor conducted therein. "Home" renders the workspace casual. Unlike austere corporate settings of investment firms that lay bare the banks' solitary focus on profit, examined by Karen Ho (2009), contemporary tech firms and co-working spaces that infuse the office with the comforts of home only further recode work commitments as matters of personal desire rather than professional obligations. "Home" makes the line between the professional and personal domains ever more porous. As these changes render "work" more challenging to recognize and therefore "work hours" more difficult to calculate, proper compensation becomes even more difficult to allocate.

"Home" likewise stages the office as a space of care and community in a time when ties between employees and organizations they work for are increasingly becoming more threadbare. Co-working companies, the firms that rent space to a flexibly employed workforce that generally does not qualify for workplace benefits accorded to full-time employees, most conspicuously expose the lauded human-centric approaches to the tech office as a design aesthetic rather than as a meaningful corporate intervention, one that in fact deflects attention away from corporate responsibility to develop more beneficial systems of employee support. Indeed, as the home-like workspace, with comfortable lounges and kitchen cupboards filled with dishes and coffee mugs, visually personalizes the office as it telegraphs the intimate pleasures of work, it symbolically decouples structural factors and institutional assistance from professional trajectories. The image and the accoutrements of the office as home thus act as a smokescreen that distracts knowledge workers from examining too closely the structural conditions of employment that make achieving stability, employment security, and, yes, even the ever-elusive but constantly promised work–life balance less possible.

The trend for designer offices modeled on sophisticated homes developed alongside spiking real-estate prices in tech centers such as San Francisco and New York. Well-heeled digital professionals have of course contributed to the gentrification and the corresponding skyrocketing housing costs in these regions. However, those working in the tech sector, particular those just starting out or who increasingly find themselves insecurely employed, have also felt these effects. While real-estate developers started to address the housing crisis by investing in compact, dorm-style dwellings designed for busy young professionals hustling with a passion who, presumably, were rarely home (Bowles, 2018), TV channels such as HGTV marked the trend with upbeat programing that showcased young couples and families enthusiastically downsizing to designer, trailer-sized "tiny homes." I also saw techies in my social media network occasionally circulate mock apartment listings that lampooned as they highlighted these converging phenomena. The San Francisco-based photographer Scott Hampton played on this idea in a playful photo series. His photographs feature dumpster containers, manholes, or park benches all marked with a "For Rent" sign that facetiously recommends these sites as affordable and conveniently located dwellings in the city center boasting great views of fountains and local restaurants (Editors, 2014).

In this difficult housing market, office space designed to look like the nicer, brighter, more stylish home that the flexibly employed knowledge workers in the tech sector increasingly struggle to afford has a disciplinary quality. The homey and design-forward office does not only beckon with its cozy appeal but with a promise of a better tomorrow where the hard work of those frantically hustling with a passion may pay off and become parlayed into the ultimate manifestation of the American Dream: an equally stylish home of one's own.

Knowledge professionals, however, derive an entirely different set of benefits from the stylish, homey office. In this context, co-working spaces do more than just aestheticize professional instability as a desirable feature of professional life and as a personal preference. While co-working companies seek to attract people through a connation with domestic comfort, they remain compelling because they confer a greater level of professionalism on those who today choose or are increasingly obliged to work outside of the confines of a corporate office. Under the dueling pressures of expanding modes of flexible employment and the rise of snack-filled, well-designed corporate headquarters among Silicon Valley's tech giants, demonstrable access to fashionable working space has emerged as an expedient means of bolstering one's professional image. As sociologist David Grazian (2020) notes in his study of co-working companies such as WeWork, contemporary office arrangements do not only provide small business owners, freelancers, and consultants with a functional place to carry out their jobs. They also make it possible for the growing numbers of flexibly yet precariously employed knowledge workers to continue to source authority from familiar business accoutrements, indicating by their growing popularity that materiality still matters in a dematerialized digital economy. As one participant in Grazian's study noted, "when you work at WeWork, you're paying money so you can feel like you're working at

Google" (p. 12). One is paying money to look like they are working at Google, too, as the aesthetic correlation not only raises one's own self-confidence in an uncertain business environment but helps to elevate personal esteem in the eyes of clients and investors alike. The emergence of the sleek, centrally located co-working facilities as a valued tool of professional impression management has likely displaced some of the appeal of the run-down subur- ban garage as the idealized site of technological invention, which has for- mally dominated the popular tech startup imaginary. Signaling the shift, startup entrepreneurs whose headquarters I would visit during fieldwork, offices that often didn't yet have the aspirational sheen of Google or WeWork, routinely apologized to me for workspaces they perceived to be too remote or too plain.

This context offers additional ways to understand why forums such as QS have gained popular attention. For many of my interlocutors, the fact that QS was expressly situated as a social rather than as a professional gathering was not its only draw as a safe-for-work hobby. The forum was an attractive site and pastime for those hustling with a passion because it presented as an amateur forum configured by corporate trimmings. My interlocutors regularly remarked on the fact that they appreciated QS as "very professionally done." The corporate settings in which gathering were held indeed were some of the key elements that ratified QS as a work-safe extracurricular activity. In add- ition to the branded elements and the stylized structure of QS discussed earlier, the business air was explicitly secured through the borrowed equity of the corporate office. Yes, some early QS events were occasionally held in cafes or even organizers' living rooms, the first most notably hosted by Kevin Kelly in his own home. This original connection with the figure of home bolstered the reputation of QS as a grassroots community organized by and for technophiles (Chapter 1). However, despite the staging of QS as an idea that was birthed at home, most of the meetings I attended during the course of my research in cities such as New York City, Boston, Washington DC, and San Francisco took place in corporate offices. These furthermore tended to be the workplaces of companies affiliated with digital entrepreneurialism in some form: tech startups, venture capital incubators, co-working offices.[6] The QS website even recommends that organizers look for ways to host their gatherings in such venues. These functions, moreover, all took place after hours, during the workweek, and in metropolitan centers with convenient access to the urban professional elite.

These sites carried benefits for corporate hosts and attendees alike. On the one hand, in keeping with the office fashions of Silicon Valley that aim to style the workplace on the intimate aesthetics of home, QS helped to endorse the companies where these events were held as spaces for socializing and entertainment, not just work. On the other hand, the official setting played a legitimizing function for digital professionals attending forums such as QS. While some of my interlocutors occasionally felt nostalgic for the more intimate feel of home-bound get-togethers, many expressed that the corporate locations were what put QS into a more desirable (read professional) light. This environment, I often heard, made QS feel more credible and respectable than just a "bunch of geeks getting together."[7]

The forum's explicit affiliation with corporate spaces was helpful to those hustling with a passion because it rendered QS as not just a recognizable hobby but an activity that could be reputably highlighted within a professional profile. It only further legitimized the forum as a dependable social activity whose put-together aesthetic could positively reflect on its attendees. It is in this additional way that QS supplied extracurricular entrepreneurs pressured to hustle with a passion with a useful safe-for-work hobby, that is, a reputation-building pastime that could be meaningfully channeled toward professional ends. For these reasons, too, QS serves as a suitable interface with such business dynamics.

More Work for Members

In the final analysis, the burden of hustling with a passion also complicates Elon Musk's workplace math. The extended hours that tech executives such as Musk require of their employees do not account for the all-consuming levels of nonwaged, dual extracurricular labor of personalizing the professional while professionalizing the personal that technologists are routinely compelled to take on in addition to their day jobs. Indeed, the dismissive and judgemental tone of his commentary featured at the start of this chapter only further underscores that the contemporary extracurricular entrepreneurs who hustle with a passion increasingly invest their energy into this unrecognized affective labor which invisibly compounds the time they commit to their careers as it reorients their lives around their jobs.

QS assumes a twofold role in this taxing professional context. In equipping technologists with a safe-for-work hobby, a useful narrative frame, as well as a templated event that helps to supplement their self-promotional labor, it supplies some of the means necessary to hustle with a passion, promising to make that work more manageable. At the same time, QS impacts tech professionals in the same way that household appliances affected women performing housekeeping labor in the home: it multiplies rather than reduces their work. Ruth S. Cowen (1983) has argued that modern inventions such as the washing machine and the dishwasher did not reduce women's domestic workload. Despite their labor-saving potential, these machines paradoxically only amplified housework. While these appliances did make chores such as doing laundry or washing dishes easier to complete, their availability and popularity also raised societal expectations around cleanliness, ultimately elevating the overall time and energy women in particular were expected to devote to managing their homes. Similarly, QS assists technologists in the labor of managing a professional image anchored in impassioned hustling as it further intensifies the affective and unwaged work required to sustain it. Like social media platforms that applicants use to manage their professional personas or the home-like amenities offered by co-working companies and technology firms, QS both alleviates and acerbates this work, inadvertently contributing to the very same problems that it helps to resolve.

When QS acts as a mechanism that enables technologists to extract value from their social activities, it also further devalues technologists' efforts. Those who contribute to QS may often be broadly guided by a range of business motives – looking to QS as a site of ethnographic consumer research, as a forum through which to stay on top of industry trends, as a space to connect with industry insiders and build business prospects, or, as discussed in this chapter, as a forum through which to bolster one's professional credentials. However, especially when framed in the casual and altruistic language of community in ways that echo with the promises of the "sharing economy,"[8] QS continues to recast community organizing as extracurricular pursuits that are located to the side of work. Like other modes of immaterial labor performed by technologists, these uncompensated personal investments are often assumed to pay dividends in other ways and at later dates, in the form of knowledge or insights gained, connections made, resume credits procured, or business leads prospected. At the same time, the terms that have installed QS as a convivial hobby forum also continue to normalize the employment volatility and insecurity that have rendered these forms of after-work socializing an important facet of a professional trajectory.

QS, therefore, cannot be understood only as a forum that showcases and celebrates data-driven rationality as it spells out new opportunities for data-driven businesses, as pundits and commentators frequently propose (see Introduction). It's also a construct that reflects turbulent business dynamics that render this affective labor necessary. As a forum that helps to situate technologists as people for whom the professional is also personal while continuing to instrumentalize worker fraternizing, QS represents a growing industry imperative to render sociality and community a requisite, not simply a desirable part of digital labor. Indeed, although scholars such as Tiziana Terranova (2000) have long highlighted free work as a constitutive part of tech capitalism, QS indicates how the expanding insecurity, flexibility, and neoliberalization of the workplace have only further expanded affective and unwaged labor as a fundamental part of the tech sector. Tending to communities such as QS has emerged as another form of care work that now sustains the digital economy. Technologists called to draw on their own resilience, creativity, and passion in an insecure work environment rely on forums such as QS as mechanisms of personal endurance in ways that once again privatize professional challenges and mask structural obstacles. At the same time, QS reveals that community does not only represent an alternative form of resource management in the neoliberal workplace. It exposes community as an organizational form that has become thoroughly commoditized.

5

The New Normal

The conversations, comments, and ideas one encounters in forums such as the Quantified Self (QS) offer alternative means to understand another recurring thematic of the tech industry that can otherwise appear both ambitious and parochial: social mobility and agility facilitated by "interoperable" digital devices. At any given time, digital executives are liable to speak of such broad-reaching benefits of connected gadgets, as Beau Wilder, for instance, did at a regional technology trade show. As he expounded on the merits of networked wearables to a room of about fifty computer engineers, marketers, and data scientists at the Wearable Tech Expo 2015, he confidently predicted that "in the future, we will live in a frictionless world." To illustrate the point, he paused over a PowerPoint slide featuring a stock photograph of a crowded urban street with the words "The New Normal" emblazoned at its bottom (Figure 5.1). The image depicts a phalanx of cars and people framed by office buildings with a billowing white cloud, or perhaps car exhaust, rising over the street's horizon. Though this photograph is largely blurry, the lens focuses on a pair of business professionals, one dressed in a discreet black dress, the other in a well-fitted black suit. Each is shown directing their gaze at a portable device rather than at the street even as they continue to move with apparent resolve. Meanwhile, the soft outlines of the crowd heighten the sense of forward momentum as the effect suggests that the busy camera only momentarily stalled the movements of these hurried city passersby. This scene, Wilder explained, illustrates the advancing "new normal," a future where wearables and sensor-enabled devices will usher in a "frictionless world" mediated by seamlessly connected digital tools.

Wilder may have delivered these words as an announcement, but in this room, such talk wasn't news. Those listening to him speak themselves routinely narrativize the possibilities of interoperable self-monitoring devices in similar terms. This hyperbolic vision forms part of a familiar tech sector

Figure 5.1 A slide from Beau Wilder's presentation. 2015 Wearable Tech Expo.

strategy, one that expresses technological achievements in terms of their idealized social functions. His words point to the improved capacities of the infrastructure that today supports the smooth relay of electronic signals as they conflate devices whose signals link without friction with effortless social experiences enabled by these very tools. In this image, the nodes that pepper the page and operate as beacons guiding the crowd through the heavy photographic fog allegorize the doubled technological and social application of interconnected gadgets.

This techno-social imaginary is also not without historical precedent. Some of these sentiments reproduce the views of mid-twentieth century cyberneticians who first started to envision people and computers as really "brothers under the skin" (Hayles, 1999). In a set of conferences convened between 1945 and 1960 in New York City, this eclectic group of mathematicians, psychologists, and social scientists debated whether the cognition of both humans and computers was fundamentally mediated by a computational logic. While these ideas remained hotly contested among cyberneticians themselves, they gained broader acceptance in the ensuing decades, especially as influential figures such as Stewart Brand helped to enter these concepts into wider social circulation (Turner, 2008; see also Chapter 1). By 1985, Donna Haraway reflected on the degree to which this outlook had entered both popular and industry lexicon. "Our best machines are made of sunshine," she wrote, summarizing the rhetoric. "They are all light and clean because they are nothing but signals, electromagnetic waves, a section of a spectrum, and these machines are eminently portable, mobile." Although she cautioned readers to remember an already overlooked fact in tech sector discourse: "people are nowhere near so fluid, being both material and opaque" (p. 294).

And yet, the associations technologists continue to establish between digital and social mobility are not only overconfident industry predictions to be critiqued. If we are to understand social experiences in terms of their mechanical functions, this rhetoric can also point to alternative parallels between technological imaginaries and working bodies. Haraway, for example, proposed to see devices that in her day were fast becoming smaller and less noticeable, that is, as "light and clean" as electromagnetic signals, as models of labor that was equally being rendered ephemeral and invisible – particularly the work of low-wage laborers creating these gadgets in factories that were out of sight and far away from the people purchasing them. In the new equivalence Haraway established technology continues to represent human capacities, albeit in ways that depart from typical tech sector tributes.

This chapter similarly argues that the enthusiastic connections executives such as Wilder make between digital gadgets and human experience can be read as something other than exaggerated expectations of digital executives. In addition to constituting the public face of data (see Chapter 2) or expressing a more literal hope for a well-networked technological future, ongoing investment in frictionless interoperability and the repetitious nature of such talk point to something else: the symbolic value of movement without interference in the (work) lives of technologists themselves.

On some level, this perspective connects with an even longer historical view. Wilder's hopeful vision remains well tethered to the aims of early-twentieth-century efficiency engineers, who used then novel techniques and technologies to remove everything and anything that stood in the way of people working with the same predictable efficiency as industrial machines. Like Wilder, early scientific managers saw themselves as people ushering in a new normal. In many ways, today's digital executives extend the legacy of practitioners who once presented themselves as innovators who turned to the photo camera and early biometric tools to discipline laboring bodies.

However, the fetishistic fixation of present-day digital professionals on the benefits of technological seamlessness should be analyzed as something more than a narrow commitment to corporate efficiency. This talk can instead be read as a marker of the pressures, aspirations, and anxieties experienced by those making these tools in ways that are both familiar and new. Contemporary digital professionals do not just dutifully reanimate the productivity-oriented mindset of the Progressive Era and then recast these propositions as major industry news. Spend enough time with those working in the tech sector and you're likely to see these lofty projections not just as tedious recitals of century-old predictions but as indexes and instruments of a different circuitry of social and economic connections technologists today often hope that digital devices that link without friction can help establish.

In this work, QS once again provides a useful entry point to the additional social mechanics powering the self-tracking sector and the digital professionals working therein. As this chapter examines the relationship of effortlessly interoperable devices to digital work, it turns to QS as an interface that reflects the professional journeys, concerns, and aspirations of those making self-tracking devices. The discussions that surfaced in QS gatherings do not only reveal tech sector executives as intellectual descendants of scientific managers. They also demonstrate how the fantasies and aesthetics of mobility invoked most clearly in corporate promotional materials are informed by technologists' own preoccupations with social and professional momentum and the hope that self-tracking devices may restore dynamism to lives otherwise overburdened by excess – especially in a demanding job market.

Frictionless interoperability has a particularly pressing appeal in a flexible work environment. This chapter therefore concludes by exploring how wearable devices that connect without issues more directly model as they help coordinate the work of those hustling with a passion. QS acts as an important interface to these dynamics as well. It helps manifest some of the personal connections that shape the tech sector. As it offers extracurricular entrepreneurs some of the more practical means of realizing the agile and well-networked professional mobility that this work requires, it also exemplifies the plasticity demanded of those employed in the present-day digital economy.

Efficiency Engineers and Their Legacy

Some of the similarities between the social imaginary of contemporary wearables developers and the concerns of early-twentieth-century scientific managers are instructive. Efficiency engineers of this period may not have spoken of the impact of seamlessly connected gadgets. They did, however, dream of eliminating "waste" with the aid of analog devices such as the stopwatch and the photo camera. Like the talk of modern-day technologists, these aspirations were as pragmatic as they were moralizing. Wilder conjures a "frictionless" universe where any resistance has been removed from technological connections, and, relatedly, from social experiences. Turn-of-the-twentieth-century productivity specialists shared the parallel goal of eliminating any wasteful gestures that stood in the way of optimal comportment. Crucially, both discourses are explicitly centered around the needs of employers; they express labor-maximizing philosophies that route concerns about individual mobility around the demands of work.

The moral qualities of thwarted momentum and its impact on work are especially resonant in the writing of Frederick W. Taylor, the progenitor of scientific management. In the very first pages of his foundational manual, *The Principles of Scientific Management*, originally published in 1911, Taylor warned of the cost of unexamined work routines as he compared wasteful gestures made by day laborers to a depleting natural resource: "We can see our forests vanishing, our water powers going to waste ... but our larger waste of human effort, which goes on every day through such of our acts as are blundering, ill-directed or inefficient, and which Mr. Roosevelt refers to as a lack of 'national efficiency,' are less visible, less tangible and are but vaguely appreciated" (p. 4).

Frank Gilbreth, Taylor's protégé and rival, also ardently condemned what he saw as the corrosive effects of wasted movement. In the work *Fatigue Study: The Elimination of Humanity's Greatest Unnecessary Waste, A First Step in Motion Study*, which he published together with his wife Lilian Gilbreth some eight years after Taylor penned his manual, the Gilbreths wrote:

> In Motion Study we stated: "There is no waste of any kind in the world that equals the waste from needless, ill-directed, and ineffective motions." It is an aspect of wasted motions that we are discussing here. Wasted motions mean wasted effort and wasted time. One of the results of this waste is unnecessary fatigue, caused by unnecessary effort expended during time that must, as a result, be wasted. Time, a lifetime, is our principal inheritance. To waste any of it is to lose part of our principal asset. (1919)

Operating at a time of growing suspicion of "subjective" judgement, efficiency engineers such as Taylor and the Gilbreths proposed the time study and the motion study, respectively, as "scientific" approaches that could help managers identify and eliminate wasteful labor. The Gilbreths turned to the photo camera to document and analyze performance. Taylor's studies involved careful attention to workers' actions and the minute accounting of the amount of time it took to perform them using a stopwatch. These investigations required long periods of observation and relied on the judgement of the researcher who was now charged with deconstructing workers' movements and defining the parameters of efficient work. Still, Taylor and Gilbreth

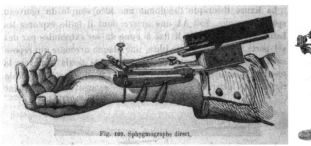

Figure 5.2 Left: Sphygmograph. (La circulation du sang à l'état physiologique et dans les maladies / par E.J. Marey. Wellcome Collection. *Source*: Wellcome Collection.) Right: Step tracker developed by Etienne Jules Marey in 1860. (lynea/stock.adobe.com.)

relegated most of the agency to their preferred technologies. While scientific managers thus themselves transformed "rule of thumb" (Taylor, 1911, p. 8) practices from wasteful to productive labor through acts of human-directed monitoring and recording, they claimed that ideal work sequences rose plainly from the data.

In Europe, Etienne-Jules Marey, a physician and an amateur engineer, undertook the study of laws that governed bodies in motion in an even more systematic fashion as he contributed to a burgeoning, and more academically entrenched, science of work. In his time, Marey invented countless biometric devices that documented the outputs of moving bodies. Most of his creations, including the sphygmograph, a hand-held device that measured pulse (Figure 5.2), and a step-monitoring tool that kept pace of gait – items that today appear as clear progenitors of modern wearables such as the Fitbit – found successful application in medicine and in the arts.[1] Despite these accomplishments, Marey was especially enthusiastic about their potential impact on work.

Like Taylor and the Gilbreths, who endorsed technological and numbers-driven tactics as more scientific, Marey saw his notational devices as mechanisms that supplied a more objective way of understanding bodies at work. And, as historian Ansen Rabinbach (1992) narrates, Marey anticipated a future where technologies such as his would create a "systematic elaboration of the economy of the working body" (p. 117). In a world where "all machines work silently with grace and waste very little energy ... we could also see a more efficient deployment of energy in the manual trades," Rabinbach quotes Marey as predicting (p. 118).

Scientific managers and scientists of work hoped to streamline the way people moved so as to improve how they worked. They carefully tracked and documented workers' activities in the hope of isolating a universal set of gestures that could then become standardized across laboring bodies through systematic training. Their observant eyes turned the corpus into a simple mechanized object that, just like machines, could be made "subject to sophisticated analytics of space and time" (p. 87). For Marey in particular, who embraced the mechanistic metaphor wholeheartedly, the body as motor was not just an analogy. He approached his analysis of mobility with an engineer's precision, interpreting the body as just another device to be meticulously tuned and improved.

Paradoxically, the closer efficiency engineers attempted to get to the body, the more their approaches created distance from it. Their tactics rationalized the body and in doing so obscured attention to the individual worker. Their scrupulous surveillance "dissolved the anthropomorphic body as a distinct entity," Rabinbach writes (1992, p. 87). Work became similarly dematerialized. As historian Elspeth H. Brown (2005) notes, under the watchful eyes of efficiency engineers, "work was no longer subject to an individual worker's control and definition; instead, it was an abstracted national resource threatened by waste and inefficiency" (p. 73). So dematerialized, individual mobility became a formal quality of labor rather than the laborer.

These period aspirations, along with their limited view of the body, continue to resonate, if not to intensify, in the pronouncements of contemporary wearables executives such as Wilder. In the same way as the efficiency engineers who modeled the laboring body on the tireless capacities of industrial machines, uninterrupted productivity is part and parcel of the frictionless universe technologists often claim connected digital devices can help deliver. That is why, similar to their predecessors, many makers of self-tracking technologies remain focused on manufacturing gadgets that discipline and regulate bodies at work.[2] These tools also do more than simply shift decision making and agency from employees to their bosses as they simulate the rhythms of continuous work. Today's wearable device makers are as likely to appeal to the neoliberal knowledge worker hustling with a passion as they are to their bosses (Gregg, 2011, 2018). As these devices now incorporate the watchful eye of the scientific manager into platform software (Beer, 2018),[3] they call on device users to take up the censuring supervisory posture themselves.

QS meetups typically offered ample access both to the devices and the rhetoric extoling the impact of wearables on productivity. One such example arrived in my inbox after I signed up for email announcements from a developer of a self-tracking application that I encountered at a QS Demo Hour. The promotional note excitedly announced the company's search for "productivity enthusiasts":

We're looking for hardcore productivity enthusiasts to join us. If you're hyper-vigilant about time, if you create routines to drive maximum focus, if you automate tasks to make sure minutes don't leak out of your day, if you're determined to reach previously unimaginable levels of productivity, if you are trying to slay time itself – we want to help you get there.

The promise to plug the "leak" of time speaks to the anxieties of contemporary executives hustling with a passion who are increasingly advised to reach "unimaginable levels of productivity" by recouping precious *minutes* as productive activity. These are the guiding principles of the relentless "productivity imperative" that today's workers experience, sociologist Melissa Gregg notes, as "an archly personal, everyday concern" (2018, p. 3).

Even when wearables are not explicitly directed at managing work processes, they leverage a mechanistic and bureaucratic vocabulary that trains device users to monitor for deficits or wasteful gestures that can impede industrious activity in ways that continue to echo the aspirations of scientific managers. For example, device platforms that connect digital monitoring with forms of accounting associated with the office – reports, budgets, balance sheets – continue to direct the attention of those aspiring to work in Wilder's frictionless world toward identifying and eliminating wasteful gestures that impede professional progress. More, as they stimulate productivity and routinely orient users toward "not just doing but doing *more*" (Gregg, 2018, p. 113, emphasis in the original), these platforms also aim to recoup even the act of generating data as industrious activity not to be wasted.[4] In speaking of the "body battery" that needs to be recharged through routines of healthy eating, exercise, and sleep, as Garmin, a watch that gathers personal biometrics, for example, does, these applications persist in taking a mechanized view of the body as they reframe everyday activities such as exercise and self-care as social practices to be perpetually rendered useful.[5] While efficiency engineers sought only to eliminate useless gestures, today's technology and technologists instead look to recover all actions – even resting, as Gregg had likewise observed in her analysis of meditation devices such as Muse – as potentially productive.

In these ways, contemporary self-monitoring applications both reflect and exceed the aims of early-twentieth-century efficiency engineers. While contemporary device makers no longer speak specifically of waste to be eliminated from work routines, their odes to seamless interoperability and digitally supported, friction-free mobility clearly follow in the legacy established by early-twentieth-century scientific managers and scientists of work. Indeed, Wilder's vision of a frictionless future that opened this chapter seems to speak directly to the "hyper-vigilant productivity enthusiasts" who are called to be continuously efficient. It is therefore fitting that the futuristic "new normal" he imagines is illustrated by a pseudo-professional scene, one in which busy executives ambitiously navigate the street without friction as their movements and workflows are presumably seamlessly coordinated by digital tools.

At the same time, in a decentralized, precarious workplace, productivity can no longer be viewed as easy to standardize. Moved by the metaphor of the machine, early-twentieth-century efficiency engineers still imagined that technologies like the stopwatch or the photo camera could help practitioners discern a set of gestures that could reliably discipline workers' bodies. Today, productivity lacks any fixed metric or authority, as Gregg notes. Contemporary appeals to "productivity enthusiasts" are thus also laced with anxiety specific to the flexible, neoliberal workplace. In this environment, the sprawling and endlessly expanding associations that digital devices make lack any anchor. These gadgets support as they mirror contemporary exigencies of work where, like the open-ended yet directionless connectivity of wearable devices, the pursuit of productivity remains a perpetually shifting target.

The Frictionless Life

Despite the apparent parallels between the aims of early-twentieth-century efficiency engineers and the promotional appeals of present-day wearables companies, contemporary technologists also channel the discourse on digital mobility toward slightly different aims. These days, tech executives hustling with a passion are as likely to talk about the possibilities wearable devices offer for affecting a more frictionless life that is not weighed down or torpedoed by burdensome chores and commitments as they are about the virtues of a continuously productive one. If anything, the discourse can be read as a response to the very same aimless productivity these technologies continue to promote.

This alternative function of WT surfaced in the subtle contrast between "efficiency," which scientific managers and scientists of work sought to stimulate, and the goals of "optimizations," which technologists I met at forums such as QS often focused on. Consider, for instance, Brandon's commentary, an engineer I met at QS15, the QS Conference and Expo that took place in 2015 in San Francisco. When I interviewed him, he first conflated the QS forum with the act of self-tracking itself, saying:

My quantified self-practice is just general self-optimization. I never really developed a good practice about self-reflection and self-awareness and all of that kind of stuff. . . . I lead a very complex life, I have many segments of my professional life, I've got different segments in my personal life. And to be able to kind of look across all of those and see where things correlate is, you know, not practical. So that's what I'm really looking for, to take all of these different data streams hopefully as they become less and less evasive, and to notice automatic things . . . So [self-optimization] essentially is finding the most efficient outcome I am looking for. . . . Being an engineer, I am always looking for shortcuts . . . I am always looking for the way that will work faster. (Brandon, 2015)

Yes, Brandon's notion of self-tracking as just "general self-optimization" appears in line with the claims set both by contemporary and turn-of-the-twentieth-century productivity experts, especially as he seems to use the words "efficiency" and "optimization" interchangeably. Twentieth-century efficiency engineers hoped to render the worker more productive through mechanized notation. And on first blush, "optimization" in this commentary speaks to the same normative and calculative goals. Indeed, like Taylor, Brandon is an engineer who by his own admission sees life, not just work processes, in a systematic way – as a collection of so many steps and "segments" to be mapped and analyzed. Interestingly, it is this plainly administrative and improvement-oriented connotation of "optimization" that Wolf and Kelly tried to guard against in naming their forum Quantified Self and not, as Wolf noted to me once, "'Optimized Self' or 'Perfected Self' or, you know, 'Become a Winner'" (Wolf, 2016).

And yet, when Brandon discusses self-tracking as a substitute for self-reflection or even as a shortcut to it, his observations suggest additional notions of optimization and its relationship to self-monitoring that exceed narrow practical ends. The shortcuts do not simply yield more efficient comportment to produce a more productive self. Connected devices also offer Brandon the means of tackling his "complex" life and of identifying meaningful correlations within it. As Brandon ultimately puts it, he sees these devices as mechanisms that can help him "hack" through the density of his commitments and allow him to get to the base of what matters.

The reenvisioned application of self-tracking tools as instruments that can help address the burdens of contemporary living matters here. Even if these devices remain oriented around the discourse of waste and bodily rationalization, they are now also described as filtering tools that promise to help their wearers navigate a middle-class life riddled by surplus and cluttered by competing demands, material excess, and perpetual incitement to escalate both performance and desire. Brandon's perspective on optimization thus also resonates with the difference communications scholar Joseph Reagle (2019) identifies between "efficiency" and "effectiveness" – a long-elusive promise of the self-help literature itself (p. 30). Efficiency is about performance, no matter the cause. Effectiveness is about working with a purpose.

These imputed functions of digital technology remain markedly idealistic and even appear as a form of "technological solutionism" (Morozov, 2013), where Brandon looks to technology rather than to structural changes or collective action to address the challenges created by capitalist modes of consumption and production. Nevertheless, his words register a present-day pathos that characterizes the social and professional predicaments of contemporary knowledge workers. Here, the purifying capacities relegated to machines mark, even if in the end they do not fully resolve, the burdens he experiences. In this way, they offer an unexpected rhetorical challenge to the aims of efficiency engineers that pushed people to continually give and make more without concern for how this emphasis impacted people's lives outside of work.

Safi spoke about the virtues of digital self-monitoring in related terms to Brandon. Initially, his attitude towards self-tracking also appeared to mirror the somatic ambitions of twentieth-century efficiency engineers. When we met at a QS meetup in Boston, for example, we chatted about the various steps he took to reduce anything that interfered with his "optimal" functioning in life. Safi explained that he took particular pains with managing what he called his "sleep hygiene," minimizing habits that proved disruptive to his nighttime rest. After a period of self-tracking, he instituted rigorous measures to streamline his life for better sleep. Anything that interfered with an effective sleep routine, including social interaction, were eliminated from his calendar. As we spoke, he consulted his watch. It was nearly a quarter to nine in the evening and he planned to leave the event early to make it home three hours before bedtime in order to put on a special set of yellow-tinted glasses that reduced his exposure to bright light (Safi, 2015).

Safi's additional reflections softened a purely pragmatic position. These surfaced as we perused the gadgets displayed during the session's Demo Hour that night. At one point, we paused at a table where an entrepreneur was showcasing a weight-training wearable gadget. According to its maker, this device was designed to reduce any gestures that did not contribute to one's weight-training goals through regimes of rigorous data collection and analysis. Certainly, this was a mechanism of which efficiency engineers of years past would have been proud. And yet, the product developer derived inspiration from a more contemporary source. This device, the entrepreneur told us, nodding to us with a knowing look, was designed to help users discover their "minimum effective dose."[6] Upon hearing this phrase, Safi responded with a broad smile. It was the type of thing he himself saw as the rightful goal of self-tracking, he later told me. I recognized the expression, too, which I heard frequently in my conversations with technologists.

The concept of the minimum effective dose, or the MED, was originally coined by Tim Ferriss, a digital entrepreneur and author of several "how-to" productivity books. The notion informed many of the self-tracking projects and products of my interlocutors both in the QS "community" and beyond it. The same day that I met Safi, for example, I visited Connor at the headquarters of a wearables startup operating out of a local WeWork. When we spoke, he explained that the device he was promoting was anchored by Ferriss's principles. Connor claimed that these ideas guided his work and personal life. In his spare time, he bridged the two online in a blog titled *Optimized Me*. Refracted through the lens of the MED, optimization meant the following to Connor:

> It's the smallest number of things you can do to get the best desired result. So, think of it in terms of medicine. If you have too little medicine, it doesn't work. It has no effect. But if you give too much, you have side effects. What is that happy medium, the smallest amount that you want with no side effects? And so, you figure that out for most things. If you want to get tan, do you have to sit in the sun for two hours? No, you're going to get burned. So maybe you just need to sit in the sun for twenty minutes to trigger the hormones that will get your skin to darken. For weight loss, it's figuring out the foods that you need to eat versus just eating vegetables all day long. So that is how I see all these different lifestyle hacking, happiness hacking, supplement, sleep – just figuring out the smallest change you can do to create a disproportionally large result. (Connor, 2015)

There are clear similarities in Ferriss's concept of the MED and Taylorist strategies. Like Ferriss, scientific managers preached workplace minimalism, promising to identify the smallest number of gestures necessary to perform any task. Both Ferriss and Taylor aim to understand and calculate the least effort necessary to complete an undertaking. Still, Ferriss's concept of the MED, especially as Connor understood it, departs from notions of efficiency as understood by twentieth-century productivity engineers. The latter sought to program the body like a machine with a routine that would allow the worker to complete any given job with as little effort as possible so as to work as long and as much as possible. Productivity was narrowly reflected through this singular instrumental aim. And although Progressive Era experts were concerned with fatigue, they explored it only to understand the limit to which managers could push their workers (Rabinbach, 1992). By contrast, Connor sees the MED, and by association optimization, as a process of moderation rather than maximization, one that yields a "happy medium" rather than the greatest possible output.

The concept of the MED is also at odds with Taylor's notion of a "fair day's work." For Taylor, "fair" was a concept established by an employer narrowly driven by profit. As sociologist Chris Grey (2005) highlights, a "fair day's work meant the maximum amount of work a person could physically do without collapsing, and a fair day's pay meant the minimum amount that could be paid to induce the worker to give this level of effort" (p. 38). Guided by his Protestant faith, Taylor approached people strictly as those whose bodies had to be tuned to the strict demands of work, rather than as human beings with desires, family responsibilities, and personal ambitions. By contrast, Ferriss proposes the MED as a kind of anti-work and anti-burnout treatise, putatively offering his followers ways to reduce their workload. He presents the MED as a self-management tool that allows people to set limits around their various commitments so that they can instead lead fuller, more multifaceted lives.

Ferriss's litany of books, mostly published under the title "4 Hour"– *The 4-Hour Work Week: Escape 9–5, Live Anywhere, and Join the New Rich* (2007); *The 4-Hour Body: An Uncommon Guide to Rapid Fat-Loss, Incredible Sex, and Becoming Superhuman* (2010); *The 4-Hour Chef: The Simple Path to Cooking Like a Pro: Learning Anything, and Living the Good Life* (2012) – endorse a message of moderation even as their range and the many different activities they encourage readers to pursue all but defeat the author's call for restraint. "Four hours," however, is as much of a practical guide as it is a commentary on social expectations. The books promise to navigate readers away from the ever-escalating cycles of productivity associated with capitalist economies, from the need to push oneself to the edge, to always work and to give just a little more.

It's not surprising that Ferriss's ideas find a welcome audience among overburdened tech executives who gather in forums such as QS. The premise that four hours is enough to learn a new skill, develop a health routine, and pursue a hobby all while building a successful career speaks to an aspirational middle-class lifestyle. These are also tempting thoughts for extracurricular entrepreneurs prompted to ceaselessly hustle with a passion, professionals for whom even twenty-four hours may not be enough to live up to the all-consuming demands of their jobs (see Chapter 4). Ferriss's books appear to offer a way out of this vicious cycle of productivity and performance as they promise a shortcut to a satisfying life. Those I spoke with thus saw Ferriss's teachings, and the concept of the MED in particular, as a critique of the socio-economic climate that constantly asked them to do more as much as a practical guide for achieving it. And they endorsed digital self-monitoring as both the literal and the metaphorical hammers that made it possible for them to "optimize" their lives in these ways, that is, to hack through the complexity and break away all that drains their energy and stands in the way of what they value.[7]

Safi explicitly saw the MED, and the practice of digital self-monitoring that supported it, as a challenge to the American "more is more" logic. In another conversation, he explained how his personal views on data gathering have changed over the years as they have become modified by Ferriss's teaching:

> I used to think, OK, if running a 10k is good, maybe I should be training for a marathon, and if running a marathon is good, maybe I should be running an ultra-marathon. And I wasn't really doing anything health promoting in the sense that I may have been operating in a world where if a little of something was good, then more of it was better. And actually, that's a very American idea. If a little of something is good, then double of that must be double as good. If I have one scoop of ice cream, then double that is better. It's very logical in many cases. But I think for me, my personal feeling was that the more I did, the better it was for me as an individual, and that led me down this idea that if I ran 10k then I can run a marathon, and if I ran a marathon, then maybe I should train to do more and more and more. It was just this idea that if something is good, then double that is doubly good.
> I laugh – even in Boston there is a SoulCycle on every corner, I just laugh when I walk by that because this is so American! This is our thing: one cycle class is good, but I am going to take six! I can say it is a very American thing to do. If you are at an all-you-can-eat, well then you eat all that you can. (Safi, 2015)

As Brandon, Connor, and Safi all point to the glut of expectations and desire that define contemporary middle-class living, one that constantly asks them to do more, they enlist self-monitoring technology to manage this overabundance, to create necessary guardrails on their time, and to reestablish connections to things that matter.

Chris Dancy, an IT professional turned "most connected man on earth" whom we met in the Introduction and in the previous chapter, tends to similarly frame digital technology as mechanisms that help produce a lighter and more streamlined existence. Rehashing the familiar promises of wearables entrepreneurs, he claims to have used data to identify and eliminate sources of friction that led him to eat healthier, loose excess weight, quit smoking, and reevaluate his relationships (Silverman, 2020). In systematically attributing his personal transformation to wearable and sensor-enabled tech, he stimulates the view that these gadgets can help clear obstructions and realign priorities of an otherwise messy and oversaturated life.

In fact, Dancy's transition from an analog "collector" to a "self-tracker" often anchors his public narrative, particularly as it is presented in the popular press. Years before he found his way to Fitbit and Twitter scraping software, he lovingly assembled oversized collages filled with paraphernalia from years gone by. Photos of these physical archives sometimes still decorate articles profiling his ample digital habit. For example, an expose about Dancy published in *Mashable* (Murphy, 2014) includes an image of him seated regally in an ornate wooden chair framed by the panels bursting with pieces of loose paper, receipts, photographs, and random artifacts pinned to them across years. An article in *Bloomberg* (Boudway, 2014) likewise presents Dancy positioned against the background of his mementos pinned to large posterboards.

In these accounts, Dancy's collages serve a specific function. They are not featured as the analog precursors to his current digital self-tracking practice. In fact, they are hardly mentioned in these articles at all. Instead, they are left to stand as visual mnemonics, as overbearing signposts of his contemporary opposite: his present, digitally streamlined life. That is because the panels chiefly impress in their mess. Filled with souvenirs from the past and tributes to places he's been, things he's seen, or challenges he's overcome, they appear as chaotic, nostalgic shrines to a bygone era. His digital data, however, are associated with futuristic purity and order. The boards overflow with tchotchkes – a muddle of kitsch culled from personal memorabilia. The data are offered as clean, organized, perusable, and streamlined. The boards thus make an impression on the senses. The data, particularly when visualized as so many graphs and charts, are meant to appeal to one's sense of structure (Figure 5.3). In popular reporting and in Dancy's own public storytelling, the disorganized physical archives thus often serve as a foil to his digitally realigned reality. They point to the clutter he's cleared from his everyday through regimes of digital self-monitoring.

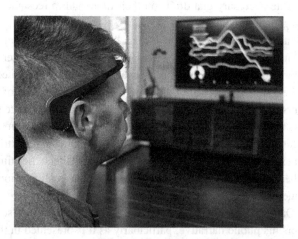

Figure 5.3 Chris Dancy as featured in Showtime series *Dark Net*. "The Dark Net" used with permission. ©2024 SHOWTIME Networks Inc. All Rights Reserved.

These associations draw additional symbolic power from the liquid metaphors that technologists tend to use when talking about data. Practitioners often talk about data as substances that "flow" between devices and bodies, and eventually "seamlessly" accrete into "streams," "pools," and "lakes," or even "oceans" of information. Where analog collections appear messy, this vocabulary sanitizes digital knowledge. Such correlations frame digitization as itself a process of washing and cleansing, of methodically removing the dirt to reveal clean knowledge buried within. By extension, water-like data exert purifying effects on the person using them.

Certainly, many people have turned to digital self-tracking out of sincere and practical desire to solve a therapeutic or a lifestyle problem (Nafus and Sherman, 2014; Reagle, 2019). At the same time, the views I encountered in forums such as QS also reflect the overburdened lives of digital executives. In part, my interlocutors' comments on digital "self-optimization," as much as Dancy's media and personal self-presentation as a technologist who has cleaned up his life with data, seem directed straight at the stereotype of the esoteric and slovenly computer programmer who has long been stereotyped as someone driven by excess: coding into the night, letting their hair and personal habits go, abdicating any regard for their physical body and social life. By contrast, people such as Dancy represent contemporary technologists who have renewed their commitments to health and wellbeing with fervor. They inhabit a world where mechanized "life hacking" has become the "self-help for the digital age's creative class" (Reagle, 2019, p. 149). In this social context, tech entrepreneurs make headlines for their extreme regimes of self-care more frequently than for their lack of interest in it (Pastis, 2023). Their tendency to rely on digital means for self-management also do not simply reflect the aspirations of those who put undue faith in systems thinking and computer logic. They echo a common frustration of those who are struggling to find their way through a world of plenty – of things to do and to buy. Little wonder that they readily endorse self-monitoring technology as a "compass," as Natasha Dow Schüll (2016) also characterizes it, that can "help individuals navigate a world of choices" (p. 13). In negotiating a release from an overburdened life via digital means, these technologists inevitably code "freedom" as the "power to delegate" (Gregg, 2018, p. 93). More broadly, their efforts, comments, and business initiatives represent the experiences of those who perceive modern excesses as friction that creates resistance to their capacity to live well.

Colin, who gave a talk on his digital self-tracking at a QS meetup in New York, echoed these sentiments. Describing a list of nearly eighty habits that he meticulously tracks on a daily basis, he emphasized that digital record keeping has helped him isolate and identify what matters most. Here, the choices about the metrics to collect rather than the metrics themselves were what truly counted. Like books lovingly organized in Walter Benjamin's (1969 [1931]) library, the choices reflected the priorities and values of their collector. Certainly, Colin kept an eye on the numbers as he catalogued some of the personal changes that he was proud of: "Stopped snoozing, stopped spinning out on news during work hours, stopped compulsively checking Facebook, increased average sleep to 7.75 hours, eliminated caffeine, meditate daily." Yet he explained that monitoring his life with the aid of digital devices meant something more than systematically adhering to mechanized notions of progress. Colin discussed self-tracking in generative terms, calling the experience a "personal evolution" and routine tracking as a "check-in with myself" that has helped him to continually reaffirm his intentions and priorities.[8] Rather than tracking to discover a problem, Colin cared about the choices he made in deciding what to monitor. The act of collecting data reconnected him with what he valued.

To be sure, self-tracking technology cannot be fully realigned one's life in the way that people I spoke with often hope for. For one, despite their numbers, sensors collect a restricted range of inputs, and even then produce data that is semantically unstable (see Chapter 2). Digital monitoring also remains both a disciplinary and a world-making activity where, in contrast to Colin's psychoanalytic view of digital monitoring, the limited affordances of wearable devices and self-tracking apps determine what can be made countable.[9] Additionally, despite the rhetoric of conservation, contemporary wearable and connected gadgets remain riddled by excess, much like the strategies proposed by early-twentieth-century scientific managers and the scientists of work always already were. The latter may have invoked the language of science to situate their practices as more authoritative, exact, and less wasteful than the "rule of thumb" workflows set by workshop gang bosses. These lofty aims, however, did not square with practice. Historian Elspeth H. Brown (2005) has stressed the paradoxical inefficiency of efficiency engineering by emphasizing that the strategies proposed by Frederick Taylor and his contemporaries were little more than competing promotional techniques of industry consultants. They were sales tactics advertised by competitors whose proliferating approaches routinely conflicted with one another, leaving a questionable impact on the professional spaces they touched. Their very quantity also ultimately defeated the possibility of creating the singularly efficient subjects their advocates promised. Makers of contemporary wearables may likewise recommend these gadgets as dispassionate observers that can parse through the thick fog of life. In a parallel manner to period efficiency engineers, however, these manufacturers produce what, in relationship to digital productivity aids, Gregg calls the "aesthetics of activity," rather than activity as such (2018, p. 82). Self-tracking tools likewise often create only the appearances of a life stripped of excess rather than an actual gateway to it. They simulate simplicity and optimization, and even the individual desire for it, without necessarily delivering it. The premise that these tools can help one to prioritize commitments and "hack" through the clutter to produce a more seamless and friction-free existence are in the end also undercut by the practical realities of digital self-monitoring. Even looking at the extraordinary amount of extra work and time that these practices often require, of which my interlocutors endlessly complained and wished to be rid of, indicates that these technologies often add new forms of labor rather than reduce individual physical or cognitive workloads.

The challenges of digital self-monitoring echo with the paradoxes of modern-day home organization trends, which gained popularity in the same period as commercial self-tracking tools. Since the mid-2000s, Marie Kondo has become the poster woman for domestic minimalism, particularly in middle-class and affluent households in the US. Kondo endorses tidiness as a general strategy for happiness as she advises people to pare down possessions only to those items that "spark joy" (2022). For Kondo, eliminating clutter does not just produce a neat home. Mirroring Colin's reflections on digital self-monitoring, Kondo recommends home organization as a strategy for crystalizing one's priorities in life. "The question of what you want to own is actually a question of how you want to live your life," Kondo guides (2022).

Kondo's approach of course overlooks the modes of privilege that regulate contemporary home organization strategies in the same way that the mostly male wearables entrepreneurs tend to take for granted the degree to which they resocialize familiar feminized labor as "innovative" masculinized solutions (Reagle, 2019). The "minimalist" aesthetic that animates both home organizers such as Kondo and self-improvement-oriented technologists also discounts that those who have experienced loss or economic precarity tend to have a less flippant relationship with their personal possessions. "In order to feel comfortable throwing out all your old socks and handbags," highlights Arielle Bernstein in an article for *The Atlantic* covering the popular appeal of organizational techniques such as the ones promoted by Marie Kondo, "you have to feel pretty confident that you can easily get new ones" (2016). Part of the invoked appeal of digital self-monitoring is its promise to make one's life more manageable. But wearables and connected devices are pitched as tools that can deliver a streamlined "new normal" by well-heeled middle-class technologists who may more readily respond to the call for digitized clarity and order because they already have much to give away. Moreover, just like with house cleaning, the possibilities with which technologists imbue these devices only help to refresh cycles of consumption, further amplifying processes of accumulation that clutter one's life with new things and responsibilities. These devices thus impede the crystalline interoperability and friction-free personal mobility their makers anticipate, producing an excess that is impossible to fully process. Even more so as digital optimization comes at the cost of endless data hoarding, which in fact contributes to actual pollution (Gabrys, 2013).

Wearable and connected devices may not be able to realign and to reorganize one's life in the ways their makers promise. Like the generic stock photograph that Wilder has used to illustrate the "new normal," wearables and self-tracking devices tend to supply a superficial solution to an actual problem. Still, even if these devices do not in the end bring about the promised personal cleanse, in rehearsing a utopic technological imaginary of a lighter and more seamless future, my interlocutors' perspectives on the MED and optimization achieved through digitization resonate as a commentary on the contemporary pressures they feel both as consumers and as digital professionals. The technological fantasy of a friction-free world invoked by Wilder and my interlocutors registers this social dilemma even if it doesn't actually remedy it.

In the early parts of the twentieth century, scientific managers and scientists of work wanted to document movement in order to purge the worker's body of wasteful gestures. Albeit in different ways, today's technologists likewise turn to digital devices to manage and resolve complexity. It is due to the sense that their dense days are obscured by an almost existential excess, however, that wearable tools are often presented by device developers as mechanisms that can restore dynamism to an oversaturated reality. Technologists discuss self-tracking gadgets as instruments that both respond to and index this late-capitalism pathos. Little wonder that these are the capabilities and qualities that they also endorse in the marketing of these tools. While digital scholars often link self-tracking with questions of control (Lupton, 2016), my interlocutors discuss and advertise these devices as liberating technologies, ones that can offer the means of achieving a moderate existence rather than just a more monitored one. Promotional images of digital technology as mechanisms that stimulate mobility without friction mirror their makers' own aspirations for an unencumbered life.

Leaning In

There is another way to understand the fantasy of seamlessness and technologists' relationship to it, however – one where self-tracking devices play an additional role as symbols of ambitions, stresses, and desires of contemporary knowledge workers. Friction-free mobility does not articulate the idealized productivity of knowledge workers or the qualities of a simplified life alone. Wilder's vision of seamless connections also reflects the fluctuating rhythms of the digital economy to which digital professionals are expected to effortlessly conform. Wearables that Wilder has enlisted in his imaginary of the future are today predominantly produced in settings marked by the fretful movements of those hustling with a passion (see also Chapter 4). The talk of smoothly linked devices thus also inadvertently transposes the pressures of technologists' own conditions of employment onto aspirational qualities of wearable tools.

These unsteady professional dynamics were all too apparent in the settings where many of my interlocutors worked. Wearable tech firms, for example, increasingly employ data analysts, computer developers, and data visualization specialists trained at one of the many short-term coding camps and academies that have become vital career retraining centers for a rapidly shifting workforce. In these settings, management philosophies such as Lean (Riles, 2011) and software development frameworks like Agile (Martin, 2002) also dominate. Lean and Agile emphasize attunement to change, cultivating an organizational and management style that is marked not only by a lack of heavy corporate structure or intransigent business plans but by a constant orientation toward modification, frequent adjustment, and change.

Wearables and self-tracking applications are additionally commonly developed in small startups funded through transient forms of capital such as crowdsourcing platforms[10] or supported by temporary startup accelerators that increasingly condition private equity investments. These firms, moreover, tend to occupy temporary offices in co-working spaces such as WeWork as they see employment trends rise and fall with changes in investment strategies or social appetites. In recent years, tech startups have hired profusely as part of the "growth" expected by investors, resulting in markets with plenty of work options (Ovide, 2022). However, the boom-or-bust style of innovation that characterizes the wearables sector, where a quick corporate buyout by larger firms is the anticipated "exit strategy" of a great number of early-stage self-tracking companies, also means that people and data change hands rapidly. During the course of my research, a number of the companies where my interlocutors worked went out of business. Only a few received additional funding or were bought by a larger firm. The trajectory is similar to the plight of companies such as Basis, Jawbone, Scanadu, and Zeo – all early digital wearable firms that initially received intense media and investor attention and modest consumer interest before going out of business. Rarer is the spectacular success of Fitbit, which was acquired by Google in late 2019.

When these firms are purchased or when they close their operations, the devices they make are either folded into existing corporate products or discontinued. The personal data collected by these devices thus often becomes corrupted or lost to users as the original devices or applications go unsupported by new parent companies. These changes reveal that Wilder's futuristic fantasy of interoperable devices that endlessly link without friction is already antithetical to the cycles of technological innovation pegged to a capricious tech market. They additionally demonstrate that the ideal of a seamlessly mobile and connected digital future says more about the erratic mode of labor that organizes the technology sector around frequent interruptions, fits, and starts than it does about capacities of self-tracking devices. The friction-free comportment Wilder envisions does indeed describe a new normal. However, it speaks more to the fluctuating experiences of technologists who rarely stay in their jobs for long. Theirs is a professional milieu where effortlessly "moving on," as Ilana Gershon (2017) puts it in a book focused on the perpetual mobility of contemporary knowledge workers, has become "the new normal."

At the Consumer Electronics Show (CES) in 2016, I was able to experience some of the rush produced by this form of agile professional mobility as I stood in the middle of an open rotunda at The Venetian hotel in Las Vegas while waiting for an industry acquaintance to arrive. Crowded conferences such as the CES allegorize as they place the mobility expected of digital professionals on display. Throughout the day, I allowed myself to become swept up by the swarm of bodies, succumbing to the seductive roar of the crowd. Carried along as though by some internal mechanism, I eagerly rushed to and from, keeping pace with the tech executives that flitted from display to display exhibiting new inventions and grandiose pronouncements of data-driven futures. Now, as I watched conference goers pour out of the hotel's every crevice, I realized that this was the first time that I could truly appreciate some of the scope of the reputed 170,000 people that descended on the Vegas strip for the CES that year, attendance numbers that were bolstered by the enthusiasm surrounding wearable and sensor-enabled tools. As white dress shirts glistened like foam in a sea of undifferentiated business attire, the momentum of the crowd called me to keep moving even as I stood still. At the time, momentarily facing the tidal wave of people as they swirled and swooshed about me felt exhilarating and even slightly defiant. My fixed posture also contrasted sharply not only with the rapid movements of conference goers making their way across the hotel lobby floor but with the position digital professionals are expected to assume when navigating their careers in the technology sector.

It's fitting, then, that "lean in" has become more than a management philosophy but a new mantra of this lithe and mobile workforce. Sheryl Sandberg, former chief operating officer (COO) of Facebook, originally developed this expression as an injunction to women in her *New York Times* best-seller *Lean In: Women, Work, and the Will to Lead* (2013). Observing that women graduate from universities at similar rates to men but remain woefully underrepresented in senior management, Sandberg controversially concluded that the disparity is a result of uneven initiative, not, chiefly, of structural or social factors. In counseling career women to confront barriers head on, Sandberg implicitly offered the concept of leaning in as a feminist alternative to the macho yet stiff, "broad-shouldered" posture that has long characterized American business. Ironically, Sandberg's message of professional female endurance is delivered through a trope dripping with sexist connotations. Leaning in, after all, is a more supple and compliant posture. Those who lean in do not stiffen against opportunities, but neither do they change the conditions in which they operate. Like a plant whose stem flexes to prevent it from breaking in a storm, they only adjust to their environment by bending with the airflow.

And yet, the feminized, supplicating, forward-directed pose Sandberg proposes may well describe the posture expected of a flexible workforce more broadly. It inadvertently allegorizes the modern power pose, the aerodynamic posture of least friction and maximum forward momentum that Wilder has also unwittingly visualized. Viewed through this lens, the seamlessly connected future that tech executives envision says less about the capacities of digital sensors than it does about the professional possibilities and anxieties of those who produce them. So, if technologists eulogize friction-free connectivity, it may be because these ideas have a distinct urgency and appeal in the unsteady professional environments in which they themselves work.

Some critics rightfully worry that contemporary self-tracking technologies only reinstate the forms of corporate surveillance that have characterized the Progressive Era – monitoring that holds bodies in check and in place (Kaplan, 2015; Wade, 2019). However, modern-day wearable devices do not simply reflect the dreams of efficiency engineers of the twentieth century that promised to adjust working bodies to the demands of work by means of rigorous tech-enabled managerial oversight. Like the tactics of Frederick Taylor and the European scientists of work, these gadgets are once again implicated in the corporate training of bodies, but with a contemporary twist. The seamlessly connected digital sensors and interoperable datasets tech makers envision, the types of tools that are enthusiastically discussed by technologists in forums such as QS, today provide an orienting symbol of a nimble workforce. The futuristic vision that digital professionals summon does not only reflect an idealistic view of digital connections but the ambitions of technologists navigating a flexible and unstable workplace. As these gadgets pivot on the dream of seamless and enduring mobility, they echo the comportment necessary to succeed in a rapidly changing and moving tech sector. The gadgets materialize the value of mobility and interoperability technologists embrace in their working lives. The lessons digital professionals making these devices ask others to learn from seamlessly connected digital tools are thus modeled on the aspirational friction-free movements of technologists themselves.

Community of Flexible Workers

Technologists might install self-monitoring devices as symbols and even as instruments of personal agility and mobility. However, it is forums such as QS, rather than the digital gadgets themselves, that ultimately facilitate the idealized connectivity and mobility of working bodies. By socializing digital professionals, and by offering developers and device makers novel spaces for fellowship, collaboration, and networking, collectives such as QS produce some of the desired professional momentum these gadgets model.

That QS helps engineer connections necessary to a flexibly employed workforce was made routinely manifest during my research in subtle and overt ways. At one New York City gathering that I attended, for example, I sat across the table from Tom. We introduced ourselves and exchanged pleasantries. He explained that he came to hear the evening's presentations because he recently left a corporate job. Now a consultant in his fifties, he struggled to create the structure that he was accustomed to when he had a steady office job. From the talks, he said, he hoped that he might learn strategies that could help him better adjust to his new unmoored status, ideas that could keep his professional life on track. But he was also there in search of connections that may lead to a job. "I'm a data scientist," he explained to me as he slipped me his business card. Maybe I knew someone at Columbia University with whom he could talk?[11] Others were there to establish professional relationships, too. Speaking about her interest in sleep tracking, Esther gave a brief presentation about her dissatisfaction with three of the devices she personally trialed. But as she spoke, "for full disclosure," she casually mentioned that she was an early investor in Basis, a once-popular wearable device that tracked steps and heart rate. "I don't know if anybody would want to do a scientific study on sleep?" she coyly asked as she wrapped up her talk, delicately probing for prospective business partnerships.[12] There were such people. The next speaker talked about his tracking habit. "I liked it so much, I'm actually making a software version of it," he announced as he concluded his presentation with a soft sales pitch.[13] Similarly, a speaker at a different meetup talked passionately about her weight loss journey mediated by self-tracking technology. During the Q&A, she made sure to mention that her success was the product of a food-logging application that she was now commercializing.[14]

QS's language of "membership" is especially interesting to consider in this context. Membership does not only articulate a sense of belonging and inclusion co-extensive with the concept of community or, as discussed in Chapter 3, as a category that produces the "consumer-centric" observational posture idealized by tech sector "vendors." The notion of membership also makes QS's professional orientation more explicit. In part, the term "member" draws on, even if inadvertently, associations with pricy members-only clubs such as Modernist in San Francisco or the Soho Club in New York City that socialize the well-heeled creative business elites and confer insider status on their affiliates. On its website, Modernist promises to put members in contact with Silicon Valley technorati. The Soho Club opened its doors in 2002 and was even featured in an episode of *Sex and the City* the same year. While the cachet of the Soho Club has since waned, replaced by stylish co-working offices as a desirable place in which to be seen conducting business, taking a meeting here, perhaps over lunch, still carries a certain amount of prestige. It telegraphs financial stability, status, and professional promise to potential business contacts and partners. Although these sites are represented as social spaces, like QS they are also known as explicit sites for professional encounters.

Certainly, membership in QS does not mean the same thing as it does in venues such as Modernist or the Soho Club. For one, the barriers to joining QS are few. One merely needs to have the means to attend QS events or the motivation to follow QS activities online. Still, the promotional and organizational work of the forum's original founders has brought a certain amount of renown and repute to group activities (see also Chapter 4). This does not only positively reflect on the professional identities of forum participants. It also attracts more people to QS sessions, thus maximizing networking possibilities.

Some scholars see QS as a response to neoliberal healthcare policies that have shifted care for the self to the patient (Nafus and Sherman, 2014). Others have analyzed QS participants as standard-bearers of a digitally connected future (Lupton, 2016). By contrast, my research indicates that QS does not simply organize the tech-obsessed. The forum helps an insecurely employed workforce to cultivate and tap into external networks of support that provide professional assistance as well as a more general sense of inclusion, feelings of belonging, and shared plight in a rapidly moving marketplace. QS offers a space where people can establish new business connections as well as friendships, and in doing so keep their professional momentum going. It's these qualities of QS membership, rather than the forum's reputation as an organizing space for technology enthusiasts, that ultimately enliven its status as a community. When understood as a product of flexible conditions of employment, QS also has to be interpreted as a forum that materializes the novel forms of care that now help to keep business connections intact so as to allow its participants to continuously adapt to the hectic rhythms of the digital economy.

Thinking about QS as a product of a fractured and unstable business climate opens onto questions of technological breakdown. While wearable and sensor-enabled devices are often discursively aligned with novelty and smooth functioning, anthropologists such as Brian Larkin (2008) remind us that both novelty and failure are "a condition of technological existence" (p. 234). In evaluating the impact of technological development on life in places such as Nigeria, Larkin explores breakdown as both a consequence and a constitutive part of technological innovation. The rhetoric of newness and progress originally helped colonial governments repackage the more sinister language of imperialism. However, despite the aspirational framework, Larkin points out that technology never really works as intended, even under the best of circumstances. It breaks, it's misused, and it requires repair. If this technological reality may get overlooked in Western centers still enchanted by the euphoria of the new and improved, it's often inescapable in places such as Nigeria, where the experience of technological collapse has long been routine. Indeed, it's produced by the very cycles of Western innovation that incessantly promise to prevent it.

The professional networking that QS facilitates also indicates that breakdown, rather than frictionless mobility, is central to the experience of US-based technological elites, albeit in a different way. It recognizes that their work often involves both forestalling and producing technological collapse. Even as technologists dream of developing "seamless" digital devices, they navigate unstable employment markets shaped by irregularity as they work through cycles of innovation marked by "disruption." While data professionals thus publicize digital monitoring as a means for achieving a slicker life, forums such as QS help to foreground the qualitative and situated nature of digital work and further underscore the volatile conditions that produce digital knowledge. The harried sociality of those involved in the business of self-tracking is a component of technology marked by uncertainty and failure. As technologists conform to industry conventions, they often produce digital devices that work through breakdown. This indeterminacy is not only a reality of an emerging field yet to be stabilized; it is the means of its existence.

Focusing on the ambitions and challenges of digital technologists made visible in spaces such as QS thus offers additional ways to appreciate how insecurity and not only Silicon Valley grandstanding shapes the imaginary of digital technology. It reveals the degree to which frictionless WT and the seamlessly connected digital futures that they aestheticized remain configured by the fretful sociality and unstable employment patterns of its makers.

6

The Promises and Failures of Digital Connections

The previous chapters have discussed the ways technologists talk about data, imagine their consumers, and connect their work with personal interests and ambitions. I have argued that this discourse offers visibility into the underlying social mechanics that shape the development of self-tracking devices and the techno-imaginaries that uphold their circulation. Throughout, the Quantified Self (QS) has served as a chief interface for accessing and interacting with the central dilemmas of digital work. Documenting the wide-ranging demands of the office, however, says little about the modes of privilege that continue to regulate innovation in the tech sector and guide how digital executives convert their affective labor into business advantage. With QS serving as a bridge to the business landscape one last time, the remaining chapter investigates these challenges.

Take a look around the room of any QS event and a clear pattern will quickly emerge. Those who frequent such functions tend to be mostly white, middle class, health-conscious, and male. Over the years, organizers have made concerted efforts to render the forum a welcoming space for a broader group of people. This chapter first looks at these strategies, interrogating the notion of difference that have informed these measures. In contrast to technologists' more clearheaded and self-aware appraisals of digitization discussed throughout this book, these approaches indicate that the tech sector often remains constrained by a much narrower view of social diversity.

This chapter primarily zeroes in on issues associated with tactics meant to redress uneven gender representation within the forum. In discussing how these well-meaning interventions often exist in tension with enduring patterns of discrimination that continue to shape the tech industry, the chapter also provides lessons for the tech sector at large. QS acts as a gateway to these challenges because solutions adopted in forums such as QS are not localized. They mirror corporate "diversity and inclusion" efforts. If the remedies proffered by QS organizers as well as tech executives often prove inadequate, it's because they frequently do little to overcome systemic biases that continue to underpin both how professionals navigate the technological arena and how they situate self-tracking technology in the public domain.

QS does not only hold up a mirror to the tech sector. I argue that it also inadvertently serves as one of its channels of exclusion. The group's efforts and struggles to foster diversity ultimately illustrate as they continue to reinforce the prejudices that shape how the self-tracking arena responds to social inequality and the uneven benefits technologists are able to reap from their impassioned hustling. In examining why these approaches have largely not succeeded neither within the group nor within the tech sector more broadly, this chapter acts as an interface to the troubled promises of inclusion that impact the organizing activities of QS and structure digital entrepreneurialism more broadly.

Difference and Simulacra

The notion of difference that typically configures QS activities was on clear view at QS15, the QS Conference and Expo convened in the summer of 2015 in San Francisco. It came through, for instance, in the efforts QS hosts undertook to address the ongoing gender disparity within the forum – and by extension within the tech sector – by developing strategies intended to expand the number of women participating in group events so as to signal that QS was a female-friendly gathering. To indicate the latter, event planners labeled conference rooms with names of female computer scientists. To satisfy the former, meetup leaders made sure the program was well balanced with female speakers and presenters, building as they did so on the efforts initially mobilized by several female QS participants who for a short time organized a female-only QS offshoot named QSXX. The entire event ultimately concluded with Gary Wolf bestowing a first-time award – a shiny blazer – on Sam De Brouwer, the co-founder of a portable medical device called Scanadu, for being a "trailblazer" in the field. The bedazzled jacket offered to De Brouwer was baggy and oversized, yet in its flashiness already seemed to awkwardly prefigure a female host. Showing surprise at the honor, the elegantly dressed De Brouwer accepted the jacket with humility. "We're up to something … let's do this," she proclaimed quietly from the stage, and, after a bit of a pause, she slipped on the shiny, ill-fitting coat.[1]

The documentary *Personal Gold*, which was screened at the close of the conference, extended this work. The film focused on the unexpected success of the American female cycling team during the 2012 London Olympic Games. Cycling, long dominated by greats such as Lance Armstrong, is not a sport known for its female athletes. During the London games, the female American team was the clear underdog. Despite the odds, the women managed not only to take the silver medal but to steal attention away from male cycling, then rocked by scandals of drug abuse. In *Personal Gold*, the audience learned that the team was led to victory by a stringent regimen of self-monitoring. With the help of their coach, the women diligently assembled data of their blood pressure, food intake, sleep quality, air purity, and even mattress firmness to craft what the cyclists described as a complete picture of their daily routine. The athletes made continuous adjustments in response to the data they collected. "Data, not doping" became their rallying cry. Data gathering emerged as a wholesome means of maximizing the team's performance, as a more natural alternative to drug use that had hitherto scandalized male cycling.[2] If performance enhancing medicine seemed prohibitive and unethical, as a shortcut that gave competitors an unfair synthetic advantage, excessive data gathering was heralded as healthy and organic. The more data the team collected, the more they felt that they were advancing toward their goal. They yearned to improve the digital inputs they monitored on their computer screens as much as they aimed to hit high marks on the scorecards of the race. Screening the film at the conference stereotypically glorified digital self-monitoring, though highlighting QS as a forum that appreciates such digital tributes was not its sole goal. It had an additional role to play. The inclusion of a film focused on the turn of female athletes toward data in the event lineup represented yet another means of symbolically diversifying group activities that in practice remained, not unlike professional sports, largely dominated by men.

In a forum comprised primarily of white, middle-class techies, organizers attempted to foster diversity in other ways as well. One way, was through food. Following the screening, the audience poured out of the venue and into the outdoors before quickly splintering into small lines queuing up for craft food trucks that conference organizers had brought in for the occasion. Generic sandwiches or pasta served with cans of soda or bottled water were the standard fare at tech functions. This setup was therefore a welcome treat. And yet, like the film, the cuisine seemed strategic. The choice of the mom-and-pop food trucks with ethnic menus appeared to be another way to inject diversity, if only for now mostly through food, into conference proceedings.

At the conference, and beyond it, the inclusive character of QS was additionally reproduced rhetorically. In particular, it was invoked through routine

Figure 6.1 QS15 conference website screenshot. http://qs15.quantifiedself.com/.

references to the international popularity of the forum. In the years since Wolf and Kelly hosted the first gathering, QS has taken on a global presence. In conference proceedings as well as during local meetups and the forum's websites, QS organizers regularly tallied the regions and countries where QS meetups were being held. This information was both practical and promotional. Such details guided people toward local gatherings as they endorsed QS as a global community that brought "advanced users and toolmakers from over 100 cities in 30 countries," as the marketing materials for QS15 proclaimed (Figure 6.1).

The titles of QS conferences that were organized with regularity on the West Coast of the United States and in Amsterdam in the years that I conducted my research between 2012 and 2017 only reinforced the message that QS was a diverse, multicultural community. Perhaps because it was developed first, and likely due to the symbolic significance of Silicon Valley as a staging ground for the international technological elite, the first conference convened in San Francisco was dubbed a "global" event. Subsequent conferences held in Amsterdam were titled "European." In between these events, the main website was generally well curated to highlight sessions and activities from places beyond central American or European cities to reaffirm QS as a worldwide happening that welcomed participants from around the globe yet transcended any firm national or cultural boundaries.

While well intentioned, these tactics generally respond to an "accretive" view of pluralism that anthropologist Terrance Turner (1993) has critiqued as a key feature of "difference multiculturalism." Turner has argued that multiculturalism presents difference merely as "a shopping mall of world cultures"

(p. 418). These strategies continue to maintain difference largely as an "object-like phenomena," as Akhil Gupta and James Ferguson (1997) have noted in their own critique of multicultural rhetoric. Unlike the fantasy of endlessly linked, baggage-free, interoperable devices and datasets that technologists tend to recognize as both an industry ideal and as a functional fiction (Chapters 2 and 5), social differences largely emerge as something to be patiently gathered together into a single, all-encompassing whole. Political philosophers[4] and anthropologists[5] have long challenged any smooth images of multicultural cohesion. They've argued that integration and a sense of belonging are products of continuous contestation and social debate, not of straightforward social accounting. The strategies organizers often undertake to render and to represent QS as an inclusive space and gathering exist in tension with these positions; they tend to simplify the challenges and politics associated with social belonging as they take some of the broader modes of discrimination and exclusion that continue to shape both QS and the tech sector for granted.

It was plain to see, for example, that the organizing activities of QS lacked the social diversity otherwise routinely asserted rhetorically. For one, despite the common staging of the forum as an international community and even as a global event, QS has remained primarily an anglophone and Euro-American phenomenon. This was evident both in the locations in which conferences took place and in the fact that English has remained the common language by means of which the "community" organizes. The grand titles of these events – "global," "European," additionally contrasted with patterns of attendance. For instance, although the term "global" suggested the West Coast conferences were a hub for those affiliated with QS the world over, the majority of people who attended these functions were located closer by. Most either traveled to these events from the United States or, more frequently, primarily from in and around the Bay Area. Meanwhile, despite the equally wide-ranging connotations of the term "European," events hosted in Europe mostly attracted participants from the Netherlands, particularly from Amsterdam, which was the key European site for such gatherings.

The inclusive facade only extends what Paul Dourish and Scott D. Mainwaring (2012) have, in a related context, called the tech sector's "colonial impulse." The authors have observed that American and European technologists often see innovation as something that flows from Western centers to global peripheries. In this construction, the West, and especially Silicon Valley and the San Francisco Bay Area, reproduces and reenacts the civilizational discourse of colonial powers, casting these sites as figurative laboratories that now incubate novel technologies and by extension the futures awaiting developing nations. QS takes on just such a role vis-à-vis its Silicon

Valley origins and its reputed global spread, and all the more so by virtue of its titular administrative entity, QS Labs. The forum's apparent worldwide appeal is often invoked to telegraph the notion that QS constitutes both a grassroots initiative that has now surpassed American borders and a universal phenomenon that cuts across cultural differences. This trajectory, however, unironically invokes QS both as a figurative and as a literal Silicon Valley innovations "lab" that cultivates practices that slowly, almost inevitably, spread to the world at large.

The notion that QS adhered to a "big tent" (Nafus and Sherman, 2013) strategy also at times undercut inclusive aims as people invoking modes of difference the forum admits often defined diversity as a function of device use rather than as an analytic that could address how social biases shape QS activities. For example, in describing her own experience with QS, one contributor, Sharon, emphasized the following:

> I was kind of surprised to see the *breadth, the variety of topics* that people track. Sometimes there would be something weird where I would go, "Oh that's a really weird thing." Totally would love to do that. I wish I had been collecting dream data for the last eighteen years. Do I want to start now? Eh, not really, but it's really cool. And then another time I may see something and think, "Why would you care to track that?" And again, it comes back to what personally interests you; what are the areas you want to work on in your own life. So, for some people, it's like, "Oh wow, I'm going to track my productivity at work; where am I spending my time." But I thought it was cool to see the *diversity.* (Sharon, 2016, emphasis added)

The miscellany of approaches as well as the sheer "breadth, the variety" of things to track were what Sharon highlighted when I asked about her first impressions of QS, as she stressed that it was "cool to see the diversity." Here, the selection of tactics and questions broached in QS sessions stood in for, or perhaps even compensated for, the ongoing social homogeneity of forum participants.

If Sharon noted the range of self-tracking methods and applications, Sagan emphasized the assortment of expertise and positions on self-monitoring he encountered at QS events, saying:

> I went to a meetup and I didn't know what it would be like. But I thought it was just so interesting, the first meetup was just so interesting because it was an interesting combination of engineers, self-trackers, entrepreneurs, scientists, skeptics, philosophers. . . . In that first meetup, there was one person who gave a talk about what was the point of tracking anything, and if you are tracking anything you are wasting your time. And it was so embraced by the community. (Sagan, 2015)

Listing what he felt to be an incongruous group – scientists alongside data skeptics, philosophers alongside entrepreneurs – Sagan conveyed the varied perspectives as the key forms of difference that were eagerly "embraced by the community." These were some of the chief qualities that indicated to participants, as another person told me, that QS constituted an "open community." And my interlocutors regularly credited forum leaders such as Gary Wolf with cultivating this type of welcoming atmosphere. Frank summarized it to me this way:

> My perception is that he [Wolf] really focuses on how he can help support an *open community*. . . . He doesn't want to force, to limit Quantified Self to the idea of "here is the gadget that will tell people what to do" and so forth. He wants to be open to those people but not limited to those people. At the same time, *he wants to be open to people who have very broad views, and some would say ridiculously broad views*, of the value of self-observation. He doesn't want to say no to them either. Present your views. Present what you are learning. But don't tell people what to do. One thing you might have seen just from the nature of Show & Tell talks is that the emphasis is very much on the first person – What did you learn? What did you do? – as opposed to being more dogmatic about telling others what to do. So again, [there is] *this spirit of encouraging an open community respectful [of] many points of view*. (Frank, 2015, emphasis added)

To participants such as Sharon, Sagan, and Frank who saw QS as a capacious idea, the at times diverging positions on self-tracking of forum participants, the range of self-tracking "experiments" they focused on, and the different tactics they employed to execute them suggested something promising. Predominantly, however, they point to openness as a mode of tolerance toward those with "very broad views and some would say ridiculously broad views of the value of self-observation," rather than as a framework for analyzing or confronting the socio-economic factors that also define QS as a community.

When QS was further conceptualized as a collective of eccentrics and tech early adopters, the rhetoric paradoxically positioned the largely male, cisgender techies as somehow themselves different, as though they were at odds with and operating on the margins of the mainstream. These associations were not only reinforced by popular media that routinely situated QS participants as unusual because they expressed interest in novel technologies (see Introduction). They were also stressed by forum contributors who regularly framed their self-tracking in the language of experimentation and therefore placed themselves on the edges of the ordinary. QS contributors often hoped to normalize interest in data at the same time as they aligned activities of group "members" with the work of a daring techno-scientific avant-garde. This discourse, along with the broader reputation of tech entrepreneurialism as heroic and risqué (Holt and Thompson, 2004),[6] which also shaped these endeavors, routinely situated the generally white, male, young, and middle-class technologists who contributed to forums such as QS as other and subversive of Western, heteronormative ideals.

As a result, even as organizers sincerely tried to make more room for difference, they ended up unwittingly reproducing simulacra. At the close of QS15, Gary Wolf lamented these effects to a group of us chatting on the sidelines while we were munching on tacos and sipping craft beer. Despite ongoing attempts to promote diversity within the forum, Wolf was disconcerted at their lack of success. Noting the enduring homogeneity, he mused pensively, "you know, the self-tracker in Bangalore probably still has more in common with those in Silicon Valley than with others from Bangalore."[7] Then he added with humor, but also with some frustration, "this conference has the largest number of fit people I've even seen," as his gaze wondered over the look-alike, trim, and well-dressed clusters of mostly white and male participants merrily socializing before us.

Gender and Self-Tracking

The solutions forum leaders have adopted reveal that those who speak in the "accretive" modality of difference multiculturalism or who conflate group diversity with the range of self-tracking projects and applications tend to interpret difference as another type of variable to be added, to be included into a broader and ever-expanding community of technophiles. If the above strategies have not reaped the intended results in QS, it is because they remain constrained by the calculative logics that shape them. These limitations are furthermore important to consider because in many ways they mirror the shortcomings of corporate strategies.

To better understand why the tactics employed by QS organizers did not succeed in fostering greater equity and diversity within the forum, I will now delve deeper into the issue of gender. In particular, I will explore how industry solutions that simply seek to insert women back into a field that has excluded them often perpetuate an accretive notion of difference while simultaneously relying on a binary model of gender. The challenges of QS organizers thus offer valuable insight into the broader limitations of corporate diversity and inclusion efforts within the tech sector. Ultimately, these challenges highlight the constraints of contemporary technological imagination and expose the reasons innovative gadgets said to be at the forefront of futuristic practices continue to reproduce and recode age-old social biases.

In orchestrating an inviting atmosphere for female participants, and in actively centering women in the presentation structure, award ceremony, and entertainment lineup of the conference, QS leaders were acting in ways similar to senior tech executives who, in response to a broader social critique of the ways science, technology, engineering, and mathematics (STEM) fields continue to marginalize women, have in recent years proposed a number of tactics intended to expand female engagement with the digital arena. During his keynote address at the Consumer Electronics Show (CES) in 2015, for instance, Intel CEO Brian Krzanich pledged to dedicate $300 million to improve staff diversity by 2020. That same year, firms such as Facebook (now Meta) also started instituting "diversity training" programs intended to "manage unconscious bias" in hiring.[3] Many of these efforts emphasized enhancing the participation and visibility of women in the field. On the heels of such pledges, women have been welcomed into tech settings with growing alacrity. In a veritable theater of inclusion, women are now enthusiastically added to corporate conference sessions and highlighted in the marketing materials of coding camps, singled out for specialized accolades and interviewed for articles, as well as extoled on panels devoted to "Women in Tech," much like Scanadu's De Brouwer had been when she was selected to receive the Trailblazer award at QS15.

The conversations I have had with women throughout my fieldwork, as well as the discourse analysis of tech sector conventions that I offer below, indicate some of the more specific drawbacks of the numbers-based remedies practiced by QS organizers and beyond. Women I have interacted with, for example, actively debate whether inclusion efforts attenuate gender bias or simply distract attention away from it. One computer programmer I spoke with felt uneasy about this mode of incorporation as she saw the well-intentioned accolades as a dubious honor. "I never realized I was the only woman in the room until I was selected for a Woman in Tech leadership role. That's when I realized I'm a 'woman in tech,'" she noted, expressing discomfort with being singled out in the tech sector in these ways.[8] In addition to pointing to the limits of an accretive notion of social justice, these worries reveal that inclusion and diversity programs often operate in the modes of tolerance that Wendy Brown (2006) has written about. Without attending to the broader gendered milieu of the technical arena, inclusion, much like tolerance, does not simply negate the disparity but helps to mark and perpetuate an unbalanced dynamic of power by further "inscribing essential otherness within the commons" (p. 46). Just as tolerance still maintains, and perhaps even strengthens, an internal power hierarchy between the tolerated and the tolerant, the women "included" into technical spheres feel marked, perhaps now even separated with greater force, as their explicit inclusion is staged both as an index of social difference and as an erasure of gender discrimination that nevertheless remains in place.

In casual conversations, my interlocutors have also noted that these approaches do not practically dismantle the inequality and uneven treatment that structure women's more routine sense of marginalization within QS as much as the tech industry at large. That is because these challenges show up for women in more mundane ways than inclusive policies currently recognize. They surface in routine practices, such as habits of dress. Women working as computer engineers or data scientists have often shared with me the pressure that they feel to mimic the normative appearance of their male counterparts. To fit in at the office, women explained that they avoid stereotyped modes of feminine self-presentation. They consciously forego wearing makeup, fashionable hairstyles, or dresses and skirts in favor of what they see as more gender-neutral clothing: plain jeans and T-shirts. Otherwise, they risk being mistaken for an administrative assistant or a junior member of the team. Stories about these moments of misrecognition abound. These experiences have become so commonplace that some have joked that jeans and a T-shirt have become the tech sector's new "power suit."

Conventional gender norms may at times appear blurred or easier to surmount in tech settings filled, as popularly imagined, with nerdy engineers themselves often viewed as on the outskirts of traditional masculinity. The casual wear favored by male programmers, epitomized by Meta's Mark Zuckerberg's fondness for hooded sweaters, may even seem to neutralize or to democratize professional attire as it replaces older, more formal and masculinized codes of corporate apparel. Nevertheless, as women's commentaries readily reveal, approaches that seek merely to add women to the corporate pool as undifferentiated bodies also make it easy to overlook the uneven gender dynamics that continue to structure women's experiences in the workplace. The principles of tolerance that shape these efforts and the accretive notion of inclusion that still inform the corporate imagination surrounding diversity, as it does QS conferences and sessions, effectively discount the dynamics of power that preclude any easy assimilation of women into still masculinized tech environments. As these approaches continue to focus on seeking women out largely as corporate bounty to be counted, they often bolster and occlude rather than help to overcome the gendered tropes and hierarchies that continue to exist at the level of practice.

The redemptive aspirations of practices that aim to rebalance gender disparities are further challenged by the fact that industry rhetoric surrounding wearables and self-tracking applications remains mediated by stereotyped ideas about women's behavior. For one, the expected "attunement" of wearables still echoes with the focused vigilance characteristic of "attachment parenting," a style of parenting where the mother in particular is encouraged to be in the constant presence of her children, for instance by carrying infants in special slings throughout the day so as to remain attentive to their minutely changing needs, as sociologist Kara Mary Van Cleaf (2016) has pointed out. When the tech sector is seen as anchored by masculinized notions of scientific rationality and detachment, women are also often recognized – and even recognize themselves – as vital conduits of emotions. On one panel at a tech conference for wearable technology (WT), for example, a female executive chided the still largely male audience for simultaneously developing technology that continued to disregard the human sensorium and for not hiring enough women who, she argued, would help incorporate these affective faculties into product design. Indeed, the claim has an institutional precedent as "affective computing," the branch of computer science that deals with emotions, was itself pioneered by the now renowned female engineer and computer scientist Rosalind Picard.

Additionally, device makers continue to draw on cliches in presenting self-tracking tools as technologies that embody, support, and even extend a gendered division of labor. One developer of a wearable that measured mood, for example, excitedly described the results of a user test in which her tool was used to resolve a conflict between a mother and a teenage daughter. The gadget alerted the mother to signs of distress the daughter was experiencing during their heated exchange by setting off a flashing red LED light embedded inside it as her heart rate and skin conductance rose past a specified level. In this case, the developer inadvertently presented the wearable as both a tool that had subsumed the emotional labor mothers are often expected to perform and as a device that may improve the quality of awareness mothers are naturally seen to possess. In doing so, this device developer articulated the gadget as something that could not only alleviate the social burden of affect management that already disproportionately falls on women's hands but, albeit unintentionally, also tacitly discipline women to become even more attuned mothers (and daughters).

Other executives made the connection between self-tracking and maternal oversight more explicitly, occasionally even promoting these mechanisms as tools that not only supplemented but altogether supplanted motherly labor. This came through in the humor and social commentary that surrounded these devices. Some joked, for instance, that wearable and Internet of Things (IoT) tools are automating "mom guilt." Occasionally, people described the digital oversight provided by wearables as "Big Mother," the benevolent, caring foil to the paternalistic and sinister Big Brother otherwise popularly associated with nefarious corporate or government surveillance (Petersen, 2015). These gendered associations surfaced in promotional activities too. The French home surveillance system Mother is exemplary in this regard because it packages its sensors in a structure that takes inspiration from the Russian *matryoshka* doll, the traditional folk symbol of maternity and fecundity (see also Schüll, 2019).[9] The system came with "cookies" that connected to the digital hub dubbed Mother. "Cookies" designated the portable sensors that people could place throughout the home to monitor anything from visitors entering the house to the consumption of actual cookies, further extending the nurturing qualities of the device. When it was first unveiled for the US market at the CES in 2015, the digital hub attracted a lot of attention. At the crowded exhibition table, I managed to ask an executive about the decision to name the device this way. "People find comfort in the fact that 'mother' is always watching," the male executive nonchalantly explained to me.[10] The makers of Mother have thus cannily rendered the popular industry metaphor literal. They knowingly transferred the stereotypically protective gaze of the mother to the mechanical device, contriving self-tracking itself as an activity that extends and perhaps even substitutes the caring watchfulness culturally expected of maternal figures.

The marketing of artificial intelligence (AI) systems intended for the home or for personal use dubbed with names such as Amazon's Alexa, Apple's Siri, and Microsoft's Cortana exemplify another variation on this theme as they establish additional connections technologists tend to make between gendered labor and technological performance. The feminized nomenclature and voice of these devices are certainly among the elements that support the gendered, domestic applications of such gadgets. These associations were further reinforced rhetorically, for example when stereotyped feminine virtues were ascribed to mechanical functions. "Confident, caring, competent loyal, helpful, but not bossy: These are just some of the words Susan Hendrich, the project manager in charge of overseeing Cortana's personality, used to describe the program's most significant character traits," an *Endgadget* article (Molen, 2014) reports. While the engineering team interviewed by the periodical stressed that Microsoft sought to instil Cortana with "human-like qualities," as the group highlighted feminized qualities such as helpfulness and affability as the central attributes of this technology, and as they explained that the program's name took inspiration from a voluptuous character in the Halo video game series, they revealed that Cortana's identity was grounded in specific gendered tropes. Given that virtual assistants are additionally advertised largely as home aids, tasked with mundane responsibilities such as searching for directions, keeping track of song lists and birthday invitations, or reordering a bar of soap, they reconnect female labor with feminized administrative and housekeeping work.

The promotional materials of business-oriented AI systems such as IBM's Watson offer an important contrast to the marketing conventions used to endorse domestic personal technology. In advertising Watson, IBM also drew on gendered connotations, but this time to style the system as explicitly male. The name Watson, for instance, established a clear connection with IBM visionary and former CEO Thomas Watson as it implicitly drew on affiliations with the studious confidant of the fictional detective Sherlock Holmes for authority. The gender of the program was further reinforced through company advertising where a narrator with a deep baritone provided voiceovers for TV commercials. Finally, these correlations were emphasized through the program's intended application. IBM has not just routinely highlighted Watson's intelligence rather than its friendliness in marketing. In one publicity stunt, for example, Watson even participated in and won a round of *Jeopardy*. In promotional videos, the company has also typically situated the program as a knowledgeable male-sounding colleague who is equally at home in the scientific laboratory as he is in the executive suite.

Watson, Siri, Cortana, and Alexa are all devices based on a similar type of machine learning and natural language processing technology that, despite the singularized connotations of their proper names, is moreover created by teams of data scientists, programmers, and engineers. In public representations, however, these tools are systematically differentiated through gendered tropes. Reinvigorating stereotyped binaries and hierarchies, applications that are gendered male are thus elevated to the professional realm. Those that are gendered female are routinely relegated to the domestic sphere and ritualistically connected with administrative work or with the labor of managing the family and the home. These associations were so commonplace in the tech sector that they even inspired the 2013 Hollywood film *Her*, where the main character falls in love with a sultry-voiced digital assistant voiced over by Scarlett Johansson. My male interlocutors repeatedly encouraged me to watch this film to better grasp the emerging realities of our data-driven future. As tech companies and communities such as QS turn to inclusive policies to address gender differences within its spheres, corporate marketing continues to tacitly reinforce an alternative gendered geography within the digital economy.

These tendencies, moreover, are not new. They only update and reanimate the tech sector's gendered past – a legacy that continues to variously shape the commercial sphere today. Certainly, the naming convention and descriptions of technological attributes reflect a much longer history of the way gender has mediated innovation (Wajcman, 1991).[11] The nomenclature, for instance, evokes the more established tradition of labeling machines, vehicles, and vessels – from ships to cars – with female names and pronouns. This move not only further invokes inventors (as it does tech users) as putatively male; it also situates device makers and operators with respect to these inventions in paternalistic terms, investing their creators and users with a sense of ownership and control by drawing on sexist and patriarchal tropes.

The framing of self-tracking and assistive technology in feminized terms also draws on the more recent history of computing. We may no longer associate the word "computer" with the embodied work of female engineers and mathematicians, who, when coding still required the physical manipulation of wires and bulbs rather than the swift entry of code written on a keyboard, programmed the machine by hand (Chun, 2011). However, the history that had explicitly intertwined the work of female coders with the inner processes of computers, creating a woman–machine assemblage to be managed by a male engineer, remains enshrined in the language of "software" and "hardware." The etymology of these terms may be as little known today as that of the word "computer." Few people, for example, can trace the terminology to the first programming textbook written by John von Neumann and Herman Goldstine, where the authors solidified the gendered correlations in expressions such as "hardware" and "software" that they defined as the "'head work' of (male) scientists, or 'planner,' and 'hand-work' of the (largely female) 'coders,'" respectively (Ensmenger, 2010, p. 15). Their effects, however, continue to linger, as evident in the feminized descriptions of technological functions offered by device developers as well as in the enduring preeminence of hardware development as the more privileged domain within the industry, and as the territory of brainy male engineers.

The asserted relationship between assistive computing and administrative duties, moreover, reactivates the still recent associations between computer use and secretarial labor. Before computers became "personal" in the 1980s, these machines were largely sold as word-processing devices whose operations were coextensive with feminized clerical work. Promotional materials of the early computer era generated by giants such as IBM liberally leveraged these tropes to frame computing as a male executive's right hand (Atkins, 2010). As these manufacturers sought to explain the value of computers to corporate managers who constituted their key clientele, advertising routinely presented this technology, and the women who operated it, as key aids of the male C-suite (Ensmenger, 2010).

In capitalizing on a similarly bifurcated imaginary, makers of self-tracking and sensor-enabled tools continue to reproduce these gendered stereotypes. In doing so, they only reinforce the very same disparities and forms of discrimination that corporate diversity and inclusion policies ostensibly aim to overcome. These stereotyped associations may at first appear at odds with the increasingly gender-balanced ways companies aim to structure and to publicly represent their engineering and computing teams. This was certainly the case in the work profiled by *Endgadget*. In a photograph that accompanied the story detailing the development of Cortana, the core team was characteristically styled as evenly split, being comprised of two female-presenting colleagues and two male-presenting ones, even though, true to tech sector fashion, all four were featured sporting short haircuts and wearing jeans. The article also predominantly quoted Susan Hendrich, "the project manager in charge of overseeing Cortana's personality" (Molen, 2014), as though to defensively highlight that the key decisions were made by a team that was female-led. Nevertheless, echoing the designs of diversity policies of the tech sector, which aim to center and add women to the field without redressing the disparities that continue to shape their experience and absence, Hendrich's commentary and the broader inclusion of female colleagues in the magazine feature did little to undo the generalizations incorporated into product design. On the contrary, the citations (as well as the delegation of the development of technological "personality" traits to female leads) underscore how Microsoft has relied on female-presenting colleagues to deliver and to legitimize stereotyped messaging.

Finally, the terminology that technologists frequently default to when discussing processes of digitization is what continues to challenge the realization of the aspirational inclusive office invoked by well-meaning corporate policies or community practices. That is because this vocabulary remains tethered to a feminized imaginary that is grounded by gendered generalizations.

Sasha, a digital entrepreneur, exemplifies and explicitly literalizes some of these industry tendencies. Of particular interest to me here are the specific terms in which Sasha had made her business pitch, all the while delivering these ideas with the practiced ease of someone who has likely uttered these words in boardrooms or conferences many times before. As we spoke about her business – a digital platform that allows people to sell the personal data they produce from self-tracking devices directly to interested corporate sponsors – she enthusiastically explained:

> So, I am out to get the girls. How do I get girls? I'm not going to get the girls by bringing in the boys and really talk about girls and boys together in the bar. I'm going to get people to go to the bar because this bar has the most awesome restroom where all of the girls gather and share lots and lots of secrets, interesting stuff about themselves that helps them get the boys. So, we could share all of this data and talk about it as individuals amongst ourselves, and then we go to the boys in the bar. My job is to win the girls.

Speaking to me as another woman, she scanned my face for signs of recognition before continuing: "I want to create a data revolution. Because it's all about us. That's when you see that a lot of the lexicon I use is about revolution.

It's about reclaiming your data. It's about re-empowerment. It's about using computational tools that companies have, for ourselves."[12]

In Sasha's usage, "girls" and "boys" were metaphors for the consumer and the corporation, respectively. She is one of several entrepreneurs working to create a platform that will enable technology users to monetize their data. She therefore deploys this language both to simplify and to visualize the difference between the individuals who will produce data using digital self-tracking gadgets and the corporations that will pay device users for this information. By staging the trade in personal data as a mating ritual between men and women, Sasha invoked a gendered framework that enabled her to conceive of her company as a feminist intervention aimed at rebalancing the power dynamics between data producers qua device users (the girls) and companies interested in purchasing said data (the boys).

The terminology of "the girls" also doubles as a euphemism for the personal data corporate clients will be able to access. And while the metaphorical bar in this configuration constitutes the marketplace where sellers and buyers mingle and trade, the site of observation and corporate desire is further gendered by orienting the masculinized corporate gaze, in this case literally, toward the female bathroom. In prototyping her venture, Sasha started in her own bathroom, connecting every item in it to a digital sensor. That is because she saw the intimate bathroom habits of women as an especially lucrative source of data – one that has remained located outside of the male gaze, and even of the (often themselves male-led) companies selling the items that women use. So, Sasha reasoned, the boys – that is, the corporate entities – would be willing to pay top dollar to users for the gender-specific data generated there.

Although Sasha enfolds sexist stereotypes into her business pitch especially vividly and opportunistically, her tactics echo the more conventional and banal language digital executives tend to use when describing both digital users and their data. For example, designers and device developers are still routinely guided to orient their work around an imagined female user when they are urged to make these gadgets "easy enough for my mom to use" or "so simple my 97-year-old grandmother can figure it out." Paradoxically, the female consumer is not typically the default "end user," as I also explore below. However, the image of an unskilled (and often elderly) woman continues to shape the aspirational usability that informs self-tracking innovation.

The language of flows, leaks, streams, oceans, and rivers that technologists commonly deploy to explain the way data move between devices and bodies extends these sexist tropes further. While there are many ways to parse these metaphors (see Chapters 2 and 5), the gendered connotations of this digital imaginary are hard to overlook. In the Euro-American imaginary, the female body has long been connected with nature and with the emission of fluids that cannot be controlled (Ortner, 1974; Butler, 1993). Now, by virtue of these feminized connotations, personal data are often naturalized as substances that likewise flow directly from people to devices. These terms effectively equate prolific data-producing digital users with fecund female bodies. Indeed, it is this conventional relationship between data and women's bodies that has enabled practitioners such as Sasha to speak about digital users as "girls" congregating in bathrooms and to describe their data in terms typically reserved for menstrual fluids (Martin, 1987).[13] In other words, to talk about people as "leaking something that is not supposed to be represented," as another wearables developer had noted in a related context.[14]

The feminized connotations of data and device users also echo in the salacious aesthetics that often mediate digital rhetoric and particularly public discussions of the promises and concerns related to digital privacy. These ideas certainly shaped the visual vocabulary of Showtime's series *Dark Net* (which explored the digital exploits of people such as Chris Dancy in one of its episodes) and its social commentary on the dangers of digital veiling and unveiling. The way the aesthetics of erotic film configured the show's marketing is especially instructive. In one of its central advertising pieces, a discussion of which opened the Preface of this book, a blindfolded androgynous figure with distinctly softened feminine features emphasizes the feminized vulnerability of contemporary tech users. In this submissive posture, the model functions as a placeholder for the modern viewer, and by extension for the everyday computer user, whose digitization the show codes through a language of sexualized passivity. Skin tone and age offer additional interpretative frames. The model's youthful, feminized whiteness casts digital representation as somehow innocent, illicit, and promiscuous, as simultaneously natural, risky, and risqué. Moreover, with only the face visible in the image, the head represents the exposed and unsuspecting person that is understood to be located off screen and that digital monitoring is expected to penetrate and reveal. Overall, this sexualized figure is conjured as a focus of the pornographic male gaze encoded in digital devices and ultimately suggests the promiscuity of digital knowledge, that is, the seductiveness of information that cannot be restrained.

In many ways, self-tracking is thus framed by a double image. On the one hand, there is the figure of the attentive and attuned mother. When viewed through this feminized lens, tools formally associated with brute rationality and control are reframed as gadgets that amplify attentiveness, sensitivity, and perceptiveness. Allusions to motherhood convert cold masculinized surveillance into vulnerable witnessing. On the other hand, there is the hyper-sexualized and prolific female body that shapes the discourse on digital (self-)monitoring, a body that is associated with forms of expression that are tinged with transgression, danger, seduction, and taboo.

Perhaps not surprisingly, despite the language that represents self-tracking and data as feminized mechanisms, activities, and substances, this technology still awkwardly accommodates actual female users. Indeed, many wearables are still often too large for women to wear as they are often not designed with the female body in mind. One of the reasons this remains so, I am often told, is that despite the availability of increasingly more compact sensors, electronics are still too large to fit into devices appropriate for a woman's generally smaller frame. The reason that the male body and therefore patterns of use continue to be seen as the minimal requirements to meet in speculative device development also reflects entrenched beliefs that to design for a man is to design for the general type, whereas to design for a woman is to design for her specific or "special" needs, for instance by developing a menstrual period tracker. Much like the cockpits in early aviation or the first airbags installed in automobiles, which were both initially designed for the average, that is the male, driver (Johnson, 2010), the cultural expectations of the "typical" wearable user thus shape the way these technologies are taken up in social life.

This can create uncomfortable moments such as the one a friend described to me when she participated in a design sprint for an Android watch held at Google's New York City headquarters. This workshop, which gathered female designers and engineers, was aimed at exploring ways the company could better design and market its wearable devices to a female audience, and, implicitly, to create additional opportunities for women to contribute to the development of WT through rapid prototyping. These types of events are part and parcel of the extracurricular work technologists hustling with a passion are widely expected to take on (see Chapter 4). To further highlight the inclusive intentions of this effort, the "sprint" was held on March 8th, International Women's Day. And yet, on that day, women worked in teams, contributing their ideas for free to a challenge intended to include women at the level of design and development as they struggled to actually comfortably fit the bulky gear onto their own hands.

The clumsy ways in which women and their labor continue to be incorporated within tech settings are not simply corporate gaffes. Despite the equitable rhetoric of accretive inclusion favored by business executives as much as by QS organizers, these examples indicate that binary and stereotyped conceptions of gendered difference continue to stratify the way men and women are situated in the tech sector. Policies and tactics aimed at incorporating women into the field therefore only superficially address the broader and more complex ways that gender continues to mediate, bifurcate, and organize the digital arena. They offer only token recognition of an ongoing problem while continuing to sustain a rigid gender hierarchy that biases how women and men show up in the digital sphere. It's one of the reasons why such tactics ultimately fall short and remain unable to adequately address this tech industry blind spot – whether within the gathering halls of QS or within the tech sector at large.

QS and the Gendered Politics of Affective Labor

In the final analysis, as a forum that both supports and extends extracurricular work of technologists hustling with a passion, QS reveals additional ironies of policies that respond to issues such as uneven gender representation from the point of view of an accretive logic of difference. In particular, in an environment where professional success now requires technologists to perform mounting amounts of free and emotional care work, such as tending to community, QS offers further insight into the way such industry expectations continue to disproportionately disadvantage women. Despite the promising rhetoric of inclusion resonant in the organizing efforts of events such as QS15, QS can be read as an interface that reflects as it facilitates the way affective demands of community-building do not only further mark the ongoing sidelining of women in the tech sector but inadvertently contribute to it. It indicates how feminized work performed by tech sector executives continues to devalue technologists' labor as it facilitates further marginalization of women in the workplace.

As an interface of this kind, QS operates in the mode of a technological prosthesis as discussed by Sarah S. Jain (1999). Digital devices, including platforms such as computer interfaces, are often conceptualized as mechanisms that broadly extend human abilities. Jain nuances these assumptions, however, as she instead calls attention to the way prosthetic devices that amplify human capacities both configure and are configured by normative assumptions. Rather than accept or reject the generic promises of the technological prosthesis, Jain encourages readers to ask a more pointed question: "which bodies are enabled and which are disabled by specific technologies?" (p. 33). Likewise, if technologists hustling with a passion now turn to forums such as QS to translate their affective and free labor into professional gains (see Chapters 4 and 5), it's important to recognize that in a social context shaped by entrenched gender hierarchies discussed throughout this chapter, these benefits remain unevenly distributed. The low number of women who engage with forums such as QS thus suggests that QS is experiencing something more than a problem of proper representation. Women's relative absence from its activities points to the broader ways in which knowledge work that requires practitioners to engage in affective labor as a strategy of career management works against women who continue to take on a larger share of this work in their personal lives and therefore may be less available to take on these extracurricular responsibilities.

That women tend to disproportionately assume free and affective labor in the home is of course a well-documented social phenomenon. Feminist scholars have long highlighted the fact that women shoulder the better part of caregiving and family-planning duties even when both partners work outside of the home (Wajcman, 2015). This literature typically seeks to recognize connections between women's nonwaged labor in the home and men's waged work in the marketplace to reclaim family life – and women's contributions to it – in economic terms (Zaretsky, 1976). It also typically defines such work as "invisible labor" both to resituate acts of care as labor as well as to highlight their characteristically obscured nature (Hochschild, 2012).

More recently, quarantine measures imposed due to the COVID-19 pandemic have temporarily thrust these uneven burdens into further relief and into the public limelight. The competing demands of family and work experienced by housebound knowledge workers during this time did not only reveal the enduring anxiety over productivity of those hustling with a passion but also the entrenched gender divide among those performing taken-for-granted housework and care work. Popular memes effectively conveyed these realities through humor. For instance, one set of images that circulated widely among working professionals in the early days of the pandemic, the COVID-19 Daily Schedule, spoke indirectly to the pressures women were experiencing at home at the start of social distancing. On the surface, memes such as the "Daily Schedule" and its subsequent "corrections" (Figure 6.2) that circulated online and on parenting forums featured an itinerary that addressed the more general familial aspirations and challenges of stressed-out parents: their desire and inability to coordinate work around leisure, thoughtful contemplation, and extended quality time. Though in their colorful aesthetic and snarky tone, these visuals already implied a rebuke of both working women and a maternal stereotype: the homemaker who ambitiously compiles unrealistic, meticulous, color-coded schedules for her kids because she has the time to do so. These images ultimately indicated that far from relinquishing women from undue social obligations stopped short by the pandemic, working from home has placed women under even greater pressure to combine the role of an ideal stay-at-home mother with the function of a dedicated career woman. More, as

(a)   (b)   (c)

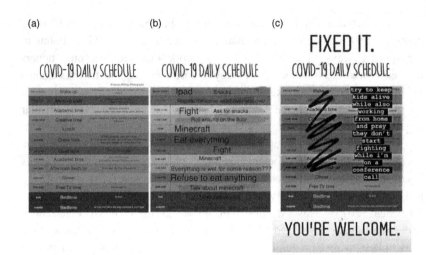

Figure 6.2 (a) Daily Schedule 1; (b) Daily Schedule 2; (c) Daily Schedule 3.

they mocked such social expectations, they voiced women's tacit desire to live up to them.

Widely reported statistics bolstered these popular appeals, indicating, for example, that women, who were frequently the default caretakers during the COVID-19 pandemic, lost or left their jobs in higher numbers compared to men, and by spring 2022, when unemployment rates showed signs of recovery, returned to work in numbers three time lower than their male counterparts (Flaherty, 2022). Even when these figures suggested that college-educated women have retained their jobs at similar rates to men (Fry, 2022), the COVID-19 pandemic also highlighted the longstanding gendered cleavages that continue to narrate how families balance housework. The "Women in the Workplace" report published by McKinsey in 2020, for example, documented that those women who lived in dual-career households with children had reported spending more time on household responsibilities since the start of the pandemic than their male counterparts, a trend that had particularly impacted women of color. In this period, women also reported considering leaving their jobs or stepping back from their work at levels 1.3 times greater than men. McKinsey estimated that there could have been as many as 100,000 fewer women in leadership roles if female executives did in fact leave their jobs at this rate, a trend that would have rolled back as many as six years' worth of gains made by women in the workplace.

The pandemic may have momentarily highlighted and even elevated the uneven distribution of these familiar duties, made all the more notable through contemporary digital communication such as meme making. Scholars, however, have also emphasized how digital technology has more consistently amplified the amount of invisible work that now has to be completed at home, the performance of which continues to be divided along familiar gendered lines. Anthropologist Jordan Kraemer (2017) has noted, for example, that digital technology has simultaneously created new types of "logistical labor" (such as managing online platforms, responding to online surveys, or searching for answers on online forums) and redefined formally waged work (customer service, user research, tech support) as uncompensated housework – a lot of which has been disproportionately absorbed by women. In the tech sector, these logistical and caretaking responsibilities additionally tend to follow women into the workplace. Women continue to take on a greater amount of affective labor in the office, often adopting the role of "office mom" who helps coordinate lunches, the empathetic colleague who listens to problems, or the social coordinator who organizes office outings (Bacon, 2013). In the tech sector, women also find more opportunities working affect-driven "people" jobs such as developing client-facing user interfaces, or, even more directly, working in human resources, communications, and client management.

So, if, among other things, QS responds to the contemporary need for technologists to take on greater amounts of affective and immaterial work outside of formal office hours, the relative absence of women in these forums highlights that the already overburdened female digital professionals may simply be less able to make time for these added commitments – especially those that, like QS, require travel and attendance at events that take place after work and far from home. The lower rates of participation of women in forums such as QS thus point to the additional ways gender continues to mediate the tech sector. While hustling with a passion is often invoked as a gender-neutral imperative, as a function of one's individual abilities, motivation, and desire, women who already perform a disproportionate amount of emotional, affective, and unwaged labor at work and at home may be less available to meet these mounting extracurricular demands of the office. This may also be why women-only networks, such as the short-lived QSXX, were unable to rebalance inequities within the forum. Rather than taking on the discriminatory practices of the tech sector in full force, such efforts continue to inadvertently particularize female engagement by relegating group activities to "female issues" without addressing the core and enduring reasons women contribute to forums such as QS – much like in the tech sector at large – in fewer numbers. Ultimately, as organizers explore strategies to symbolically include women in group activities, the modalities of participation that shape QS as a community and, in the end, as an interface to tech sector career opportunities already silently regulate who may be best positioned to take advantage of QS as a mechanism of professional transfiguration, connection, and access and therefore gain a more secure foothold in the digital economy. QS thus serves both as a means and as another example of the more subtle forms of exclusion that continue to impact how women are situated – and situate themselves – within the digital arena.

Despite the best efforts of QS organizers, much like tech executives, the inclusive remedies that promise to deliver social cohesion remain constrained by structural issues that continue to sharpen engrained biases. If these efforts ultimately come up short, it is because policies that respond only to an accretive notion of difference insufficiently address the more routine ways in which the tech sector remains male, heteronormative, and Western-centric. This presents a significant challenge for integrating anyone located outside of these privileged positions into the QS community, the tech industry, and digital innovation more broadly on equal terms.

Conclusion: Community at a Crossroads

This book has focused closely on the organizing dynamics of the Quantified Self (QS). At the same time, this has not been a book narrowly about QS. Throughout these chapters, I have explored the forum as a threshold experience that renders the labor of tech executives compatible with the demands and challenges of self-tracking entrepreneurialism. My aim here has been to understand how QS works within and in relationship to the digital economy. It's through examining how the forum intersects and interacts with this wider social and professional landscape that I have turned to QS as a central interface to the tech sector itself.

I've argued that QS has always represented something more than the ascendence of the "culture of personal data," as Wolf (2009) had first articulated it, or a robust social response to a broken healthcare system that has disenfranchised and marginalized patients, leading people to take their wellbeing into their own hands with the aid of emerging digital devices and to seek support in social collectives such as QS, as anthropologists have at times considered (Nafus and Sherman, 2014; Tamar and Zandbergen, 2016). As an interface to the tech sector, QS has offered visibility into the interplay of social factors influencing entrepreneurial activity. It has also offered insight into the alternative ways the collective has served as a link between the practice of self-tracking and the business of self-tracking.

The organizing dynamics of QS reflect some of the ways technologists both conceive of and situate personal monitoring tools in the social sphere. I've likewise examined the part QS has assumed in facilitating the interactions, exchanges, and opportunities of those working in this field. Understanding QS as an interface with the self-tracking arena therefore involved investigating the relationship between QS and the industry's conceptualizations of data, consumers, and technologists' own professional identities. Just as an interface facilitates connections, QS has enabled me to directly engage with the underlying social mechanics that support the development of self-tracking tools. As such, it has served as a central mediating platform by means of which to explore the operating social and business dynamics shaping both digital work and digital representation.

My fieldwork on the commercial role of QS has been concentrated on the group's impact and influence between 2012 and 2017. I write this book while also recognizing that QS and its relationship to the tech sector have continued to evolve since I completed my research. This is not surprising. While the language of community often invites associations with something steady that one can enter or join, there is nothing unexpected in the fact that QS has continued to shapeshift. Neither the conceptual category nor the forms of community that QS has represented have ever really been fixed. QS was an idea and a forum that were continuously brought together and renewed. This was not only a product of technologists' mercurial engagements with QS, which were evident in participants' constant trickling in and out of group activities, but also of the evolving nature of its social context and the shifting expectations of its contributors. Just as Jennifer D. Carlson and Kathleen C. Stewart note of the unsteady currents of emotions, QS has always already marked a construct that "comes apart all the time and at the same time [one where] something is (always) coming and coming together" (2014).

In the ensuing years, the forum's social and professional function has experienced a number of changes. Partially, QS and its relationship to the tech sector has been reshaped by its original founders who have continued to steer the forum into a more academic direction. Partly, its evolved application can be attributed to the developments in the self-tracking market itself. These transformations have affected the role that forums such as QS play in the digital arena.

Certainly, these changes did not take effect overnight. The shifting relevance of the forum could already be felt at QS15. This was an event initially conceptualized as a social statement, not just as another conference. "This is the age of the Quantified Self," teased promotional banners advertising the meeting on quantifieself.com. "I think Gary thought that 2015 was going to be the year where QS invites the larger community [of self-trackers and technology makers] inside. He had hoped it would be the hub where everyone would gather to talk about the buzz term he had coined," one person involved in conference organizing had shared with me.[1]

In advance of the conference, the team took steps to prepare for the anticipated robust social response. Most strikingly, while previous conferences were held in meeting rooms of mid-sized hotels that accommodated groups of several hundred, for this occasion the organizers secured Fort Mason Center for Arts & Culture – a historic and cavernous venue situated on the banks of the San Francisco Bay featuring views of the Golden Gate Bridge and the space for a group of nearly four thousand. The Festival Pavilion, the venue's main hall, also held tacit symbolic value as it sat within walking distance of the Long Now Foundation, the quirky nonprofit chaired by Silicon Valley luminaries such as Stewart Brand and Kevin Kelly, which, according to its website, is devoted to projects that "foster long-term thinking."[2] The Foundation is housed at The Interval at Long Now, a coffee shop and bar where technorati can mingle while drinking from prominently placed private bottles of whisky that register their support of the organization's mission as well as pay tribute to their nonconventional thinking. As conference goers congregated at the coffee shop in interval moments, the proximity of the Long Now Foundation to the main conference implicitly constructed QS as an equally future-forward happening.

Though a reported two thousand people ultimately walked through the doors of Fort Mason, most during the Public Exposition, the "Expo" in the QS Conference and Expo, which was opened to the general public for a discounted fee on the last day of the conference in a space designed to accommodate nearly twice as many, the rooms at times felt sparse. Notably, though two years earlier Forbes had declared premier industry functions such as the Consumer Electronics Show (CES) as "the year of the Quantified Self" (Clay, 2013) and self-tracking devices have continued to make a strong showing at these events, the QS "Expo" featured a significantly smaller number of sponsored exhibits and visitors. The lack of representatives from self-tracking companies then gaining commercial recognition, such as Fitbit, Jawbone, Misfit, and the Apple Watch, was especially noticeable. Their absence was all the more pronounced given that the opening day of QS15 coincided with the day Fitbit became a publicly traded company. I remember watching the proceedings on TV in my hotel room as I prepared to leave for Fort Mason. Fitbit's announcement inadvertently marked a moment when an event staged as a grand community coming out instead subtly signaled QS's fizzling role in the tech sector.

There were other signs as well. The New York QS meetup, for example, one of the oldest and largest groups outside of Silicon Valley, had started to convene with reduced regularity. Remarking on the change at an event that was held in one of the last weeks of 2015, some six months after QS15, Steven Dean, one of the forum's original organizers, spoke of what he felt was a "winding down" of QS. By 2017, he would step down as coordinator of the New York gathering after an eight-year run. Conferences were starting to taper off too. The last one assembled in Portland in September of 2018 with much less fanfare than the event held in San Francisco three years earlier.

Some attributed these changes to the purism with which Wolf has continued to approach forum activities (Chapter 1). At QS15, this was expressed in the way commercial self-tracking companies interacted with the "community." Despite the addition of an enlarged technology Expo, Wolf, I was told, was committed to making sure that the conference retained a sense of intimacy and DIY sensibility to set the event apart from standard tech industry functions where the main activities revolved around speeches and exhibits of paid sponsors (see Chapter 2). This came at a cost as corporations accustomed to a more prominent stage were not as motivated to officially sponsor an event where their presences would be marginalized. Over the years, the group's founders have also more firmly crystalized the forum's core mission around advocacy and legitimization of citizen science. In 2016, Wolf announced the launch of *N-of-1: The Journal of the Quantified Self* devoted to projects focused on "single subject research." In 2022, Wolf, along with several collaborators, published the book *Personal Science: Learning to Observe*, which explores the benefits of digital self-tracking. For a time, the formal entity known as QS Labs that officially supported the organizing activities of the forum even collaborated with a university in the northern Netherlands, the Hanze University for Applied Science, in establishing the Quantified Self Institute (QSI). Even though QSI has by now been folded into a broader concentration on "Personalized Digital Health," the university's website continues to indicate that "the educational programmes on Quantified Self are part of several curricula at Hanze UAS."[3] If QS was first conceived as a more capacious idea, as a hub that expressed an entire culture of personal data, the ongoing curation of QS in this more focused direction has ultimately produced the lingering perception that the self-tracking acolytes QS attracts are simply too specialized and niche, which ultimately limited industry engagement as both vendors and members.

Others, however, saw the downturn as a sign that self-tracking has, at last, reached wider acceptance. One participant I spoke with, for instance, explained that the declining interest in the forum was an indicator that self-tracking as a practice was "moving in the right direction" and was simply becoming more mainstream. "When my uncle has a Fitbit," he told me, there is less of a need to get together to talk about these gadgets. Another contributor, an avid cycler who has spent time in the Netherlands, compared self-tracking to biking in Amsterdam. "To ask what self-tracking is now," he noted, would be like "asking someone who lives in Amsterdam what it means to be a cyclist."[4] To that person, the question would seem superfluous. Like biking in Amsterdam, self-tracking has become a routine part of life, particularly for those living in the US.

These comments suggested that the "B-to-Fringe" strategy – a dictum that states that what starts "fringe" always goes mainstream, as referred to by Tim Chang, the CEO of Basis, in a staged conversation with venture capitalist Bryce Roberts at QS15 – was working. While low attendance at QS events was viewed as a budding sign of digital enthusiasm in the forum's earlier years, now its putatively dulling popular appeal suggested to these participants that ideas discussed therein were becoming an unremarkable feature of everyday life. In such a social milieux, it made sense to them that the forum would see depressed attendance because gathering to discuss these practices had become unnecessary. These participants thus read the "winding down" of QS as a sign that what was formally niche was now becoming widespread. Indeed, by resituating QS in these terms, these interlocutors highlighted the revised way in which QS now functioned as an interface to digital enthusiasm. To them, its falling relevance itself offered visibility into the upward social momentum of self-tracking tools. It's perhaps not surprising that many of these commentators were themselves executives involved in the self-tracking sector. Their view that reduced interest in all things QS somehow signaled greater social uptake rather than a rejection of digital monitoring at a time when, despite enthusiastic media attention, many technologists still candidly worried that wearables mostly remained solutions in search of problems (Chapter 3), itself reads as a projection of the tech sector's enthusiasm for this technology rather than necessarily as a reflection of its broadening social relevance.

It might also be, of course, that the waning interest in QS was a result of growing fatigue. After going strong for years in part due to the support of technologists described in this book, some felt that QS may just have run its course. By 2017, when I was winding down my own research, the forum was more than ten years old. Conversations in these spaces, I heard, started to feel repetitive. The forum's long tenure, therefore, carried mixed implications. On the one hand, the group's age testified to the success and social usefulness of this idea. At this rate, QS has outlasted many of the self-tracking companies that participants have enthusiastically discussed over the years. On the other hand, it's not surprising that the initial public and academic curiosity that for some time sustained group activities has slowed, along with the forum's momentum. After helping to jump-start some of the industry enthusiasm surrounding self-tracking technology, as discussed throughout this book, the personal investments – the uncompensated, affective labor – also took a toll. Developing this forum has been a lot of work. "Be careful unless you have a lot of time," one QS meetup host advised those who wanted to join the organizing efforts.[5]

Inevitably, these changes have altered the course QS has charted within the tech sector and for those working within it. When QS still held the promise of a community that represented a larger cultural swell, it appeared as a more fitting place from which to access the "future" consumers and therefore as a more desirable space for professional self-realization and promotion explored throughout this book. It was then that QS attracted technologists whose debates and discussions could offer insight into the organizing dynamics of the self-tracking market. While the motives first driving attendance have settled around something more restrained, the forum's salience within the tech sector has also shifted. As a result, although "quantified self" as a label for a class of self-tracking devices and as a descriptive moniker of the personal data derived from them – the idealized "data doubles" that make up data's public face that were discussed in Chapter 2 – have remained intact, QS as a forum has lost much of its former social and professional function.

It may be the case that QS no longer acts precisely as the type of tech sector interface that I had once encountered. Nevertheless, the industry practices, challenges, and promises filtered through the QS lens in this book remain germane as they speak to the more enduring subtleties of commercial wearables and the self-tracking market. These forces continue to affect and shape the sector even if they may now appear in an altered guise. Many of the dynamics that I have discussed in this book can today be observed, for instance, in the growing popularity of podcasts and webinars as the preferred media for professional self-fashioning. Their role as mechanisms of endurance and connection has grown in the wake of the COVID-19 pandemic, especially when working from home and social distancing measures have undercut the community-making aspects of in-person gatherings such as QS. It's likely that these virtual supports – and the affective investments that they demand – have become even more necessary as technologists continue to work remotely in large numbers and as employment in this arena becomes more precarious in the wake of extensive rounds of layoffs that have shaken the sector in 2023.

In particular, as a one-time instrument of the self-tracking market, QS still offers important insights into the expanding value of community in the digital economy. Scholars and popular observers exploring the social impact of QS have left the notion that the forum represents a user community largely unproblematized. This book has instead interfaced with the varied notions of "community" that QS represents as it examined the expanding role of community in the digital context.

To date, popular and academic observers have tended to treat QS either as a community of those who share an exuberance for self-tracking technology or else as a collective of disgruntled patients and citizen scientists, as this book's

Introduction explored. These assessments align with the concept of community familiar to anthropologists. Appraisals of this kind resonate, for example, with the concept of culture upheld by anthropologists in the first part of the twentieth century explored in Chapter 1. These interpretations of QS as a community tend to present the collective as a self-evident unit awaiting discovery. Indeed, the very framing of QS as a "community" produces a sense of interiority that is frequently contrasted with its constitutive outside: the media, the business executives, and the social science researchers who engage with or look in on it as though from without.

In recognizing QS as a byproduct of neoliberal policies and therefore as a community that has emerged in response to the reluctant self-reliance forced by decades of globalization, privatization, and the accompanying federal retreat from social welfare programs, the group ties that analysts interpret QS as fostering also at times resonate with concepts of community familiar to sociologists and political scientists. In qualifying QS as a collective of this kind, they inadvertently present it as a social response to the decades-old retreat into solitary individualism brought on by transformations in American public life, forms of communication, leisure, housing patterns, patterns of employment (Putnam, 2000), and, more recently, by digital technology (Turkle, 2011). QS, in this rendering, functions as yet another example of a community that has become both the focus and the locus of social action, advocacy, and care. "Society," sociologist Nicolas Rose (1996) notes, formally cohered through geography and was generally the territory of governments. Now, he observes, community has emerged as the primary mode of resource management and social organizing. Rose suggests that many now look for society to become "regenerated, and social justice to be maximized, through the building of responsible communities, prepared to invest in themselves" (p. 333). Whether QS is understood as a localized network of digital aficionados rediscovering physical connections or as a forum for marginalized patients and health advocates uniting against a common cause, these ways of seeing QS create the impression that the collective exists on the margins or at least in conversation with digital entrepreneurialism. In either case, the concept of community as it relates to QS is not itself taken into question.

This book, by contrast, has taken the presumed status of QS as a user community as a direct object of inquiry. In doing so, it has built on the work of scholars who have started to call attention to the complicated function of community in the digital context. Extending the early critique of digital theorists (Terranova, 2000), media and digital labor scholars have begun to recognize that "community" does not only characterize a vital social aggregate or express a contemporary mode of belonging and problem solving. On the contrary, they excoriate "community" as a convenient euphemism that cloaks the more sinister and exploitative practices of technology companies (Scholz, 2013; Van Dijck, 2013; Rosenblat, 2018; Zuboff, 2019). This literature highlights that organizing community is not only a response to societal changes or digital innovation. Today, doing so has also become big business. Indeed, the digerati celebrating the social value of community most vociferously are often the same ones who use the concept of community most opportunistically. The heads of companies such as Meta, Google, or Uber regularly mobilize the language of community to present technology use in altruistic and friendly terms. As they construe themselves as partners who co-construct community alongside their users, they obscure the uneven dynamics of power between producers and consumers of these tools, disguising from view how "community" deflects attention away from the exploitative ways tech companies in fact put both people's data and labor to work.

Like the scholarship that points to a double standard of community in the digital context, this book has served as an interface between popular conceptualizations of QS as a user community and its business function. I have argued that QS as a user community cannot be abstracted as a phenomenon in its own right. Much like the interface, the language of connectivity that has shaped QS masks as much as it reveals. As this work has examined the conditions of possibility that have constituted QS as a user community, it has analyzed the different ways the construct has been used descriptively, discursively, and cunningly within the tech sector.

Looking deeper at the business imperatives that have cohered QS as a collective of technophiles, as I have in this book, reveals additional connections between technologists and tech hobbyists, as well as between tech capitalism and community organizing. If digital executives readily embraced the premise that QS constituted a user community, this book has explored how this concept has been deployed within a consumer-centric business environment. This framing has enabled digital executives to situate themselves as observers divining social preferences rather than the ones determining them. It has endorsed QS as one site where tech professionals could come into direct contact with potential customers even as QS effectively supplied the very means through which they actively constructed the subjects of their product marketing. This monograph has, moreover, analyzed how the notion that QS constitutes a user community has helped technologists to realize passion as a valued professional quality. Ultimately, this book has explored how the forum responds to as it registers the larger value of digital and social connections in a flexible economy. In short, these chapters have analyzed QS as a collective that has brought technologists rather than device users together and connected them to opportunities for professional advancement as well as with each other in an increasingly neoliberal, fragmented, and turbulent employment environment.

That we cannot assess what it means to live in a data-driven world without accounting for the professional contexts in which these devices and the data they produce develop has been the key conceit of this book. Analyzing how technologists have helped to constitute rather than simply to encounter forums such as QS as a collective centered around the fetish of digital enthusiasm has offered alternative ways to appreciate the business and social function of community in the tech sector. By resurfacing these professional associations, this monograph has also investigated how the tech industry creates community rather than simply co-opts it for its own devices. From this end, it has argued that QS represents a new form of sociality derived from within the digital economy. It is when understood as a collective of this kind that QS acts as an interface, that is, as a social mechanism, that has helped digital executives to reconcile the demands of digital entrepreneurialism and as one that reflects as much as it shapes some of the ways self-tracking devices now operate.

Notes

Introduction

1 See the analysis toward the end of this chapter.
2 This verbiage represents consumer-facing reiterations of older concepts that describe connected machines. These technologies are thus occasionally still referred to as M2M or machine-to-machine interaction, although IoT technologies are seen as ones that can potentially connect an infinite range of devices and sensors, whereas M2M solutions were understood to connect only a limited cluster of sensors.
3 Some of the top meetups that I frequented included: Data Driven NYC, IoT Central, Personal Data NYC, Hardwired NYC, Wearable Tech NYC, Bots and Brains Machine Learning NYC, Volumetric Society of NYC, Consciousness Hacking NYC, NYC Open Data, Data Skeptics, NYC Women in Machine Learning & Data Science, Women Who Code NYC, and Girl Develop It NYC.
4 The development of self-tracking tools takes place, today, in a social and entrepreneurial environment where Emily Martin's (1994) observations about the value of flexibility have come to maturity. Additionally, Rosenblat (2018) highlights that the term "entrepreneur" is increasingly used to describe the work of contingent contract workers, not only the labor of those who are spearheading startup companies. As precarious labor is progressively presented as entrepreneurial labor, the framing glamorizes insecure work arrangements while displacing care and accountability, such as the provision of benefits, from employers onto employees themselves.
5 A widely cited distinction made by sociologist Whitney Erin Boesel encourages writers to differentiate between the two common uses of the expression "quantified self." Boesel notes that the expression is often used indiscriminately, as though it referred both to the work of the companies developing data-monitoring gadgets, the so-called "quantapreneurs," as well as to the device users who convene on a regular basis to share their experiences with self-tracking tools. To avoid the confusion between these two groups of people, she advises to mark their differences by writing the former in lowercase letters and the latter using title case (Boesel, 2013).
6 Field notes, December 2015, on file with the author.
7 For further discussion of the promises of "intimate self-surveillance," see Hong, 2016.
8 The metaphor of the body as a machine has a long historical precedent. (See Rabinbach, 1992; Crary, 1999.)

9 Daston and Galison (2007) first developed the concept of "mechanical objectivity" to historicize the concept of objectivity. The historians show that notions of truth and the relationship between knowledge and the experts producing it have shifted over time. In the middle of the nineteenth century, just as a range of mechanized devices, including the photo camera, started making their way into the scientific laboratory, a new regime of truth began to take shape. Earlier models of scientific expertise relied on visionary qualities of the scientific genius who could decipher ideal form from the imperfect earthly matter he encountered. By contrast, mechanical objectivity rendered the individual observer an imperfect and a hopelessly flawed witness while it endowed mechanized tools with the capacity to strip away convention or bias to directly access brute, naked facts.

10 Developers of early wearables often dramatized this technology as a figurative armor, valorizing the conspicuousness of these tools. Innovators of wearable computing such as Steve Mann and Thad Starner, who are recognized today as key founders of wearable computing, endorsed this view. In the 1990s, they also helped to draw enthusiasm and curiosity for the field by creating an experimental club at MIT dubbed the Borg club in a salute to the figure of the suited cyborg. Members of the Borg club committed to irreverently wearing their bulky heads-up displays on a regular basis, inviting rather than shunning public scrutiny and attention. For Mann, in particular, the fact that these devices were noticeable held critical potential. He originally developed his own head-worn piece as a political commentary intended to call out rather than to enable what he perceived as the expanding regime of public surveillance. Mann called this form of self-monitoring, which was "undertaken by an entity not in a position of authority," "sousveillance" (Ali and Mann, 2013).

11 Field notes, July 2015, on file with the author.

Chapter 1

1 For additional reflections on the intersection of Quantified Self and Stewart Brand's techno-utopianism, see Boesel, 2013; Hong, 2016; Ruckenstein and Pantzar, 2017.

2 Field notes, June 2015, on file with the author.

3 Joseph Reagle distinguishes between two types of lifestyle hackers, the geeks and the gurus, in the book *Hacking Life: Systematized Living and Its Discontents*. Both geeks and gurus share a rational worldview and embrace an ethos of experimentation for self-improvement, but they differ in their roles and influence. Geeks are the everyday hackers, exploring and optimizing their own lives through hands-on experimentation. Gurus are the select few who have ascended to the level of guide – popular authors and teachers who have amassed a large readership and online following.

4 In textual analysis conducted by Ruckenstein and Pantzar (2017), the authors found that the expression "quantified self" was used in forty-one *Wired* magazine articles across sixty issues published between 2008 and 2012 alone.

5 Andreas Hepp uses the term "imaginative 'haze'" to describe the influence of collectives such as QS on the tech sector at large. He argues that their impact lies in the effect they have on the social reception of technology, not in any specific economic contributions.

6 Bronislaw Malinowski's (1914) opening to the now classic book *Argonauts of the Western Pacific: An Account of Native Enterprise and Adventure in the Archipelagos of Melanesian New Guinea* has by now become one of the most famous descriptions of ethnographic entry.

Chapter 2

1 Field notes, on file with the author.
2 Field notes, May 2016, on file with the author.
3 Field notes, May 2016, on file with the author.
4 For a fuller discussion of how entrepreneurs view open standards, see Andrew L. Russell (2014). For an industry perspective on interoperability, see discussion in David Rose (2015).
5 While the citywide water pipes and sewer systems on the surface appear to be objective feats of engineering, Joyce argues that the hydraulic infrastructure in cities such as London and Manchester emerged as a major and largely unacknowledged "arm of government" (2003, p. 69). The water pipe was a key conduit of liberal values. The desire for freedom was constructed by these infrastructural developments as well as symbolized the freedom of the liberal subject.
6 Field notes, 2015, on file with the author.
7 The Social Media Collective (SMC) collated "Metaphors of Data: A Reading List," documenting both popular uses of digital metaphors and scholarly reflections on these metaphors: https://socialmediacol-lective.org/reading-lists/metaphors-of-data-a-reading-list/.
8 Field notes, 2015, on file with the author.
9 Field notes, 2015, on file with the author.
10 Field notes, 2016, on file with the author.
11 In her classic text *Purity and Danger: An Analysis of Concepts of Pollution and Taboo*, Douglas (1966) insists that cleanliness and dirt are not binaries but rather socially relative categories. For example, shoes on the table are not dirty in and of themselves – they become dirty only when they appear as "matter out of place" (p. 50).
12 For an additional discussion of the contradictory pressures between art and business experienced by advertising "creatives," see Hackley and Kover (2007).
13 Field notes, 2015, on file with the author.
14 Mike Fortune explores the ambitions of private companies working at the intersection of genomics, life sciences, and entrepreneurialism in the book *Promising Genomics: Iceland and deCODE Genetics in a World of Speculation*.
15 Other ways that wearables businesses align themselves with medical science, such as by designing light and sleek product packaging, only compound the impression that these tools are equivalent to those produced for scientifically advanced, sterile laboratory or medical environments.

Chapter 3

1 In "Justice for Data Janitors," Lilly Irani examines the largely unrecognized contributions of low-wage and low-status workers to the tech sector who perform tasks such as scanning and digitizing books. Mary L. Gray and Siddharth Suri likewise discuss the "ghost," that is the invisible labor of people working a stream of low-paying and short-term "gig" jobs in the tech sector. These workers contribute to tasks such as training of algorithms, data cleaning, and data labeling.
2 Tom Boellstorff has noted that tech executives now more frequently speak of "community" rather than of networks and networking. The shift is evident in

Mark Zuckerberg's 2017 public manifesto, a message which he titled "Building Global Community." Although the 2010 Hollywood film describing the rise of Facebook was still titled *The Social Network*, Zuckerberg has chosen the word "community," which, Boellstorff calculates, he used in the manifesto a grand total of eighty times (see Boellstorff, 2017).

3 Field notes, on file with the author.

4 This is the term TikTok uses to demarcate its users.

5 In the article "But My Customers Are Different," Donna Flynn, an anthropologist employed in the private sector, discussed a contradiction she encountered in her work with Microsoft. As an ethnographer, Flynn's focus was on conducting research with Microsoft's business customers. However, product managers had a hard time accepting her findings because her descriptions of them did not match their own expectations. When presented with research, the findings were routinely rejected with the claim that "these are not my customers." In this article, Flynn explores the structural and cultural reasons that shaped this response.

6 For example, John Cheney-Lippold (2011) describes how digital platforms create what he calls an "algorithmic identity" – identity based on one's online history and its interaction with marketing categories rather than individual self-selection. He writes that "online, a category like gender is not determined by one's genitalia or even physical appearance. Nor is it entirely self-selected. Rather, categories of identity are being inferred upon individuals based on their web use" (p. 165). Sofia Noble (2018) has relatedly explored how search algorithms are influenced by private interests, leading to biased results that tend to favor whiteness and marginalize people of color, in the book *Algorithms of Oppression: How Search Engines Reinforce Racism*.

7 For example, Theodor M. Porter (1995) has explored the appeal of numbers and quantitative reasoning in business and government in the now classic work *Trust in Numbers: The Pursuit of Objectivity in Science and Public Life*. Marilyn Strathern's edited volume *Audit Cultures* (2000) has similarly examined the diverse regimes of numerical accountability that have developed in government, education, and business.

8 Field notes, October 2015, on file with the author.

9 Schüll (2016) describes the ambitious PR of companies such as Fitbit and HAPIfork and explores how this corporate discourse constructs the "self as database."

10 Margaret Mead (1963 [1935]) originally made this distinction between small-scale and large-scale societies to justify her own study. In the opening of the study *Sex and Temperament in Three Primitive Societies*, she explains: "I have studied this problem in simple societies because here we have the drama of civilization writ small, a social microcosm alike in kind, but different in size and magnitude, from the complex social structures of people who, like our own, depend upon a written tradition and upon the integration of a great number of conflicting historical traditions" (p. ix).

11 Dougla B. Holt and Craig J. Thompson (2004) identify a dominant masculine archetype in American media and popular culture, which they called "the man of action hero." The man of action is an idealized figure that is based both on rebellion and conformity. This figure acts out against the status quo as he works to take his seat at its head. According to the authors, tech entrepreneurs (just like movie superheroes) are prototypical men of action. They rail against corporate power and celebrate disruption, only to create companies that ultimately reaffirm existing power structures.

Chapter 4

1 Anna later retitled it "Personal Report" on her website: www.annanicanorova.com.
2 For additional analysis of the neolibearal self managed as a business, see Feher, 2009, 2018; Gershon, 2014, 2017; Gregg, 2018).
3 Griffin notes that this expression has been adopted both as a tagline by Nike, the brand that has been telling its acolytes for years to "Just Do It," and as the title of a book by Daymond John, an entrepreneur who is a regular contributor to the popular business show *Shark Tank*.
4 Richard Florida's concept of the "creative class" refers to a social and economic group comprised of knowledge professionals, artists, and educators that, according to him, are among the key drives of modern-day innovation and economic growth.
5 Anand Sharma, the founder of a data-aggregating platform called Gyroscope, exemplifies some of the ways entrepreneurs routinely fold the personal with the professional. In a talk he gave at the QS conference in 2015 titled "From April Zero to Gyroscope," for instance, Sharma talked about Gyroscope as a hobby he has started to monetize. The trajectory of Gyroscope as a product that emerged from an individual pastime mirrors the ways Sharma has discussed his business in the industry press. Here, too, he presents Gyroscope as a business that has organically grown from his own experiences. In this case, the personal softens and authenticates the commercial. It recodes the transactional and distant nature of the sale pitch into an intimate offering.
6 The QS meetups I attended in Boston were generally hosted at Microsoft's Cambridge NERD (New England Research and Development) Center, where Microsoft not only offered free use of their conference space but also generously catered an impressive, healthy set of snacks for attendees. In New York and in Washington, DC, events were often held in WeWork locations, a popular co-working site where entrepreneurs and freelances rent offices and share facilities.
7 Field notes, May 2016, on file with author.
8 See also Rosenblat (2018) on the sinister aspect of the sharing economy. Rosenblat has analyzed how companies such as Uber invoke the rhetoric of sharing and desire to recast occupations like driving as monetizable hobbies or as hitherto uncompensated forms of sociality, rather than as professions worthy of a proper wage. This type of messaging is particularly palpable in Uber's marketing materials where it presents the "archetypal millennials – young, unattached, looking for adventure" as the prototypical drivers (p. 35). Marketing tactics that conceptualize driving as a passion project of budding entrepreneurs or as a lifestyle choice of millennials on the prowl for fun experiences distract from the reality that driving does not only offer supplemental income for fun-loving youngsters with time to spare. It's also necessary income that pays for mortgages, medical expenses, or college tuition.

Chapter 5

1 For example, Marey helped settle the longstanding debate among equestrians on whether all four hooves of a galloping horse ever left the ground at the same time – they did (Rabinbach, 1992).
2 For a further discusion of the expanding role digital self-tracking plays in the workplace, see see Karen Levy's 2016 book, *Data Driven: Truckers, Technolog, and the New Workplace Surveilance*, which describes the growing use of digital

monitoring and biometrics in the truckign industry. Mainstream publications have also examined the impact of biometric monitoring on courier and delivery services (Kaplan, 2015), Amazon distribution facilities (Yeginsu, 2018), and the tech office (Connolly, 2020).

3 David Beer discusses both the ambitious vision and the pervasive role data analytics now play in contemporary corporate life in a a book aptly titled the *Data Gaze: Capitalism, Power, and Perception.*

4 For an in-depth discussion of the way technology companies have commoditized and monitized social experience, see Shoshana Zuboff's (2019) *The Age of Surveillance Capitalism: The Fight for a Human Future at the New Frontier of Power.*

5 See also Chris Till (2014) who argues that contemporary digital self-tracking devices are transforming leisure activities like exercise into a form of uncompensated work.

6 Field notes, 2015, on file with the author.

7 For a more detailed discussion of the concept of hacking and its relationship to digital self-monitoring, see Joseph M. Reagle's (2019) book *Hacking Life: Systematized Living and Its Discontents.*

8 Field notes, April 2016, on file with the author.

9 For a discussion of the role algorithms play in determining users' identity, see John Cheney-Lippold (2017) who explores how algorithms shape both our sense of self and the world around us. Amrute (2020) also discusses how algorithmic systems that we use to guide our daily experiences carry the residue of history as they remain shaped by deep-seated colonial logics.

10 Crowdsourcing platforms such as Kickstarter.com, where people can offer small financial support to a rising venture (often in exchange for early access to a finished product rather than equity), have become an increasingly popular supplement to more formal venture capital money. Venture capital firms in fact often only invest in companies that have first gathered sufficient popularity and money through a crowd-funded platform. For many institutional investors, these early money-raising schemes act as initial "proof of concept." Startup accelerators are programs often hosted by larger companies. Companies typically invest "seed money," often taking an equity stake in the fledgling business, and providing financial, administrative, and marketing support to a "class" of early-stage entrepreneurs for a period of one or two years.

11 Field notes, April 2016, on file with the author.

12 Field notes, April 2016, on file with the author.

13 Field notes, April 2016, on file with the author.

14 Field notes, April 2016, on file with the author.

Chapter 6

1 Field notes, 2015, on file with the author.

2 This equivalence is not without precedent. Fred Turner has already explored some of the interconnections between hallucinatory drug use and computer technology that originated in the 1960s counterculture. The New Communalists first explored frontier living and drug use as modes of achieving a more authentic state of being, ideas that later became transposed onto personal computing as well (see Turner, 2006).

3 See Facebook, "Managing Unconscious Bias," Facebook.com, https://managingbias .fb.com/.

4 For example, Ernesto Leclau and Chantal Mouffe (1985) see political harmony and consensus as masking problems instead of eradicating them. See also Fraser, 1990.

5 For an example of a work critiquing multiculturalism, see Povinelli, 2002. Informed by her work with indigenous people of Belyuen, an Aboriginal community of the Northern Territory of Australia located in the middle of the Cox Peninsula, Povinelli explores the struggles the Australian indigenous population faced in claiming legal recognition of land titles. This analysis embeds a larger critique of the politics of recognition that implies the construction of the very thing to be recognized. In exploring the competing Western and indigenous categories through which an idea of indigeneity is formed, Povinelli examines the material and legal repercussions of dueling social classifications, a contest that also complicates the construction of a national narrative of Australia premised on inclusive and equitable multiculturalism. Her work exposes the degree to which multiculturalism is driven by power and often ends up repeating the injustice it is meant to correct.

6 Holt and Thompson discuss the tech entrepreneur as the "most potent" example of a modern masculine archetype they call the "man-of-action hero." Men of action derive their heroic status from fearless demolition. They "practice creative destruction in order to create powerful new companies" (p. 428).

7 Field notes, June 2015, on file with the author.

8 Field notes, July 2015, on file with the author.

9 Schüll (n.d.) also describes the insidious responsiveness of sensors that play on maternal stereotypes in the article "The Sense Mother." She highlights how the staged intimacy of this oversight is often framed by marketers as less threatening and more desirable than the cold and impersonal glare of the "big brother."

10 Field notes, 2015, on file with the author.

11 In the chapter "Technology as Masculine Culture," sociologist Judy Wajcman explores how "the traditional conception of technology is heavily weighted against women" (p. 137). This includes the social privileging of technology invented or used by men. However, it also includes a correlation between notions of "manliness" and technological prowess.

12 Interview with the author, June 2015.

13 In *The Woman in the Body: A Cultural Analysis of Reproduction*, Martin discusses how women's reproductive organs and processes such as menstruation and menopause are often seen negatively, as something over which women have little control.

14 Field notes, 2016, on file with the author.

Conclusion

1 Field notes, 2016, on file with the author.

2 https://theinterval.org/about/

3 https://quantifiedself.com/blog/quantified-self-institute/

4 Field notes, 2015, on file with the author.

5 Field notes, 2014, on file with the author.

Bibliography

Agha, A. (2006). *Language and Social Relations*. New York: Cambridge University Press.

Ali, M. A., and Mann, S. (2013). The Inevitability of the Transition from a Surveillance-Society to a Veillance-Society: Moral and Economic Grounding for Sousveillance. *2013 IEEE International Symposium on Technology and Society* (ISTAS).

Amrute, S. (2020). Bored Techies Being Casually Racist: Race as Algorithm. *Science, Technology, & Human Values, 45*(5), 903–933.

Anderson, B. (1983). *Imagined Communities: Reflections on the Origin and Spread of Nationalism*. New York and London: Verso.

Andrejevic, M. (2013). Estranged Free Labor. In T. Scholz (ed.), *Digital Labor: The Internet as Playground and Factory* (pp. 149–164). New York: Routledge.

Anonymous. (2016). Interview with the Author (Y. Grinberg, Interviewer).

Armstrong, P. K., and Kotler, P. T. (2018). *Principles of Marketing*. Harlow: Pearson.

Asad, T. (1993). *Genealogies of Religion: Discipline and Reason of Power in Christianity and Islam*. Baltimore, MD, and London: Johns Hopkins University Press.

Asif, A., and Wortham, S. (2005). Discourse across Speech Events: Intertextuality and Interdiscursivity in Social Life. *Journal of Linguistic Anthropology, 15*(1), 1–5.

Atkins, P. (2010). *Computer*. London: Reaktion.

Bacon, L. (2013, January 24). Tech Companies, Stop Hiring Women to Be the Office Mom. *Quartz*. https://qz.com/47154/tech-companies-stop-hiring-women-to-be-the-office-mom

Barbrook, R., and Cameron, A. (1996). Californian Ideology. *Science as Culture, 6*(1), 44–72.

Baudrillard, J. (1994). *Simulacra and Simulation*. Ann Arbor: University of Michigan Press.

Bauman, Z. (2000). *Liquid Modernity*. Oxford: Blackwell Publishers.

Beer, D. (2018). *The Data Gaze: Capitalism, Power and Perception*. London: Sage Publications.

Ben. (2015, June). Interview with the Author (Y. Grinberg, Interviewer).

Benjamin, W. (1969 [1931]). Unpacking My Library. In *Illuminations* (pp. 59–68). New York: Schocken Books.

Berg, M. (2017). Making Sense of Sensors: Self-Tracking and the Temporalities of Wellbeing. *Digital Health, 3*, 1–11.

Bernstein, A. (2016, March 25). Marie Kondo and the Privilege of Clutter. *The Atlantic.*

Bilton, N. (2016, October). Exclusive: How Elizabeth Holmes's House of Cards Came Tumbling Down. *Vanity Fair.*

Boellstorff, T. (2017, February 27). Zuckerberg and the Anthropologist: Facebook, Culture, Digital Futures. *Culture Digitally.* https://culturedigitally.org/2017/02/zuckerberg-and-the-anthropologist-facebook-culture-digital-futures/

Boesel, W. E. (2013, May 22). What Is the Quantified Self Now? *Cyborgology.* https://thesocietypages.org/cyborgology/2013/05/22/what-is-the-quantified-self-now

Boudway, I. (2014, June 5). Is Chris Dancy the Most Quantified Self in America? *Bloomberg.* www.bloomberg.com

Bourdieu, P. (1996). *The State Nobility: Elite Schools in the Field of Power.* Stanford, CA: Stanford University Press.

Bourdieu, P. (1999 [1975]). The Specificity of the Scientific Field and the Social Conditions of the Progress of Reason. In M. Biagioli (ed.), *The Science Reader* (pp. 31–50). New York: Routledge.

Bowker, G. C., and Star, S. L. (2000). *Sorting Things Out: Classification and Its Consequences.* Cambridge, MA: MIT Press.

Bowles, N. (2018, March 4). Dorm Living for Professionals Comes to San Francisco. *The New York Times.*

Brandon. (2015, July). Interview with the Author (Y. Grinberg, Interviewer).

Brown, E. H. (2005). *The Corporate Eye.* Baltimore, MD: Johns Hopkins University Press.

Brown, N. (2005). Shifting Tenses: Reconnecting Regimes of Truth and Hope. *Configurations, 13*(3), 331–355.

Brown, W. (2006). *Regulating Aversion: Tolerance in the Age of Identity and Empire.* Princeton, NJ: Princeton University Press.

Brunton, F., and Nissenbaum, H. (2015). *Obfuscation: A User's Guide for Privacy and Protest.* Cambridge, MA: MIT Press.

Butler, J. (1993). *Bodies That Matter: On the Discursive Limits of "Sex."* New York: Routledge.

Butler, J. (1997). *The Psychic Life of Power: Theories in Subjection.* Stanford, CA: Stanford University Press.

Callon, M., and Muniesa, F. (2005, August). Economic Markets as Calculative Collective Devices. *Organization Studies, 26*(8), 1229–1250.

Carlson, J. D., and Stewart, K. C. (2014, July 2). The Legibilities of Mood Work. *New Formations, 82*, 114–133.

Carreyrou, J. (2015, October 16). Hot Startup Theranos Has Struggled with Its Blood-Test Technology. *The Wall Street Journal.*

Carreyrou, J. (2018). *Bad Blood: Secrets and Lies in a Silicon Valley Startup.* New York: Knopf.

Case, A. (2012, July 28). Get Ready for CyborgCamp Portland 2012! Nov 3rd from 9:30am–6pm. *CyborgCamp.* http://cyborgcamp.com/2012/07

Case, A. (2014, August 24). Speaker Announcement: Chris Dancy! *CyborgCamp.* http://cyborgcamp.com/author/caseorganic/page/3

Cassidy, J. (2006, May 7). Me Media: How Hanging Out on the Internet Became Big Business. *The New Yorker.*

Cetina, K. K. (1999). *Epistemic Cultures: How the Sciences Make Knowledge.* Cambridge, MA: Harvard University Press.

Chen, A. (2018, September 13). What the Apple Watch's FDA Clearance Actually Means. *The Verge.* www.theverge.com/2018/9/13/17855006/apple-watch-series-4-ekg-fda-approved-vs-cleared-meaning-safe

Chen, C. (2022). *Work Pray Code: When Work Becomes Religion in Silicon Valley.* Princeton, NJ: Princeton University Press.

Cheney-Lippold, J. (2011). A New Algorithmic Identity: Soft Biopolitics and Modulation of Control. *Theory, Culture & Society, 28*(6), 164–181.

Cheney-Lippold, J. (2017). *We Are Data: Algorithms and the Making of Our Digital Selves.* New York: NYU Press.

Christin, A. (2020). *Metrics at Work: Journalism and the Contested Meaning of Algorithms.* Princeton, NJ: Princeton University Press.

Chun, W. H. (2008). *Control and Freedom.* Cambridge, MA: MIT Press.

Chun, W. H. (2011). *Programmed Visions: Software and Memory.* Cambridge, MA: MIT Press.

Clay, K. (2013, January 6). CES 2013: The Year of The Quantified Self? *Forbes.*

Clifford, J. (1986). Introduction: Partial Truths. In J. Clifford, and G. E. Marcus (eds.), *Writing Culture: The Poetics and Politics of Ethnography* (pp. 1–26). Berkeley, CA: University of California Press.

Clifford, J. (1988). *The Predicament of Culture: Twentieth-Century Ethnography, Literature, and Art.* Cambridge, MA: Harvard University Press.

Clifford, J., and Marcus, G. E. (eds.) (2011). *Writing Culture: The Poetics and Politics of Ethnography.* Berkeley, CA: University of California Press.

Clynes, M. E., and Kline, N. S. (1960, September). Cyborgs and Space. *Astronautics,* pp. 26–76.

Coleman, G. (2013). *Coding Freedom: The Ethics and Aesthetics of Hacking.* Princeton, NJ: Princeton University Press.

Collins, H., Evans, R., and Weisel, M. (2017). STS as Science or Politics? *Social Studies of Science, 47*(4), 580–586.

Connolly, R. (2020, December 14). The Pandemic Has Taken Surveillance of Workers to the Next Level. *The Guardian.*

Connor. (2015, April). Interview with the Author (Y. Grinberg, Interviewer).

Cowan, R. S. (1983). *More Work for Mother: The Ironies of Household Technology from the Open Hearth to the Microwave.* New York: Basic Books.

Cranny-Francis, A. (2008, August). From Extension to Engagement: Mapping the Imaginary of Wearable Technology. *Visual Communication, 7*(3), 363–382.

Crary, J. (1999). *Suspensions of Perception: Attention, Spectacle, and Modern Culture.* Cambridge, MA: MIT Press.

Dancy, C. (2015, April). Interview with the Author (Y. Grinberg, Interviewer).

Dancy, C. (2016, January). Interview with the Author (Y. Grinberg, Interviewer).

Dancy, C. (2017). *Mindful Cyborg.* www.chrisdancy.com

Daston, L., and Galison, P. (2007). *Objectivity.* Princeton, NJ: Princeton University Press.

De Kosnik, A. (2013). Fandom as Free Labor. In T. Scholz (ed.), *Digital Labor* (pp. 98–111). New York: Routledge.

Douglas, M. (1966). *Purity and Danger: An Analysis of Concepts of Pollution and Taboo*. New York: Routledge.

Dourish, P., and Bell, G. (2014). "Resistance Is Futile": Reading Science Fiction alongside Ubiquitous Computing. *Personal and Ubiquitous Computing*, *18*(4), 769–778.

Dourish, P., and Mainwaring, S. D. (2012). Ubicomp's Colonial Impulse. Ubicomp 12 Proceedings of the 2012 ACM Conference on Ubiquitous Computing (pp. 133–142).

Dreyfus, H. L. (1990). *Being-in-the-World: A Commentary on Heidegger's Being in Time, Division I*. Cambridge, MA: MIT Press.

Dumit, J. (2004). *Picturing Personhood: Brain Scans and Biomedical Identity*. Princeton, NJ: Princeton University Press.

Dumit, J., and Nafus, D. (2018). The Other Ninety Per Cent: Thinking with Data Studies, Creating Data Studies. In D. Knox and D. Nafus (eds.), *Ethnography for a Data-Saturated World* (pp. 252–274). Manchester: Manchester University Press.

Editors, T. B. (2014, March 20). Parody Photos of the SF Rental Market Are Darkly Funny. *The Bold Italic*. https://thebolditalic.com/parody-photos-of-the-sf-rental-market-are-darkly-funny-the-bold-italic-san-francisco-249cafd0e520

Edwards, P. N. (1996). *The Closed World: Computers and the Politics of Discourse in Cold War America*. Cambridge, MA: MIT Press.

Ellerbrok, A. (2011). Playful Biometrics: Controversial Technology through the Lens of Play. *Sociological Quarterly*, *52*(4), 528–547.

Elsden, C., David, K. S., and Durrant, A. (2016). A Quantified Past: Toward Design for Remembering Personal Informatics. *Human–Computer Interactions*, *31*(6), 518–557.

Emrich, T. (2016, January 11). The Biggest Wearable Trends We Saw at CES 2016. *Mobile Syrup*. https://mobilesyrup.com/2016/01/11/wearable-tech-trends-from-ces-2016/

Ensmenger, N. (2010). Making Programming Masculine. In T. J. Misa (ed.), *Making Programing Masculine* (pp. 115–141). Hoboken, NJ: John Wiley & Sons.

Esther, K. (2015, March). The Spy Who Fired Me. *Harper's Magazine*.

Ettarh, F. (2018, January 10). Vocational Awe and Librarianship: The Lies We Tell Ourselves. *In the Library with the Lead Pipe*. www.inthelibrarywiththeleadpipe.org/2018/vocational-awe/

Eubanks, V. (2015). *Automating Inequality: How High-Tech Tools Profile, Police, and Punish the Poor*. New York: St. Martin Press.

Fairbanks, A. M. (2008). Funny Thing Happened at the Dog Run. *The New York Times*.

Fawkes, P. (2014). The Future of Wearable Tech: Key Trends Driving the Forms and Function of Personal Devices. PSFK.

Federici, S. (1975). *Wages against Housework*. New York: Power of Women Collective.

Feher, M. (2009). Self-Appreciation; or, the Aspirations of Human Capital. *Public Culture*, *21*(1), 22.

Feher, M. (2018). *Rated Agency: Investee Politics in a Speculative Age*. Princeton, NJ: Princeton University Press.

Ferriss, T. (2007). *The 4-Hour Work Week: Escape 9–5, Live Anywhere, and Join the New Rich*. New York: Crown Publishing Group.

Ferriss, T. (2010). *The 4-Hour Body: An Uncommon Guide to Rapid Fat-Loss, Incredible Sex, and Becoming Superhuman*. New York: Crown Publishing Group.

Ferriss, T. (2012). *The 4-Hour Chef: The Simple Path to Cooking Like a Pro, Learning Anything, and Living the Good Life*. Seattle, WA: Amazon Publishing.

Ferriss, T. (2013, April 3). The First-Ever Quantified Self Notes (Plus: LSD as Cognitive Enhancer?). https://tim.blog/2013/04/03/the-first-ever-quantified-self-notes-plus-lsd-as-cognitive-enhancer/

Finley, K. (2013, February 22). The Quantified Man: How an Obsolete Tech Guy Rebuilt Himself for the Future. *Wired*.

Fitbit. (2020, 11 November). www.fitbit.com/global/us/home

Flaherty, A. (2022, March 16). Women Lost Jobs at a Higher Rate in the Pandemic. Many Still Haven't Returned. *ABC News*.

Florida, R. (2002). *The Rise of the Creative Class and How It's Transforming Work, Leisure, Community and Everyday Life*. New York: Basic Books.

Flynn, D. K. (2010). "My Customers Are Different!": Identity, Difference, and the Political Economy of Design. In M. Cefkin (ed.), *Ethnography and the Corporate Encounter: Reflections on Research in and of Corporations* (pp. 41–58). New York and Oxford: Berghahn Books.

Forrester Research (2014). The Data Digest: Five Urgent Truths about Wearables. www.forrester.com/blogs/14-12-09 the_data_digest_five_urgent_truths_about_wearables/

Fortun, M. (2008). *Promising Genomics: Iceland and deCODE Genetics in a World of Speculation*. Chicago, IL: University of Chicago Press.

Foucault, M. (1990). *The History of Sexuality*. New York: Vintage Books.

Foucault, M. (2008). *The Birth of Biopolitics: Lectures at the Collège de France, 1978–1979*. New York: Picador/Palgrave Macmillan.

Frank. (2015, June). Interview with the Author (Y. Grinberg, Interviewer).

Fraser, N. (1990). Rethinking the Public Sphere: A Contribution to the Critique of Actually Existing Democracy. *Social Text, 25/26*, 56–80.

Fry, R. (2022, January 14). Some Gender Disparities Widen in the U.S. Workforce during the Pandemic. *Pew Research Center*. www.pewresearch.org/short-reads/2022/01/14/some-gender-disparities-widened-in-the-u-s-workforce-during-the-pandemic/

Gabrys, J. (2013). *Digital Rubbish*. Ann Arbor: University of Michigan Press.

Galison, P. (1997). *Image and Logic: A Material Culture of Microphysics*. Chicago, IL: University of Chicago Press.

Gartner. (2015). Gartner's Hype Cycle for Emerging Technologies. www.gartner.com/en/newsroom/press-releases/2015-08-18-gartners-2015-hype-cycle-for-emerging-technologies-identifies-the-computing-innovations-that-organizations-should-monitor. This Gartner report is archived and is included for historical context only.

Geertz, C. (1973). *The Interpretation of Cultures*. New York: Basic Books.

Gerdau, A. (2014, August 19). A Life in Data: Nicholas Feltron's Self-Surveillance. *The New York Times*.

Gershon, I. (2014, November). Selling Yourself in the United States. *Political and Legal Anthropology Review, 37*(2), 281–295.

Gershon, I. (2017). *Down and Out in the New Economy: How People Find or Don't Find Work Today*. Chicago, IL: Chicago University Press.

Gilbreth, F. B., and Gilbreth, L. M. (1919). *Fatigue Study: The Elimination of Humanity's Greatest Unnecessary Waste. A First Step in Motion Study*. New York: The MacMillan Company.

Gitelman, L. (2013). *Raw Data Is an Oxymoron*. Cambridge, MA: MIT Press.

Goodin, D. (2011, January 25). Passenger Cleared after TSA Checkpoint Stare-Down: Man Fought the Law and the Man Won. *The Register*. www.theregister.com/2011/01/25/passenger_acquitted/

Graham, S., and Marvin, S. (2001). *Splintering Urbanism: Networked Infrastructures, Technological Mobilities and the Urban Condition*. New York: Routledge.

Gray, M. L., and Suri, S. (2019). *Ghost Work: How to Stop Silicon Valley from Building a New Global Underclass*. Boston and New York: Houghton Mifflin Harcourt.

Grazian, D. (2020). Thank God It's Monday: Manhattan Coworking Spaces in the New Economy. *Theory and Society*, *49*(5), 991–1019.

Gregg, M. (2011). *Work's Intimacy*. Cambridge, MA: Polity Press.

Gregg, M. (2018). *Counterproductive: Time Management in the Knowledge Economy*. Durham, NC: Duke University Press.

Grey, C. (2005). *A Very Short Fairly Interesting and Reasonably Cheap Book About Studying Organizations*. London: Sage Publications.

Griffin, E. (2019, January 26). Why Are Young People Pretending to Love Work. *The New York Times*.

Grossman, L., and Vella, M. (2014, September 11). Never Offline: The Apple Watch Is Just the Start: How Wearable Tech Will Change Your Life – Like It or Not. *Time*.

Gupta, A., and Ferguson, J. (1997). Beyond "Culture": Space, Identity, and the Politics of Difference. In A. Gupta and J. Ferguson (eds.), *Culture, Power, Place: Explorations in Critical Anthropology* (pp. 33–51). Durham, NC: Duke University Press.

Hacking, I. (1998). Making Up People. In M. Biagioli (ed.), *Science Studies Reader* (pp. 161–171). London and New York: Routledge.

Hackley, C., and Kover, A. J. (2007). The Trouble with Creatives: Negotiating Creative Identity in Advertising Agencies. *International Journal of Advertising*, *26*(1), 63–78.

Halpern, O. (2014). *Beautiful Data: A History of Vision and Reason since 1945*. Durham, NC: Duke University Press.

Haraway, D. (2001). A Cyborg Manifesto: Science, Technology, and Socialist-Feminism in the Late Twentieth Century. In D. Bell and B. M. Kennedy, *The Cybercultures Reader* (pp. 291–324). London and New York: Routledge. First published in 1985 in the *Socialist Review*.

Hartmans, A., and Leskin, P. (2020, April 13). The Rise and Fall of Elizabeth Holmes, the Theranos Founder Awaiting Trial on Federal Charges of "Massive Fraud." *Business Insider*. www.businessinsider.nl/theranos-founder-ceo-elizabeth-holmes-life-story-bio-2018-4?international = true&r = US

Hayles, K. N. (1999). *How We Became Posthuman: Virtual Bodies in Cybernetics, Literature, and Informatics*. Chicago, IL: University of Chicago Press.

Helmreich, S. (2009). *Alien Ocean: Anthropological Voyages in Microbial Seas*. Berkeley, CA: University of California Press.

Henderson, R. (2020). *Reimagining Capitalism in a World on Fire*. New York: Hachette Book Group.

Hepp, A. (2020). The Fragility of Curating a Pioneer Community: Deep Mediatization and the Spread of the Quantified Self and Maker Movements. *International Journal of Cultural Studies*, *23*(6), 932–950.

Ho, K. (2009). *Liquidated: An Ethnography of Wall Street*. Durham, NC: Duke University Press.

Hochschild, A. (1997). *The Time Bind: When Work Becomes Home and Home Becomes Work*. New York: Metropolitan Books.

Hochschild, A. (2012). *The Managed Heart*. Berkeley, CA: University of California Press.

Holland, P. (1991). Introduction: History, Memory, and the Family Album. In J. Spence and P. Holland (eds.), *Family Snaps: The Meaning of Domestic Photography* (pp. 5–18). London: Virago Press.

Holt, D. B., and Thompson, C. J. (2004, September). Man-of-Action Heroes: The Pursuit of Heroic Masculinity in Everyday Consumption. *Journal of Consumer Research*, *31*(2), 425–440.

Hong, S.-h. (2016, September 1). Data's Intimacy: Machinic Sensibility and the Quantified Self. *communication +1*, *5*(1), Article 3. https://openpublishing .library.umass.edu/cpo/article/13/galley/13/view/

Hookway, B. (2014). *Interface*. Cambridge, MA: MIT Press.

Hwang, T., and Levy, K. (2015, January 20). The 'Cloud' and Other Dangerous Metaphors. *The Atlantic*.

Irani, L. (2015, January 15). Justice for Data Janitors. *Public Books*. www.publicbooks .org/justice-for-data-janitors/

Irani, L. (2019). *Chasing Innovation: Making Entrepreneurial Citizens in Modern India*. Princeton, NJ: Princeton University Press.

Jain, S. S. (1999, winter). The Prosthetic Imagination: Enabling and Disabling the Prosthesis Trope. *Science, Technology, & Human Values*, *24*(1), 31–54.

John. (2016). Interview with the Author (Y. Grinberg, Interviewer).

John, L. and Jackson, J. (2005). *The Real Black: Adventures in Racial Sincerity*. Chicago, IL: University of Chicago Press.

Johnson, D. (2010). Sorting Out the Question of Feminist Technology. In L. Layne, S. Vostral, and K. Boyer (eds.), *Feminist Technology* (pp. 36–54). Champaign, IL: University of Illinois Press.

Joyce, P. (2003). *The Rule of Freedom: Liberalism and the Modern City*. London: Verso.

Jurgenson, N. (2014). View from Nowhere. *The New Inquiry*. https://thenewinquiry .com/view-from-nowhere/

Kaplan, E. (2015, March). The Spy Who Fired Me. *Harper's Magazine*.

Kelly, K. (1994). *Out of Control: The New Biology of Machines, Social Systems, & the Economic World*. New York: Basic Books.

Kelly, K. (1999). *New Rules for the New Economy: 10 Radical Strategies for a Connected World*. New York: Viking Penguin.

Kelly, K. (2011, June 26). The Technium. https://kk.org/thetechnium/the-quantifiabl/

Kemper, S. (2001). *Buying and Believing*. Chicago, IL: Chicago University Press.

Knox, H., and Nafus, D. (eds.) (2018). *Ethnography for a Data-Saturated World*. Manchester: Manchester University Press.

Kondo, M. (2022). *Kon Mari*. https://konmari.com/about-the-konmari-method/

Kramer, J. (2017, November 2). Logistical Labor: Stop Doing Companies' Digital Busywork for Free. *Scientific America*. www.scientificamerican.com/article/stop-doing-companies-rsquo-digital-busywork-for-free/

Kristensen, D. B., and Ruckenstein, M. (2018). Co-evolving with Self-Tracking Technologies. *New Media & Society*, *20*(10), 3624–3640.

Kurzweil, R. (2005). *The Singularity Is Near: When Humans Transcend Biology*. New York: Penguin Group.

Labov, W. (1972). *Sociolinguistic Patterns*. Philadelphia, PA: University of Pennsylvania Press.

Labov, W. (1966). *The Social Stratification of English in New York*. Cambridge: Cambridge University Press.

Lakoff, G., and Johnson, M. (1980). *Mataphors We Live By*. Chicago, IL: Chicago University Press.

Lakoff, G., and Johnson, M. (1999). *Philosophy in the Flesh: The Embodied Mind and Its Challenge to Western Thought*. New York: Basic Books.

Larkin, B. (2008). *Signal and Noise: Media, Infrastructure, and Urban Culture in Nigeria*. Durham, NC: Duke University Press.

Latour, B. (1988). *Science in Action: How to Follow Scientists and Engineers through Society*. Cambridge, MA: Harvard University Press.

Latour, B. (2004). Why Has Critique Run out of Steam? From Matters of Fact to Matters of Concern. *Critical Inquiry*, *30*, 225–248.

Latour, B. (2005). *Reassembling the Social: An Introduction to Actor-Network Theory*. New York: Oxford University Press.

Lawrie, I. (2019). Becoming a Real Data Scientist: Expertise, Flexibility and Lifelong Learning. In H. Knox and D. Nafus (eds.), *Ethnography for a Data-Saturated World* (pp. 62–81). Manchester: Manchester University Press.

Lazar, A., Koehler, C., Tanenbaum, T. J., and Nguyen, D. H. (2015). Why We Use and Abandon Smart Devices. In *Proceedings of the 2015 ACM International Joint Conference on Pervasive and Ubiquitous Computing* (pp. 635–646). New York: Association for Computing Machinery.

Lazzarato, M. (1996). Immaterial Labor. In M. Hardt, and P. Virno (eds.), *Radical Thought in Italy: A Potential Politics* (pp. 133–147). Minneapolis and London: University of Minnesota Press.

Leclau, E., and Mouffe, C. (1985). *Hegemony and Socialist Strategy: Towards a Radical Democratic Politics*. New York and London: Verso.

Lemov, R. (2017). Archives of the Self. In L. Daston (ed.), *Science in the Archives* (pp. 247–270). Chicago, IL: Chicago University Press.

Levy, K. (2016). *Data Driven: Truckers, Technology, and the New Workplace Surveilance*. Princeton, NJ: Princeton University Press.

Lewis, G. (2022, August 11). Industries with the Highest (and Lowest) Turnover Rates. www.linkedin.com/business/talent/blog/talent-strategy/industries-with-the-highest-turnover-rates

Lupton, D. (2013). Quantifiying the Body: Monitoring and Measuring Health in the Age of mHealth Technologies. *Critical Public Health*, *23*(4), 393–403.

Lupton, D. (2016). *The Quantified Self*. Cambridge, MA: Polity Press.

Lyon, D. (1994). *Electronic Eye: The Rise of Surveillance Society*. Cambridge, MA: Polity Press.

Maheshwari, T. H. (2020, November 25). "Thumb-Stopping," "Humaning," "B4H": The Strange Language of Modern Marketing. *The New York Times*.

Mahmood, S. (2001). Feminist Theory, Embodiment and the Docile Agent: Some Reflections on the Egyptian Islamic Revival. *Cultural Anthropology*, *16*(2), 202–236.

Malefyt, T. d. (2003). Models, Metaphors, and Client Relations: The Negotiated Meaning of Advertising. In T. d. Boeran (ed.), *Advertising Cultures* (pp. 139–164). London: Bloomsbury Academic.

Malefyt, T. d. (2018). Magic of Paradox: How Advertising Ideas Transform Art into Business and the Ordinary in the Extraordinary. In T. d. Malefyt and B. Morean (eds.), *Magical Capitalism: Enchantment, Spells, and Occult Practices in Contemporary Economies* (pp. 163–190). New York: Palgrave Macmillan.

Malefyt, T. d., and Moeran, B. (2020 [2003]). *Advertising Cultures*. New York: Routledge.

Malinowski, B. (2014 [1922]). *Argonauts of the Western Pacific: An Account of Native Enterprise and Adventure in the Archipelagoes of Melanesian New Guinea*. New York: Routledge.

Mann, S. (n.d.). *Five Significant Contributions to Research*. http://wearcam.org/contributions.pdf

Mark. (2015). Interview with the Author (Y. Grinberg, Interviewer).

Markell, P. (2003). *Bound by Recognition*. Princeton, NJ: Princeton University Press.

Markovits, D. (2019, September 15). How Life Became an Endless, Terrible Competition. *The Atlantic*.

Martin, E. (1987). *The Woman in the Body: A Cultural Analysis of Reproduction*. Boston, MA: Beacon Press.

Martin, E. (1994). *Flexible Bodies: Tracking Immunity in American Culture from the Days of Polio to the Age of AIDS*. Boston, MA: Beacon Press.

Martin, E. (2009). *Bipolar Expeditions: Mania and Depression in American Culture*. Princeton, NJ: Princeton University Press.

Martin, R. C. (2002). *Agile Software Development: Principles, Patterns, and Practices*. New York: Pearson.

Marwick, A. E. (2013). *Status Update: Celebrity, Publicity, and Branding in the Social Media Age*. New Haven, CT, and London: Yale University Press.

Mazzarella, W. (2003). *Shoveling Smoke Advertising and Globalization in Contemporary India*. Durham, NC: Duke University Press.

Mazzarella, W. (2020 [2003]). Critical Publicity/Public Criticism: Reflections on Fieldwork in the Bombay Ad World. In B. Moeran and T. D. Malefyt (eds.), *Advertising Cultures* (pp. 55–74). New York: Routledge.

McCallum, J. (2020). *Woked Over: How Round-the-Clock Work Is Killing the American Dream*. New York: Basic Books.

McKinsey. (2020). *Women in the Workplace*. https://womenintheworkplace.com/2020

McLuhan, M. (1964). *Understanding Media: The Extension of Man*. Cambridge, MA: MIT Press.

Mead, M. (1963 [1935]). *Sex and Temperament: In Three Primitive Societies*. New York: HarperCollins.

Molen, B. (2014, June 4). Her Name Is Cortana. Her Attitude Is Almost Human. *Endgadget*. www.engadget.com/2014-06-04-cortana-microsoft-windows-phone.html

Mondelez International. (2020, November 11). *Announcing a New Approach To Marketing*. www.mondelezinternational.com/News/New-Approach-to-Marketing-Humaning

Morozov, E. (2013). *To Save Everything, Click Here*. Philadelphia, PA: PublicAffairs.

Morozov, E. (2014). *To Save Everything, Click Here: The Folly of Technological Solutionism*. New York: PublicAffairs.

Murphy, S. (2014a, March 13). Meet the "Most Connected Man" in the World. *Mashable*. https://mashable.com/archive/most-connected-man-in-world-chris-dancy

Murphy, S. (2014b, August 21). The Most Connected Man Is You, Just a Few Years From Now. *Mashable*. https://mashable.com/archive/most-connected-man#Sr.mDDNZOkqG

Musk, E. (2018, November 26). https://twitter.com/elonmusk/status/1067175527 180513280?lang=enhttps://twitter.com/elonmusk/status/1067175527180513280? lang=en

Nader, L. (1974 [1969]). Up the Anthropologist: Perspectives Gained from Studying Up. In D. Hymes (ed.), *Reinventing Anthropology* (pp. 284–311). New York: Vintage Books.

Nafus, D. (2014). Stuck Data, Dead Data, Disloyal Data: The Stops and Starts in Making Numbers into Social Practices. *Distinktion: Scandinavian Journal of Sociology*, *15*(2), 208–222.

Nafus, D., and Sherman, J. (2013, March 26). The Quantified Self Movement Is Not a Kleenex. *Platypus*. https://blog.castac.org/2013/03/the-quantified-self-movement-is-not-a-kleenex/

Nafus, D., and Sherman, J. (2014). This One Does Not Go Up To 11: The Quantified Self Movement as an Alternative Big Data Practice. *International Journal of Communication*, *8*, 1784–1794.

Neff, G., and Nafus, D. (2016). *Self-Tracking*. Cambridge, MA: MIT Press.

Newport, C. (2021, 16 August). Why Are So Many Knowledge Workers Quitting? *The New Yorker*.

Nicanorova, A. (n.d.). *Anna Nicanorova*. www.annanicanorova.com/

Noble, S. (2018). *Algorithms of Oppression: How Search Engines Reinforce Racism*. New York: NYU Press.

Ogilvy, D. (1976). *Confessions of an Advertising Man*. New York: Ballantine Books.

Olen, H. (2022, November 14). How the Pandemic Ended America's Bad Romance with Work. *The Washington Post*.

Ortlieb, M. (2010). Emergent Culture, Slippery Culture: Conflicting Conceptualizations of Culture in Commercial Ethnography. In M. Cefkin (ed.), *Ethnography and the Corporate Encounter: Reflections on Research in and of Corporations* (pp. 185–212). New York and Oxford: Berghahn Books.

Ortner, S. B. (1974). Is Female to Male as Nature Is to Culture? In M. Z. Rosaldo and L. Lamphere (eds.), *Woman, Culture, and Society* (pp. 68–87). Stanford, CA: Stanford University Press.

Ortner, S. B. (2010). Access: Reflections on Studying Up in Hollywood. *Ethnography*, *11*(2), 211–233.

Ovide, S. (2022, June 14). Tech Hiring Is Still Bonkers. *The New York Times*.

Pasquale, F. (2015). *The Black Box Society: The Secret Algorithms That Control Money and Information*. Cambridge, MA: Harvard University Press.

Pastis, S. (2023, July 12). Tech CEO Who Takes 61 Pills a Day and Eats 70 Pounds of Veggies a Month to Stay Young Forever Says He's Never Been Happier: "I Pity the Previous Version of Me." *Fortune*.

Peter. (2015). Interview with the Author (Y. Grinberg, Interviewer).

Petersen, A. H. (2015, January 1). Big Mother Is Watching You. *Buzz Feed*. www .buzzfeed.com/annehelenpetersen/the-track-everything-revolution-is-here-to-improve-you-wheth

Pietra, J. L., and Rowell, C. (2019, October 14). Creating Workplace Community through a Human-Centric Approach. www.wework.com/ideas/research-insights/ expert-insights/creating-workspace-community

Poor, A. (2015, January). CES 2015 Recap: Wearables and Displays. *Display Daily*. https://displaydaily.com/ces-2015-recap-wearables-and-displays-2/

Porter, T. M. (1995). *Trust in Numbers: The Pursuit of Objectivity in Science and Public Life*. Princeton, NJ: Princeton University Press.

Povinelli, E. (2002). *The Cunning of Recognition: Indigenous Alterities and the Making of Australian Multiculturalism*. Durham, NC, and London: Duke University Press.

Priestley, T. (2015, August 18). Why Every Tech Company Needs a Chief Evangelist. *Forbes*.

Puschmann, C., and Burgess, J. (2014). Big Data, Big Questions: Metaphors of Big Data. *International Journal of Communication*, 8, 1690–1709.

Putnam, R. D. (2000). *Bowling Alone: The Collapse and Revival of American Community*. New York: Simon & Schuster.

Rabinbach, A. (1992). *The Human Motor: Energy, Fatigue, and the Origins of Modernity*. Oakland, CA: California University Press.

Rajan, K. S. (2006). *Biocapital: The Constitution of Postgenomic Life*. Durham, NC: Duke University Press.

Reagle, J. M. (2019). *Hacking Life: Systematized Living and Its Discontents*. Cambridge, MA: Massachusetts Institute of Technology.

Richards, N. M., and King, J. H. (2013, September 3). Three Paradoxes of Big Data. *Stanford Law Review*, 66(41), 41–46.

Riles, E. (2011). *The Lean Start-up: How Today's Entrepreneurs Use Continuous Innovation to Create Radically Successful Businesses*. New York: Crown Publishing Group.

Roberts, S. (2008, September 11). First Meeting of the Quantified Self Meetup Group. *Seth's Blog: Personal Science, Self-Experimentation, Scientific Method*. sethroberts.net

Rose, D. (2014). *Enchanted Objects*. New York: Scribner.

Rose, N. (1996). The Death of the Social? Re-figuring the Territory of Government. *Economy and Society*, 25(3), 327–356.

Rosenblat, A. (2018). *Uberland: How Algorithms Are Rewriting the Rules of Work*. Oakland, CA: University of California Press.

Rubio, F. D. (2020). *Still Life: Ecologies of the Modern Imagination at the Art Museum*. Chicago, IL: University of Chicago Press.

Ruckenstein, M. (2014). Visualized and Interacted Life: Personal Analytics and Engagements with Data Doubles. *Societies*, 4(1), 68–84.

Ruckenstein, M., and Pantzar, M. (2017, March). Beyond the Quantified Self: Thematic Exploration of a Datthat Paradigm. *New Media & Society*, 19(3), 401–418.

Ruckenstein, M., and Schüll, N. D. (2017). The Datafication of Health. *Annual Review of Anthropology, 46*, 261–278.

Russell, A. L. (2014). *Open Standards and the Digital Age: History, Ideology, and Networks*. New York and London: Cambridge University Press.

Ryan, S. E. (2014). *Garments of Paradise: Wearable Discourse in the Digital Age*. Cambridge, MA: MIT Press.

Safi. (2015, April). Interview with the Author (Y. Grinberg, Interviewer).

Sagan. (2015, September). Interview with the Author (Y. Grinberg, Interviewer).

Sandberg, S. (2013). *Lean In: Women, Work, and the Will to Lead*. New York: Alfred A. Knopf.

Schüll, N. D. (2012). *Addiction by Design: Machine Gambling in Las Vegas*. Princeton, NJ: Princeton University Press.

Schüll, N. D. (2016). Data for Life: Wearable Technology and the Design of Self. *BioSocieties, 11*(3), 1–17.

Schüll, N. D. (2019). The Data-Based Self: Self-Quantification and the Data-Driven (Good) Life. *Social Research, 86*(4), 909–930.

Schüll, N. D. (n.d.). The Sense Mother. *Theorizing the Contemporary, Fieldsights*.

Scholz, T. (2013). *Digital Labor*. New York: Routledge.

Seaver, N. (2017). Algorithms as Culture: Some Tactics for the Ethnography of Algorithmic Systems. *Big Data & Society, 4*(2).

Senft, T. M. (2013). Mricocelebrity and the Branded Self. In J. Hartley, J. Burgess, and A. Bruns (eds.), *A Companion to New Media Dynamics* (pp. 346–354). Hoboken, NJ: Blackwell Publishing.

Sharon. (2015, October). Interview with the Author (Y. Grinberg, Interviewer).

Sharon. (2016, July). Interview with the Author (Y. Grinberg, Interviewer).

Silverman, M. (2020, March 30). How Chris Dancy Quantified His Bad Habits to Quit Smoking and Lose 120 Pounds. *The Daily Dot*. www.dailydot.com/debug/2-girls-1-podcast-chris-dancy/

Sismondo, S. (2017). Casting a Wider Net: A Reply to Collings, Evans and Weinel. *Social Studies of Science, 47*(4), 587–592.

Star, S. L., and Griesemer, J. (1989). Translation and Boundary Objects: Amateurs and Professionals in Berkeley's Museum of Vertebrate Zoology. *Social Studies of Science, 19*(3), 387–420.

Starosielski, N. (2015). *The Undersea Network*. Durham, NC: Duke University Press.

Stewart, K. (2007). *Ordinary Affects*. Durham, NC: Duke University Press.

Stoltzfus, J. (2022). *Graphical User Interface (GUI)*. www.techopedia.com/definition/5435/graphical-user-interface-gui

Strathern, M. (2000). *Audit Cultures: Anthropological Studies in Accountability, Ethics and the Academy*. New York: Routledge.

Sunderland, P., and Denny, R. M. (2007). *Doing Anthropology*. London and New York: Routledge.

Tamar, S., and Zandbergen, D. (2016, March 9). From Data Fetishism to Quantifying Selves: Self-Tracking Practices and the Other Values of Data. *New Media and Society, 19*(11), 1695–1709.

Taussig, K.-S., Hoeyer, K., and Helmreich, S. (2013). The Anthropology of Potentiality in Biomedicine. *Current Anthropology, 54*, S3–S14.

Taylor, F. W. (1911). *The Principles of Scientific Management.* New York: Harper & Bros.

Tenen, D. (2017). *Plain Text: The Poetics of Computation.* Stanford, CA: Stanford University Press.

Terranova, T. (2000). Free Labor: Producing Culture for the Digital Economy. *Social Text, 18*(2), 33–58.

TikTok. (2021, September 28). Enter TikTok World and Meet the Next Era of Marketing. https://newsroom.tiktok.com/en-au/enter-tiktok-world-and-meet-the-next-era-of-marketing-anz

Till, C. (2014). Exercise as Labor: Quantified Self and the Transformation of Exercise into Labor. *Societies, 4*(3), 446–462.

Trouillot, M.-R. (1995). *Silencing the Past: Power and the Production of History.* Boston, MA: Beacon Press.

Trouillot, M.-R. (2003). Adieu, Culture: A New Duty Arises. In M.-R. Trouillot (ed.), *Global Transformations* (pp. 97–116). New York: Palgrave Macmillan.

Tsing, A. L. (2005). *Friction: An Ethnography of Global Connection.* Princeton, NJ: Princeton University Press.

Tsing, n. L. (2007). Becoming a Tribal Elder, and Other Fantasies of Green Development. In M. Dove and C. Carpenter (eds.), *Environmental Anthropology: A Historical Reader* (pp. 393–422). Malden, MA: Blackwell.

Turkle, S. (2011). *Alone Together: Why We Expect More from Technology and Less from Each Other.* New York: Basic Books.

Turkle, S. (2015). *Reclaiming Conversation: The Power of Talk in a Digital Age.* New York: Penguin Press.

Turner, F. (2006). *From Counterculture to Cyberculture: Steward Brand, the Whole Earth Network, and the Rise of Digital Utopianism.* Chicago, IL: Chicago University Press.

Turner, T. (1993, November). Anthropology and Multiculturalism: What Is Anthropology that Multiculturalists Should Be Mindful Of. *Cultural Anthropology, 8*(4), 411–429.

Turrentine, L. (2014, December 17). CES 2015: Here's Everything You Need to Know. *CNET.* www.cnet.com/tech/tech-industry/ces-2015-everything-you-need-to-know/

Vaynerchuk, G. (2009). *Crush It! Why Now Is the Time to Cash In on Your Passion.* New York: HarperCollins.

Van Cleaf, K. M. (2014). *Blogging through Motherhood: Free Labor, Femininity, and the Re-production of Maternity,* PhD Dissertation. New York: City University of New York.

Van Cleaf, K. M. (2016). Our Mothers Have Always Been Machines: The Conflation of Media and Motherhood. In J. Daniels, K. Gregory, and T. M. Cotton (eds.), *The Digital Sociology Handbook* (pp. 449–463). New York: Policy Press.

Van Dijck, J. (2013). *The Culture of Connectivity: A Critical History of Social Media.* Oxford and New York: Oxford University Press.

Van Dijck, J. (2014). Datafication, Dataism, and Datavalance: Big Data between Scientific Paradigm and Ideology. *Surveillance and Society, 12*(2), 197–208.

Vertesi, J. (2014, April 24). Theorizing Big Data Plenary Discussion. Talk delivered at Theorizing the Web Conference, Brooklyn, New York.

Viseu, A., and Suchman, L. (2010). Wearable Augmentations: Imaginaries of the Informed Body. In J. Edwards (ed.), *Technologized Image, Technologized Bodies* (pp. 161–184). New York: Berghahn Books.

Wade, L. (2019, November 21). The 8-Hour Workday Is a Counterproductive Lie. *Wired.*

Wajcman, J. (1991). *Feminism Confronts Technology.* New York: Wiley.

Wajcman, J. (2015). *Pressed for Time: The Acceleration of Life in Digital Capitalism.* Chicago, IL: University of Chicago Press.

Watson, S. (2015, February 18). Data Is the New "_". *Dis Magazine.*

Weber, M. (2012 [1905]). *The Protestant Ethic and the Spirit of Capitalism.* New York and London: Routledge.

Whitehouse, B. (2016, October 20). Founder of Wearable Experiments Shares Her New Vision for the Quantified Self. www.psfk.com/2016/10/billie-whitehouse-wearable-experiments-technology-quantified-self.html

Wikipedia. (2022, October 12). History of the Graphical User Interface. https://en.wikipedia.org/wiki/History_of_the_graphical_user_interface

Wikipedia. (2022). Homebrew Computer Club. https://en.wikipedia.org/wiki/Homebrew_Computer_Club

Williams, A. (2013, 26 May). The Power of Data Exhaust. *TechCrunch.* https://techcrunch.com/2013/05/26/the-power-of-data-exhaust/

Wolf, G. (2008, September 10). Quantified Self Inaugural Show & Tell! *Meetup.com.* www.meetup.com/quantifiedself/events/8526229/

Wolf, G. (2009, June 22). Know Thyself: Tracking Every Facet of Life, from Sleep to Mood to Pain, 24/7/365. *Wired.*

Wolf, G. (2010, April 28). The Data-Driven Life. *The New York Times.*

Wolf, G. (2016, June). Interview with the Author (Y. Grinberg, Interviewer).

Wolf, G. (2016, June 9). Introduction to Quantified Self Public Health Symposium 2016. *Medium.* https://medium.com/@quantifiedself/introduction-to-quantified-self-public-health-symposium-2016-2ba6b532eddd

Wolf, G. (2022). *Personal Science: Learning to Observe.* Victoria, British Columbia: Leanpub.

Yeginsu, C. (2018, February 1). If Workers Slack Off, the Wristband Will Know. (And Amazon Has a Patent for It.) *The New York Times.*

Zaretsky, E. (1976). *Capitalism, Family, and Personal Life.* New York: Harper and Row.

Zemrani, L. (n.d.). *Laila Zemrani.* www.lailazemrani.com/bio

Zuboff, S. (2019). *The Age of Surveillance Capitalism: The Fight for a Human Future at the New Frontier of Power.* New York: Hachette.

Zuckerberg, M. (2012). Founder's Letter, 2012. *Facebook.* https://m.facebook.com/nt/screen/?params = %7B%22note_id%22%3A261129471966151%7D&path = %2Fnotes%2Fnote%2F&paipv = 0&eav = AfYQtluzMYKZDC0Tvze0YsdW3XySDmQAI8HpEGUhfeQ7dCZuYUUL2NfaCRSgV-vlOkg&_rdr

Index

211